Howard Martin

Head of Humanities
Poynton County High School
Cheshire

THE FRIENDLY SOCIETY OF IRON FOUNDERS OF ENGLAND, IRELAND AND WALES.

7 Britain Since 1700: The Rise of Industry

M
Macmillan Education

For Claire and Rachel

© Howard Martin 1988

First published 1988

Published by
MACMILLAN EDUCATION LTD
Houndmills, Basingstoke, Hampshire RG21 2XS
and London
Companies and representatives
throughout the world

Designed by Wendi Watson

Printed in Hong Kong

British Library Cataloguing in Publication Data
Martin, Howard
Britain since 1700: The rise of industry
—(History in the making; v. 7)
1. Great Britain—Social conditions
I. Title   II. Series
941.07   HN385
ISBN 0–333–45949–0

Series Preface

Changes in the teaching of history over the last decade have raised many problems to which there are no easy solutions. The classification of objectives, the presentation of material in varied and appropriate language, the use and abuse of evidence and the reconsideration of assessment techniques are four of the most important. Many teachers are now encouraging their pupils individually or in groups to participate in the processes and skills of the professional historian. These developments have led naturally to the National Criteria for History for the General Certificate of Secondary Education, which seek to stimulate interest in the past through the acquisition of knowledge and the development of appropriate skills and concepts.

History in the Making seeks to develop these skills and concepts within a secure framework of historical knowledge from the first years of secondary school onwards. The first five volumes form a firm foundation for the GCSE approach. Now three new volumes have been written specifically for GCSE syllabuses in **Modern World** and **British Social and Economic** history.

Each chapter in all the volumes has four major components.

1 **The text** This provides the basic framework of the chapters, and although the approach is essentially factual, it is intended to arouse and sustain the interest of the reader of average ability. It recognises, and seeks to convey, the fascination of the good tale and the drama of human life, individual and collective. The text of the two new volumes has been written specifically to cover the information required for GCSE syllabuses in British Social and Economic History and Modern World History.

2 **The illustrations** These have been carefully selected to stand beside the written pieces of evidence in the chapter, and to provide (so far as is possible) an authentic visual image of the period/topic. Photographs, artwork and maps are all used to clarify and support the text, and to develop the pupil's powers of observation.

3 **Using the evidence** This is a detailed study of the evidence on one particular aspect of the chapter. Did the walls of Jericho really come tumbling down? Was the death of William Rufus in the New Forest really an accident? What was the background of the torpedoing of the *Lusitania*? These are the sort of questions which are asked, to give the pupil the opportunity to consider not only the problems facing the historian, but also those facing the characters of history. Different forms of documentary evidence are considered, as well as archaeological, architectural, statistical, and other kinds of source material; the intention is to give the pupil a genuine, if modest, insight into the making of history. The pupil's ability to empathise with people in the past is particularly valued.

4 **Questions and further work** These are intended to test and develop the pupil's reading of the chapter, and in particular the **Using the evidence** section. Particular attention is paid to the development of historical skills, through examination and interpretation of evidence.

The differences between primary and secondary sources, for example, are explored, and concepts such as bias in evidence and its limitations. By applying the skills which they have developed, pupils may then be able to formulate, at a suitable level and in appropriate language, ideas and hypotheses of their own.

History in the Making is a complete course in eight volumes, to meet the needs of pupils between the ages of 11 and 16 (in other words up to and including the first public examination). However, each volume stands by itself and may be used independently of the others; given the variety of syllabuses in use in schools today this flexibility is likely to be welcomed by many teachers. *The Ancient World* and *The Medieval World* are intended primarily for 11–13-year-old pupils, *The Early Modern World 1450–1700*, for 12–14-year-olds, and *British Social and Economic History* and *World Conflict in the Twentieth Century* for GCSE examination candidates.

It is our hope that pupils will be encouraged, within the main topics and themes of British, European and World History, to experience for themselves the stimulus and challenge, the pleasure and frustration, the vitality and humanity that form an essential part of History in the Making.

John Jones

Note that volumes 7 and 8 in the series form a continuum on *British Social and Economic History*: the approach is thematic rather than strictly chronological, so both volumes are necessary for a complete coverage of the period.

Contents

A note on money values and measurements   9

Introduction
Population growth and change 1700–1985   10

Change in the countryside 1700–1914
1   The revolution in agriculture 1700–1815   22
2   Prosperity and depression: agriculture 1815–1914   42

The industrial revolution
3   Textiles in the industrial revolution   56
4   The iron industry: entrepreneurs in action   74
5   Coal in the industrial revolution   88
6   Power: the impact of steam   102
7   Revolution in transport: roads and canals to 1830   114
8   Railways: the communications revolution   138

Working conditions
9   Pauper apprentices: a study of working conditions   164
10   The fight to improve working conditions   172

Working-class reaction to change
11   Luddism and machine-breaking 1811–12   191
12   The working class and political change 1815–48   198
13   Trade unions 1750–1914   218

The 'Workshop of the World'
14   Industry and trade 1700–1870   244

Index   263
Acknowledgements   266

List of Maps

Where the people lived, 1700   15
Where the people lived, 1801   15
England as affected by Enclosure Acts   35
Aston Blank before enclosure   37
Aston Blank after enclosure   37
James Caird's division of the country in 1851   45
Main textile-making areas in 1750   59
Location of Cromford   73
Charcoal blast furnace sites, beginning of eighteenth century   75
Main British iron-producing areas, 1750–1850   82
Coalfields of England and Wales, 1830   90
Transport network serving the Poynton Collieries by 1850   100
Boulton and Watt engines in England and Wales, c. 1800   110
West Riding woollen mills using steam-power by 1800   111
Routes: the River Severn and the Potteries   114
Kendal in 1698 as centre for packhorse trains   115
Transport difficulties of the Potteries   129
Main canals and navigable rivers, 1830   133
A section of the Oxford Canal   137
Transport links between Liverpool and Manchester in 1830   140
Railways completed by 1849   147
Railway competition at Derby   148
The Northbury line   152
The Atlantic slave trade   248

A note on money values and measurements

Money values have been kept in old money. In most cases the modern equivalent has been added in brackets. The table gives some of the main equivalents.

Old money			New pence
2.4d		=	1p
6d		=	2½p
12d	= 1 shilling	=	5p
	10 shillings	=	50p
240d	= 20 shillings	= £1 =	100p

Imperial units of length and weight have also been retained with metric equivalents added in the text where this has been thought relevant, or as margin notes.

WEIGHT

Imperial units	Metric equivalent
1 ounce	28 grams
16 ounces = 1 lb	about ½ a kilo
2.2 lb	1 kilo
14 lb = 1 stone	6.4 kilos
112 lb or 8 stone = 1 hundredweight	about 50 kilos
20 hundredweights = 1 ton	about 1000 kilos

LENGTH

Imperial units	Metric equivalent
12 inches = 1 foot	30 centimetres
3 feet = 1 yard	
39.4 inches	1 metre

Using the evidence: population growth

No accurate population figures exist before the first census was taken in 1801. There are, however, estimates and a reasonably accurate count for Scotland in 1755.

In 1695 Gregory King, a civil servant, used tax returns to estimate a population for England and Wales of about 5 500 000. By 1750 this had probably climbed to between 6 000 000 and 6 500 000. The figure for Scotland in 1755 was 1 265 000.

	Total number of persons (millions)		Total number of persons (millions)
1801	10.5	1901	37.0
1811	12.0	1911	40.8
1821	14.0	1921	42.8
1831	16.3	1931	44.8
1841	18.5	1941	—
1851	20.8	1951	48.9
1861	23.1	1961	51.2
1871	26.1	1971	54.0
1881	29.7	1981	54.0
1891	33.0.		

Table 1   Population figures for England, Wales and Scotland, 1801–1981

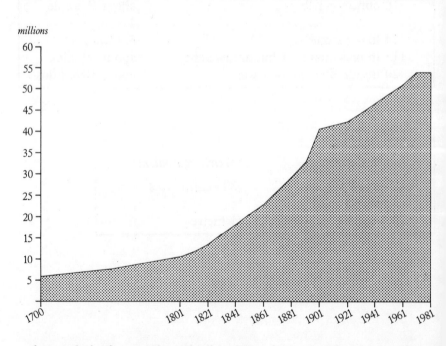

Table 2   The rate at which the population increased, 1700–1981

A population's growth or decline depends on the birth rate and the death rate. The birth rate is the number of babies born in a year per 1000 people in the population; the death rate is the number of people who die per 1000 people.

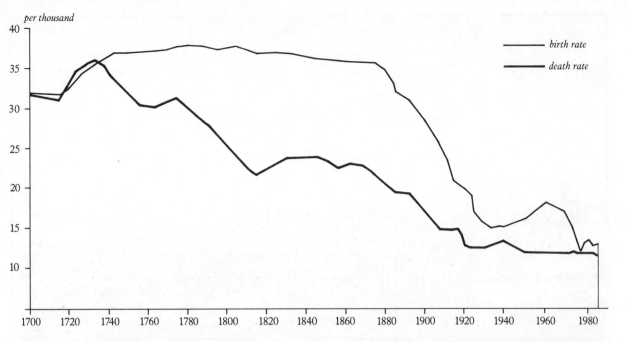

per thousand

1 Study Tables 1 and 2.
   (a) Briefly explain what happened to Britain's population in this
   period.
   (b) By how much did the population grow in these periods?
   1750–1801; 1801–1851; 1851–1901; 1901–1951.
   When was growth at its most rapid? What has happened to the rate
   of growth since 1900?
2 Now study Table 3.
   (a) Briefly explain what happened to the birth rate and the death rate
   in this period.
   (b) How does this chart help to explain the changes in the rate of
   population growth between 1700 and 1980?

*Table 3   The birth rate and the
death rate for Britain from the early
eighteenth century to the 1980s*

The eighteenth-century population explosion

Historians do not agree about the causes of the population explosion
that began about 1750. Table 3 should have told you that the birth rate
increased just before 1750 and then remained at a high level until about
1870. A fall in the death rate seems to have begun about 1750. The rate
fluctuated in the mid-nineteenth century but there was surplus of births
over deaths. These changes are signs of what was happening. They do
not provide an explanation.

The crucial time was the mid-eighteenth century. Historians and
demographers have carefully studied the problem, but their answers
are rarely in agreement.

Probably the falling death rate was more important than the high
birth rate. It seems that life expectancy at birth in 1700 was about 30

Life expectancy: the average age
to which an individual can expect
to live

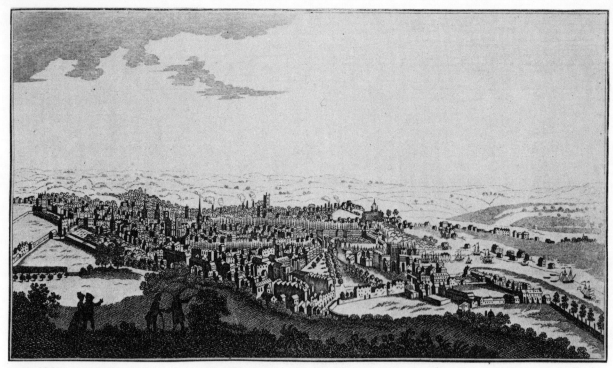

Bristol in the mid-eighteenth century. Apart from London, towns were still small places

years. A century later it had increased to 40 years. It was low because so many children died in infancy or childhood. During the century this high infant mortality rate fell slightly. More children survived into adulthood, married and produced children.

Some possible reasons for the rising birth rate and the falling death rate are given in the two charts.

A falling death rate

Disease was the main cause of death. In the eighteenth century there were no great epidemics. Smallpox remained a killer but its effects were slowly becoming less severe. The spread of inoculations may have helped but natural immunity was also spreading.

Famine and disease were partners. Those weakened by hunger, particularly children, are more susceptible to disease. A better-fed population can resist its attacks more effectively. In the 1730s, 1740s and 1750s there was a series of exceptionally good harvests. People had plenty to eat. Bad years in the second half of the century and the high prices that resulted did not mean famine. By then transport links had improved sufficiently to ensure that although there might be local shortages there was no actual starvation.

Medical improvements made little contribution to the falling death rate. Hospital conditions were appalling. there were about fifty in Britain in 1800. They only treated casualty and non-infectious cases. Infection was rife. It was the lucky patient who came out better, or who even died from the actual illness he had gone in with. The new lying-in hospitals for expectant mothers were dens of infection. In the mid-

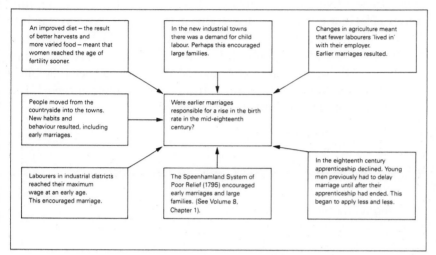

An improved diet – the result of better harvests and more varied food – meant that women reached the age of fertility sooner.

In the new industrial towns there was a demand for child labour. Perhaps this encouraged large families.

Changes in agriculture meant that fewer labourers 'lived in' with their employer. Earlier marriages resulted.

People moved from the countryside into the towns. New habits and behaviour resulted, including early marriages.

Were earlier marriages responsible for a rise in the birth rate in the mid-eighteenth century?

Labourers in industrial districts reached their maximum wage at an early age. This encouraged marriage.

The Speenhamland System of Poor Relief (1795) encouraged early marriages and large families. (See Volume 8, Chapter 1).

In the eighteenth century apprenticeship declined. Young men previously had to delay marriage until after their apprenticeship had ended. This began to apply less and less.

The rising birth rate, this was a consequence of early marriages. Some of the reasons suggested by historians and demographers for this change are highlighted on the chart. Why are they only ideas and hypotheses?

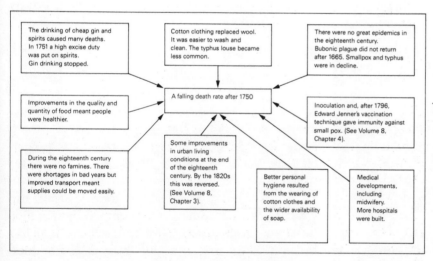

The drinking of cheap gin and spirits caused many deaths. In 1751 a high excise duty was put on spirits. Gin drinking stopped.

Cotton clothing replaced wool. It was easier to wash and clean. The typhus louse became less common.

There were no great epidemics in the eighteenth century. Bubonic plague did not return after 1665. Smallpox and typhus were in decline.

Improvements in the quality and quantity of food meant people were healthier.

A falling death rate after 1750

Inoculation and, after 1796, Edward Jenner's vaccination technique gave immunity against small pox. (See Volume 8, Chapter 4).

During the eighteenth century there were no famines. There were shortages in bad years but improved transport meant supplies could be moved easily.

Some improvements in urban living conditions at the end of the eighteenth century. By the 1820s this was reversed. (See Volume 8, Chapter 3).

Better personal hygiene resulted from the wearing of cotton clothes and the wider availability of soap.

Medical developments, including midwifery. More hospitals were built.

There is much debate amongst historians and demographers on the significance of these factors. They cannot really explain why the death rate fell

nineteenth century doctors were still advising mothers to have their babies at home. Only in the twentieth century did improved medical knowledge and techniques have a significant effect on the death rate.

The craze for cheap gin in the 1740s was an urban vice mainly confined to London. It did add to the mortality figures but its ending cannot have had an important effect on the national figures.

A gradual improvement in the standard of living through the eighteenth and nineteenth centuries contributed to an increased healthiness. Better food, a more varied diet, a more certain food supply, brick houses, more hygenic habits all combined to make this possible. Nevertheless living conditions were dirty and squalid. It was not until about 1750 that births exceeded deaths in the major towns. It was 1800 before this happened in London and Middlesex. The population of towns was increased by migration, not by births. Average infant mortality in the country at large remained at around 150 per 1000 births for most of the nineteenth century. It was much higher in towns. Life expectancies in urban slums were under 20 years.

Using the evidence: Gin Lane and Beer Street

1 Compare the two pictures.
(a) What does Hogarth blame the gin craze for? Refer to the illustration in your answer.
(b) How would things improve in 'Beer Street'? Again refer to the illustration in your answer.
2 Does 'Gin Lane' give an accurate portrayal of London life in the mid-eighteenth century? Explain your answer.

These scenes show eighteenth-century London as William Hogarth saw it ('Gin Lane') and as he thought it should be ('Beer Street')

3 Is there any evidence in the pictures which could be used to date
them?
4 Which explanation for the falling death rate could these prints be
linked with?
5 What other reasons are there to explain the growth in Britain's
population in the eighteenth and early nineteenth centuries? Why do
historians and demographers disagree about them?

The changing distribution of the population

Daniel Defoe noted in the 1720s that England south of the River Trent
was 'the most populous part of the country, and definitely fuller of great
towns, of people, and of trade'.

The area around London was the most densely populated, followed
by the southern counties in a broad band from Devon to Norfolk.
England was predominantly an agricultural country and these areas
contained the best farming land.

London, with almost 600 000 people, outstripped the next largest
towns, Bristol and Norwich, which had about 25 000–30 000. Most
people still lived in the countryside or small rural centres although
places like Manchester, Liverpool, Newcastle-upon-Tyne and Birmingham were beginning to attract a greater population.

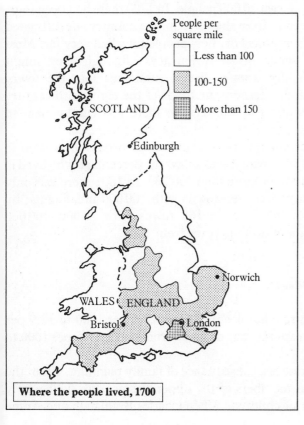

Where the people lived, 1700

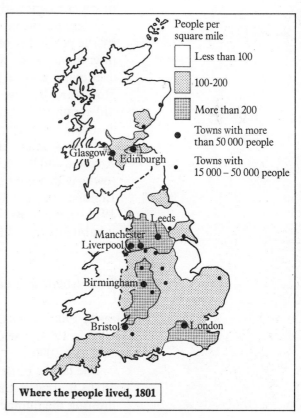

Where the people lived, 1801

Table 4   A population of town dwellers

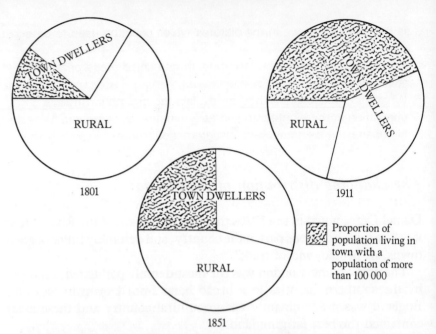

1801

1851

1911

Proportion of population living in town with a population of more than 100 000

By 1801 industrial change was having an effect. The counties and towns which had grown most rapidly in population were, with the exception of London, on the coalfields (see Map 2, page 15). There were almost one million people in London, but Liverpool, Manchester, Glasgow, Edinburgh and Birmingham had 70 000 or more. There were nineteen towns with at least 20 000 people. In 1700 there had been four.

These people moved in from the surrounding countryside, attracted by the possibility of employment. Few people travelled very far. Most migrations were a series of short journeys although they might eventually take a family from a distant rural area into the town. However, the new arable farming methods of the eighteenth century did require large numbers of workers, so there was employment to absorb a large proportion of the rural population increase.

Table 4 shows the change from a rural to an urban population in England and Wales. The shaded area shows the percentage who lived in towns with a population of more than 100 000. In 1801 there was only London. In 1851 there were ten towns with 100 000 inhabitants; by 1911 there were 36. There were 165 towns with 20 000–100 000 inhabitants in 1911, a tenfold increase from 1801.

The twentieth century

Since 1900 the birth rate has declined from 28.6 per 1000 to 12.9 per 1000 in 1984. The death rate has dropped from about 17.5 per 1000 to 11.5 per 1000.

The falling birth rate is a consequence of family planning. From the 1870s it appears that members of the upper classes were deliberately limiting the number of children. When Charles Bradlaugh and Annie

Besant, however, advocated birth control for all at that time they were accused of immorality.

During and after the First World War knowledge of contraceptive devices filtered down to all social classes. Amongst the middle classes they were quickly adopted. In the 1920s and the 1930s the choice was frequently between a baby and a Baby Austin. The car and a better standard of living often won. The easy availability of the contraceptive pill from the late 1960s confirmed the trend to smaller families amongst all social classes. An average family size of six children in the 1890s had become two children by the 1950s.

The continued fall in the death rate prevented population decline. Medical developments and improved welfare provision were responsible for this. Vaccines were discovered against the old childhood killer-diseases, diptheria, measles, whooping cough and polio. The BCG vaccine, discovered in 1906, has effectively eliminated tuberculosis, a major nineteenth-century killer. School medical inspection began in 1907. Under the Welfare State children in the 1980s are fitter, taller, heavier and better developed than their predecessors one hundred years ago.

Infectious diseases were the killers of the nineteenth century. Modern antibiotics can combat most infectious diseases. The effects of penicillin, the first antibiotic, were observed by Alexander Fleming in 1928. Howard Florey and Ernest Chain proved its value by their research work between 1939 and 1941. Mass production began in 1942 under pressure of wartime needs. Today's major killers are cancers and heart disease.

The conurbations

By 1900 conurbations had grown up. These are urban areas where towns join each other with no country between. In the 1901 census 40 per cent of the population lived in the seven conurbations:

Central Clydeside
Greater London
Merseyside
South East Lancashire
Tyneside
West Midlands
West Yorkshire

This had fallen to 33 per cent in the 1971 census and all the conurbations showed a further loss of inhabitants in 1981. Greater London has had the greatest reduction from 8.2 million in 1951 to 6.7 million thirty years later.

London's loss has not reduced population in the South East. Commuters have just moved out into the pleasanter home counties, all of which have had large population increases. Regions of declining industries, the North, Yorkshire, the North West and Wales have also experienced a relative decline in population.

The age-structure of the population

These age-pyramids show the numbers of males and females in different age groups.

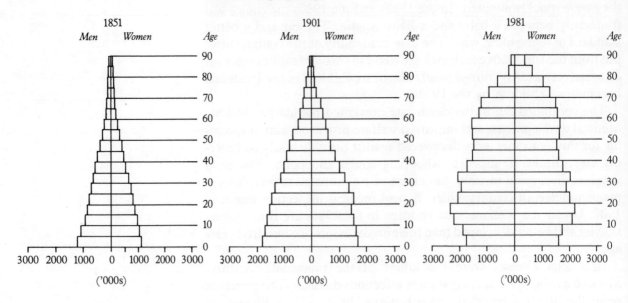

Questions

1 What can you deduce about life expectancy in 1851?
2 Compare the 1851 and 1981 pyramids. What changes have taken place in the make-up of the population?
3 How do you explain these changes?
4 What problems for society does an increasingly elderly population present?

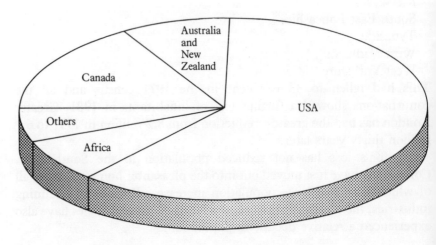

About 14 million people emigrated from the British Isles between 1800 and 1914. The chart shows where they went. Why do you think the United States was the most popular destination?

Immigration

Throughout the last two hundred years immigrants have settled in Britain. There have been three main waves of immigrants, the Irish in the nineteenth century, Jews escaping from persecution in Russia and Eastern Europe around 1900 and immigrants from the New Commonwealth since the 1950s.

Immigrant communities have always faced prejudice and resentment. The Irish in the mid-nineteenth century were the poorest of the working class. Escaping from hunger and poverty in Ireland they lived in the worst slums. Little Ireland in Manchester was notorious for its filth and squalor. Irishmen did the worst jobs. They had a reputation for drunkenness and violence in an age in which both were common.

Local working people resented the Irish, especially when times were hard. The Irish were prepared to work for starvation wages. In June 1852 there were three days of anti-Irish rioting in Stockport. Out of a population of 60 000 about 14 000 were Irish. In Irish streets houses occupied by the English were marked with chalk and undamaged. The rest were invaded and wrecked. The Irish population was driven out of the town. Two Roman Catholic chapels were destroyed, one Irishman was killed.

Successive failures of the potato crop in the late 1840s caused a disastrous famine in Ireland. Many emigrated to England and Scotland to escape its consequences

The attack on the Chapels, which seems, at first sight, to suggest the impression that religious animosity might have had a good deal to do with the matter, we think is easily explained by the circumstances, that when the passions of the English got fairly excited, and they found how little there was in the shape of furniture to be destroyed in the wretched Irish dwellings they sacked, they felt the vengeance taken so utterly inadequate as to the provocation and insults they had received that they very probably attacked and demolished the Chapels as the only property belonging to the Irish which was of any value, and the loss of which would be a serious detriment or annoyance to their adversaries.

Stockport Advertiser, June 1852

Our readers must have observed that the man who was killed was an Irishman; the 50 wounded, many of them very seriously, were Irishmen; the 114 prisoners were all Irishmen; the chapels that were gutted were all of them Roman Catholic; the houses that were ransacked and half-destroyed were all those of Irishmen. . . . How shall we solve this enigma? Were the Irish gutting their own chapels, breaking one another's heads, and turning their own houses inside-out?

The Times, June 1852

Question

Which side does each of these newspaper comments sympathise with? Explain your answer by referring to the sources.

Multi-racial triumph: the British team celebrate their 4 × 400 metres relay victory at the 1986 European Games

Similar passions were stirred up by the arrival of immigrants from the West Indies, India, Pakistan and Bangladesh. Prejudice in these cases was further complicated by differences of colour. Many immigrants were attracted to Britain by its shortage of labour in the 1950s. They were often encouraged to come by the British authorities; 1961 was the peak year with 136 000 immigrants. The 1962 Immigration Act reduced the numbers entering.

There had always been coloured communities in the ports but now districts of many cities became their homes; 1958 witnessed the first serious race riots in Notting Hill, London, an indication of growing tension between different racial communities. The first Race Relations Act was passed in 1966. It set up a Race Relations Board to end discrimination.

Problems remain. Coloured communities are often concentrated in the most deprived inner city areas. Unemployment amongst young black Britons is higher than amongst whites. The police and other authorities are accused of discrimination. Becoming a multi-ethnic community is not an easy process.

The importance of population growth

The eighteenth-century population growth, continuing through into the nineteenth, provided the workforce and a market for the Industrial Revolution. In its turn industrial growth encouraged growth in population.

A rapidly growing population created serious problems. Agriculture had to expand to satisfy new demands for food. Rapidly expanding towns and cities contained squalid and disease-ridden slums. There were too many people to be treated in the old ways.

Farmers responded to the challenge successfully. Industrialists benefited from a growing workforce and home market. With a greatly expanded population, government had to intervene to set new standards in health, education and other fields.

Change in the countryside 1700–1914

1 The revolution in agriculture 1700–1815

Thomas Coke of Holkham, Norfolk, inspects his Southdown sheep. Every year he invited his tenants, neighbours and fellow landowners to join him at the sheep-shearing. New methods and ideas were discussed and exchanged

a guinea was worth £1.05

A stone is a measure of weight. It is 14lb or about 7 kilos. Was the weight of the pig exaggerated? Look at Source D

Using the evidence: new ideas on the farm, 1800

As you read the sources and study the pictures, list all the points which suggest farming was changing at the end of the eighteenth century.

A

B Arthur Young, the leading agricultural writer of his time, explains why there was a renewed interest in agricultural change in Norfolk at the end of the eighteenth century.

About this time also, Mr Coke . . . began his sheep-shearing meetings. . . . The scarcities, and consequent high prices, brought immense sums into the country, and enabled farmers to exert themselves with uncommon vigour. South Down sheep came in about the same time. A disposition was established, that would not readily reject a proposal merely because it was new. . . .

General View of the Agriculture of the County of Norfolk, 1804

C In 1800 the Duke of Bedford held a four day sheep-shearing festival at Woburn Abbey. Here are some of the events. Coke's gatherings were very similar.

. . . the company proceeded in a grand cavalcade to the New Farm-yard . . . for the purpose of inspecting the sheep-shearing, at which five of the best hands . . . were employed. They then proceeded to the building . . . for examining the ewes that are to be let for the next season. . . .

The certificates were then opened by his Grace and a Committee, of the different candidates for the prize of fifty guineas [£52.50], to be given by his Grace for encouraging the introduction of the Leicester and South Down breed of sheep into Bedfordshire. . . .

. . . A very fine hog . . . was shown, which was supposed to weigh about a hundred stone . . . His Grace then conducted the company to a paddock . . . to see some select Devonshire oxen . . . to the water meadow . . . where there were some very fine Devonshire cows. . .

. . . Several improved implements in husbandry were exhibited. . . .

. . . The company . . . proceeded to a fallow field . . . where experiments were tried by five different ploughs. . . . Experiments were made with Mr Leicester's scuffling harrows . . . his Grace . . . having offered a premium of twenty guineas [£21] to the person who should produce at this sheep-shearing, the best and most newly invented implement in agriculture. . . .

husbandry: farming

Farmer's Magazine, 1800

D

A proud owner displays his prize Durham Shorthorns. What seem to be the main features of these beasts?

E

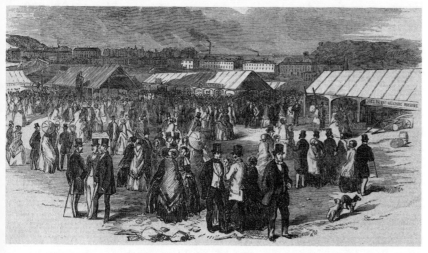

The show organised by the Bath and West of England Agricultural Society, 1853

1 How were Thomas Coke and the Duke of Bedford encouraging new farming methods and ideas by their sheep-shearing festivals?
2 How would you describe the animals in source D? Why do you think its owner was painted with them?
3 What reasons for the interest of farmers in new ideas are suggested in source B?
4 What is the connection between the event described in source C and the agricultural show illustrated in source E? Explain your answer.

An agricultural revolution?

The rapid population growth of the eighteenth and nineteenth centuries meant more food had to be grown. In addition an expanding transport system dependent on the horse required vast quantities of fodder. The achievement of Britain's farmers in the hundred years after 1750 was that they increased production to satisfy these new demands. It has been estimated that in 1850 home-produced grain fed 80 per cent of the population. This was mainly due to an increase of the cultivated acreage, but new methods and techniques also played their part. All this was done with only a slightly enlarged labour force.

Historians have written about an 'Agricultural Revolution' which accompanied the Industrial Revolution. The changes that took place, however, were very gradual and often had roots stretching back into the sixteenth and seventeenth centuries. Moreover, the pace of change varied from county to county, often from one village to the next. While oxen were still ploughing in Sussex, elsewhere the steam engine was making its first appearance on the farming scene. In 1850 a surprised James Caird watched ox-teams ploughing on the Sussex Downs using wooden ploughs which had been superseded by improved models during the previous century.

Industrial change depended on machines. New machinery played a limited role in improving agricultural productivity before the 1850s. Farming continued to employ a large workforce – about 2 000 000 in 1851.

Farming in the early eighteenth century

Travelling throughout the farmland of England in the 1720s Daniel Defoe noted farming's regional specialisations. Already London acted as a magnet, drawing its supplies of grain, meat, cheese and other produce from all over the country. Cattle driven from the Scottish Highlands were fattened up in Norfolk for sale in London, whilst the Essex marshlands were the destination of the cattle driven from Wales. Defoe saw turkeys and geese driven on foot from Norfolk and Suffolk or travelling on carts,

> . . . with four stories or stages, to put the creatures in one above another, by which invention one cart will carry a very great number; and for the smoother going they drive with two horses a-breast, like a coach . . . changing horses they travel night and day; so that they bring the fowls 70, 80, or 100 miles in two days and one night. . . .

He described orchards and hop fields in Kent, corn growing in Essex and at Wey Hill in Wiltshire 'the greatest fair for sheep . . . that this nation can show'; where five hundred thousand animals changed hands.

store sheep: kept for fattening

> . . . the sheep sold here are not for immediate killing, but are generally ewes for store sheep for the farmers, and they send for them from all the following

counties, Berks, Oxford, Bucks, Bedford, Hertford, Middlesex, Kent, Surrey and Sussex. . . .

Covent Garden in the late eighteenth century. Fruit, vegetables and flowers from a wide area were sold in this London market

In Suffolk,

The county around Ipswich, as are all the counties so near the coast, is applied chiefly to corn, of which a very great quantity is continually shipped off for London, and sometimes they load corn here for Holland. . . .

At Woodbridge, in the same county, there was a

. . . considerable market for butter and corn to be exported to London . . . The butter is barrelled, or often pickled up in small casks, and sold, not in London only, but I have known a firkin of Suffolk butter sent to the West Indies. . . .

firkin: a barrel holding about 28 kilos

Somerset sent cattle and cheddar cheese to London whilst horses went to the Midlands. Cider from Hereford reached the capital in large quantities. The excellent grazing in Cheshire ensured a plentiful supply of milk for the cheese that county produced

. . . in such quantities, and so exceeding good, that as I am told from very good authority, the city of London only takes off 1400 ton every year; besides the 8000 ton which they say goes every year down the Rivers Severn and Trent . . . besides the quantity ship'd both here, and at Liverpool, to go to Ireland and Scotland. . . .

Developing industrial areas also attracted produce from a wide area. Defoe went to Halifax in the West Riding and found

. . . their corn comes up in great quantities out of Lincoln, Nottingham, and the East Riding, their black cattle and horses from the North Riding, their sheep and mutton from the adjacent counties everyway, their butter from the East and North Riding, their cheese out of Cheshire and Warwickshire, more black cattle also from Lancashire. . . .

A Tour Through the Whole Island of Great Britain, 1726

Although there were many small subsistence farmers merely producing enough to feed their families with an occasional surplus for sale in local markets, Defoe provides evidence that farmers and landowners were producing for wider markets. These were the people who would adopt new methods and techniques if they proved to be profitable.

The new ideas

Eighteenth-century innovations were of three types – new crops and rotations, improved breeding methods, and new agricultural techniques.

1 New crops and rotations

In 1700 the vast majority of farmers, whether in the open fields or on enclosed farms, followed a rotation of crops, which had come down from the Middle Ages almost unchanged. Every third year, land would be left fallow with the cattle and sheep turned on to it to revitalise it with their manure.

Richard Weston had written about turnip cultivation in the mid-seventeenth century. Clover was another new crop being grown in Norfolk at that time. Lord 'Turnip' Townshend's successful improvement of his Raynham estates in Norfolk using turnips and clover popularised them. By 1750 new rotations using turnips, clover or other grasses were becoming common.

The Norfolk four-course rotation alternated the grain crops with turnips, a root crop, and clover, which put nitrogen into the soil. It was widely adopted in East Anglia because it suited the area's sandy soils. Sheep were turned onto the turnip fields in the winter. They ate the crop and by careful management manured the land for the next grain crop. Clover was also a highly nutritious fodder crop. More animals could be kept, and selective breeding became more possible.

Arthur Young was in Suffolk in 1784:

arable: crop-growing

July 23, crossed Sampford hundred to Woolverston; I had a great inclination to be informed of the management in this part of the county . . . The management is exceedingly masterly; the soil dry and sandy, all arable, . . . Their course is 1 turnips, 2 barley, 3 clover, 4 wheat. I was pleased with finding that all the dung they can raise is spread on their turnip land . . . They know so well the importance of this application of manure, that they buy large quantities at Maningtree from London, which costs 12s [60p] a five-horse load at the quay, and 20s [£1] by the time it is on the land. . . . Kentish chalk is also purchased . . . with which they form composts. They feed the turnips on the land with bullocks and sheep . . . the clover supports all the stock of the farm. . . .

Tours in England and Wales, Tour to Woodbridge etc. July 1784
from the Annals of Agriculture

Turnips, however, were vulnerable to pests, so swedes and mangel-wurzels emerged as alternative root crops. By the end of the century it was becoming apparent that too much clover could damage the soil, and other grasses were coming into the rotation.

Since the turnip needed a well-drained soil it did not flourish on the heavy clays of the Midlands. Ley farming was practised here. Several years of grain crops were followed by a lengthy period when the field lay under turf grazed by cattle.

The new rotations increased food production by eliminating the wasteful fallow year. Land was used more productively and more efficiently.

The traditional method
A triennial rotation

The rotations

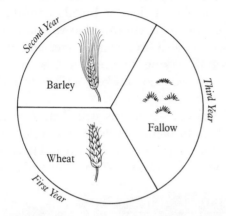

Norfolk four course rotation
A four year rotation

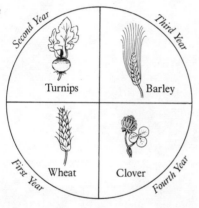

Ley farming
This cycle took
twelve years
to run through

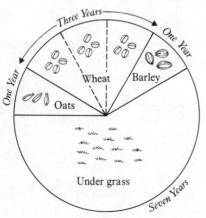

Based on W. Marshall, *Rural Economy of the Midland Counties* (1790)

2 Selective breeding

Robert Bakewell (1725–95), of Dishley in Leicestershire, has had the highest reputation of all the eighteenth-century breeders but he was one amongst many and his new breeds were not particularly successful.

On his Dishley farm he pioneered breeding methods which were to be widely adopted. At the beginning of the century it was probably four to five years before a sheep or bullock was sufficiently fattened for the butcher. Bakewell aimed to breed a sheep that would fatten quickly. The result was his New Leicester breed. Unfortunately, although weight was put on quickly, the mutton was very fatty and could only be sold at low prices. He also bred shire horses and experimented with cattle, unsuccessfully trying to build a new breed based on the longhorn. These proved poor milkers and were unsatisfactory beef animals.

The annual ram-letting at Robert Bakewell's Dishley Farm. What kind of sheep are they? Why is there such a demand to hire them?

Others used Bakewell's methods with better results. About 1780 John Ellman and Jonas Webb developed the highly successful Southdown sheep, good for both mutton and wool, whilst in the North East the Colling brothers bred good beef cattle out of shorthorn stock.

Bakewell was much in demand, entertaining many noble visitors on his farm and advising great landlords on their breeding policies. His success made him a wealthy man: in 1789 his ram 'Two Pounder' earned 200 guineas in breeding fees. Other farmers copied his methods and experimented for themselves. In 1784 Arthur Young found a Mr Toosey who only farmed seventy acres but,

. . . has been some years a very attentive practiser of Mr Bakewell's cattle-husbandry. . . .

His cattle are of Bakewell's breed . . . The bull which he calls 'Twopenny' from that of Bakewell's . . . is . . . a very fine one, particularly in the breadth and straitness of his back, the barrel carcass, and the short leg. He leaps cows at half a guinea, at which rate many have been brought to him. . . . In tying up all his cattle, Mr Toosey copies Bakewell's system. . . . The sheep are equally well made with the cattle; some few he sells for the breed, but gets from 30s [150p] to £3 for two-year-old wethers from the butchers.

wether: a castrated ram

A practice in which this gentleman is perfectly original, is that of stall-feeding his sheep in winter. . . .

Upon occasion of straw and stubble being scarce, Mr Toosey bedded all his cattle with sand, and found that . . . it did very well. . . .

Tours in England and Wales; Tour to Woodbridge etc. July 1784

3 Improved farming techniques

In 1768 Arthur Young made his first tour of Norfolk and enthused about everything he saw.

All the country from Holkham to Houghton was a wild sheep walk before the spirit of improvement seized the inhabitants, and this glorious spirit has wrought amazing effects: for instead of boundless wilds and uncultivated wastes inhabited by scarce anything but sheep, the country is all cut into enclosures, cultivated in a most husbandlike manner, richly manured, well peopled, and yielding a hundred times the produce than it did in its former state.

Southern Tour, 1768

Three years later he explained how this change had been brought about.

The great improvements have been made by means of the following circumstances:

FIRST By inclosing without assistance of Parliament.
SECOND By a spirited use of marle and clay.
THIRD By the introduction of an excellent course of crops.
FOURTH By the culture of turnips well hand-hoed.
FIFTH By the culture of clover and ray-grass.
SIXTH By landlords granting long leases.
SEVENTH By the country being divided chiefly into large farms.
The Farmer's Tour through the East of England, 1771

Norfolk was the county where the most extensive improvement had taken place, and, as Young suggests, it was more than a change in rotations and crops.

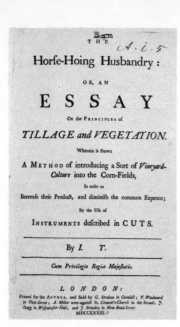

THE
Horſe-Hoing Husbandry:
OR, AN
ESSAY
On the Principles of
TILLAGE and VEGETATION.
Wherein is ſhewn
A Method of introducing a Sort of *Vineyard-Culture* into the Corn-Fields,
In order to
Increaſe their Product, and diminiſh the common Expence;
By the Uſe of
Instruments deſcribed in CUTS.

By I. T.

Cum Privilegio Regiæ Majeſtatis.

LONDON:
Printed for the Author, and Sold by G. Strahan in Cornhill; T. Woodward in Fleet-Street; A. Miller over-againſt St. Clement's-Church in the Strand; J. Stagg in Weſtminſter-Hall; and J. Brindley in New-Bond-Street. MDCCXXXIII.

The title page of Jethro Tull's book on farming methods. Where did he get his ideas from?

The light sandy soils were improved by the addition of marl, a type of clay. Added to the thin Norfolk soils it improved water retention. Dug from pits where it occurred near the surface, marl was carried to the farm by the wagonload. Marling was expensive – it would cost about £2 an acre – but many landlords were prepared to pay this, whilst others bound tenants to marl their land as a condition of their lease.

Marling was not new, but it was re-discovered in the eighteenth century and became an essential part of farming in Norfolk and Suffolk. Lord Townshend was said to have introduced it into Norfolk but there is evidence that it was used earlier. Townshend was an improver, not a transformer of farming methods.

In the 1720s Defoe saw Essex farmers spreading vast quantities of chalk from Kent and Sussex on their land. Lime and chalk were used as fertilisers and to improve drainage on heavy clay soils. The extension of the canal network across the Midlands gave farmers access to cheap lime. Lime kilns were frequently sited near canals.

Agricultural writers in the eighteenth century stressed the importance of manuring the land. Farmers diligently conserved the supplies produced by their own animals and grazed sheep on the turnip fields in carefully controlled patterns. All this was supplemented by 'town muck' brought out by road or river, and, after the 1760s, by canal.

New machines played no part in these eighteenth-century changes on the farm. Jethro Tull (1674–1741) did invent a horse hoe and a seed drill. He had an active, enquiring mind and experimented with new methods on his land in Berkshire. Although many of his ideas were mistaken, he did believe in the importance of hoeing between rows of turnips to keep down weeds and to aerate the soil. His horse-drawn hoe was designed to break the soil deeper than the hand hoe, and his seed drill enabled him to sow his seeds in straight lines with the minimum

Tull's seed drill

waste. The seed drill was a good idea but it was the end of the century before successful examples were manufactured, and hand-hoeing of root crops still employed large numbers of labourers a hundred years after Tull's death.

Cheap iron made the manufacture of machines possible, but progress was bound to be slow until specialised firms began to make farm implements. During the eighteenth century farmers depended on local craftsmen working with traditional materials. Early in the nineteenth century, agricultural-machinery firms like Ransome of Ipswich appeared and a wider range of farm machinery was soon available. Nevertheless the most common farm machine before the 1830s remained the mechanical thresher, powered by hand, horse or even, on a few progressive farms, by a steam engine. Andrew Meikle's machine quickly became popular after its appearance in 1786.

4 Spreading the new ideas

Arthur Young (1741–1820), the leading agricultural journalist, had not made a success of his farming ventures as a young man. In 1788, however, he inherited the family estate at Bradfield in Suffolk and was able to conduct his own agricultural experiments. He made his first 'tour' in 1767. Young visited a district and then wrote about the things he saw, commenting on the state of farming. By 1771 he had published his *Southern*, *Northern* and *Eastern Tours*.

In 1784 Young began to edit the *Annals of Agriculture*. All the latest progressive methods were discussed in its pages and he continued to make his tours, reporting his findings to his readers. He could write as a practical farmer but the circulation of the *Annals* was never very large – no more than 400 copies. It probably had very little direct influence on the ordinary farmer, but Young could inspire by his own enthusiasm and interest and he probably achieved more by personal contact and discussion than through his writings. A French visitor touring Suffolk with him in 1784 saw him at work.

It is incredible how intelligent the farmers are, even the small farmers. . . . I have seen a hundred of them talking with Mr Young on the principles of their calling, making suggestions and recounting their experiences for three-quarters of an hour or an hour; they never fail to win Mr Young's admiration, though he was well used to it.

A constant stream of visitors made their way to Bradfield but not all were impressed. In December 1784 George Culley, a breeder from the North East wrote:

. . . people that devote their time to writing cannot act or execute; his sheep are scabbed, his cattle ill-chosen and worse managed, in short he exhibits a sad picture of mismanagement.

In 1793 Young became Secretary to the Board of Agriculture. The Board was to encourage the discussion of new ideas, solve technical problems, and protect the interests of landowners and farmers.

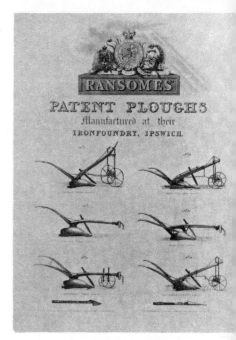

There was a wide choice of ploughs to suit all soils

Arthur Young

Unfortunately it was not official, its funds were inadequate and its reports were not widely read. Within ten years in had collapsed.

Landowners were the best placed to encourage progressive methods on their estates. In Norfolk Thomas Coke (1750–1842) of Holkham Hall was a renowned agricultural pioneer much praised by Arthur Young. He gave his tenants long leases but carefully laid down the farming systems and rotations they had to adopt. He used oil cake as a cattle feed and encouraged the use of sainfoin and other fodder crops as alternatives to clover. He introduced Southdown sheep to Norfolk and further improved the breed. About 1790 he began his annual sheep-shearing meets, private agricultural shows which did much to spread knowledge of the new farming.

Questions

1 Briefly describe the contributions made by Lord Townshend, Robert Bakewell and Jethro Tull to the development of agriculture in the eighteenth century.
2 Do you think that they deserve the reputation they have had as the great pioneers of farming change? Explain your answer.

Enclosure

At the beginning of the eighteenth century much of the arable land in the midland counties of England was still farmed in the medieval 'open' fields. Increasingly, improving landowners and farmers wanted to change. It was very difficult to adopt the new farming methods in the open fields.

Many Midlands villages were still surrounded by three huge open fields and the common land where most inhabitants had grazing rights. Usually each farmer's land was scattered through the open fields in strips. Each year one field was left fallow, grazed over by the village animals to manure it and restore its fertility. Farming was a communal activity. All grew the same crops, whilst ploughing and harvesting were community activities when equipment and labour were shared. On the commons all the villagers' animals mingled together. Selective breeding and stock improvement was impossible. New crop rotations could only be tried if all the farmers agreed.

The answer was enclosure. This was not new in the eighteenth century. For centuries local landowners had enclosed land by agreement amongst themselves, or one landowner might purchase a neighbour's land and then enclose it. In open-field villages farmers often agreed to form their land into compact units by exchanging their strips of land.

These methods were slow. In the eighteenth century improving landlords turned to enclosure by Act of Parliament. This was expensive but it was quick and it enabled the large landowner to steamroll over any opposition from small landowners.

Enclosure by Act of Parliament – the process

1 Owners of largest proportion of land agree. Usually they were the owners of four-fifths of the land. At Wigston Magna, Leicestershire, this was 20 out of 99 landowners. Elsewhere it was often fewer. In many cases the petition was signed by one landowner or by the chief landowner and the vicar.

2 Those in agreement petitioned Parliament for an Act. After 1774 they had to give public notice to the rest of the community.

3 The Bill was referred to a committee of the House of Commons. Opponents had to present their case at this stage. This was difficult for small landowners and villagers distant from London. Opposition was only successful if a powerful or important landowner was against the enclosure proposal.

4 The Act was passed.

5 Enclosure commissioners arrived in the village. They had to decide on claims to land in the enclosed village. They drew up field and farm boundaries, laid out roads and ditches, altered the course of streams and rivers.

6 The cost of enclosure had to be met. All who received land had to contribute to the legal fees, the commissioners' expenses and the fencing of land given to the church in compensation for the abolition of tithe payments. The cost of hedging and ditching had to be added to this. Average cost at the end of the eighteenth century was 28 shillings (140p) an acre. A smallholder with about 20 acres had to find from £50 to £70 at Wigston Magna.

Using the evidence: the problem of the open fields

A In this extract Arthur Young expresses the improving farmer's horror at the waste and conservatism of the open fields.

19 July 1791. Taking the road from Cambridge to St Neot's, view for six or seven miles the worst husbandry I hope in Great Britain. All in the fallow system, and the loss of time, and the expense submitted to, without the common benefit, these fallows are overrun with thistles. . . .

. . . all the way from Cambridge, must be classed amongst the ugliest counties in England. The lands mostly open field, at 6s. an acre. The management very bad, much strong clay, and some fallows not yet ploughed; the course

1 Fallow, ploughed thrice; breaking up . . . Two stirrings. . . .
2 Wheat, produce 14 or 15 bush. per acre. . . .
3 Oats or beans.

About St Neot's a vast improvement by an inclosure, which took place 16 years ago. . . .

A Month's Tour to Northamptonshire, Leicestershire, 1791

But were open-field farmers always as bad as this?

B In 1785 Young had viewed the open fields at Royston.

The farmers are sensible, intelligent men, for they agree amongst themselves to sow turnips instead of fallowing on many of their lands; and also sainfoin by keeping off their sheep in the spring. It succeeds excellently, has been worth at one cutting £7 an acre. . . . They also use much oil-cake on their land. . . .

Annals of Agriculture, V, 1785

1 What does source A reveal about the farming methods in open fields?
2 Arthur Young was impressed by what he saw at Royston. Was open-field farming always inefficient and wasteful? Use the evidence from both sources in your answer.
3 'About St Neot's a vast improvement by an inclosure' – what does this comment tell us about Young's attitudes and opinions?

Many large landowners enclosed to increase their rents. If farmers were producing more and making greater profits the landlord had to get his share. Enclosure made farming more efficient and productive. Farmers were able to adopt the new rotations and could keep improved flocks of sheep or herds of cattle.

Farms were made into convenient units and the pattern of farm buildings surrounded by fields was set. Drainage could be improved and a planned road system made movement easier. Most important of all, however, at a time of growing population, more land was brought under cultivation, especially during the high price years of the French Wars. Marginal land on the Sussex Downs, for instance, previously only poor sheep runs, was ploughed up for arable.

bush: a bushel. Unit of measurement for grain

About 6 million acres of open fields, commons and waste were enclosed, nearly half of that wasteland made productive for the first time. Around 4000 Enclosure Acts were passed between 1750 and 1850, mainly in the 1760s and 1770s (900 Acts) and during the French Wars from 1793–1815 (2000 Acts), when grain prices were high.

Harvest time in the open fields at Cambridge about 1730. Arthur Young visited them in 1791

Questions

1 The map shows the areas most affected by Enclosure Acts. Were they needed all over the country? Why not? What conclusion can you draw about farming systems before enclosure in the Midlands?

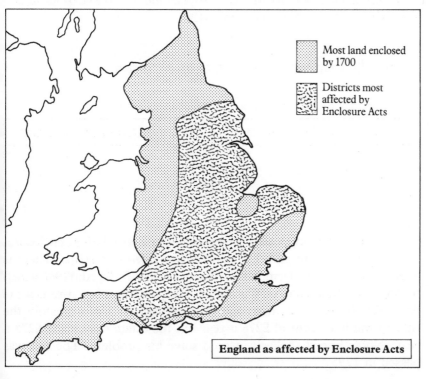

Most land enclosed by 1700

Districts most affected by Enclosure Acts

England as affected by Enclosure Acts

From: The Agricultural
Revolution 1750–1880 by J. D.
Chambers & G. E. Mingay

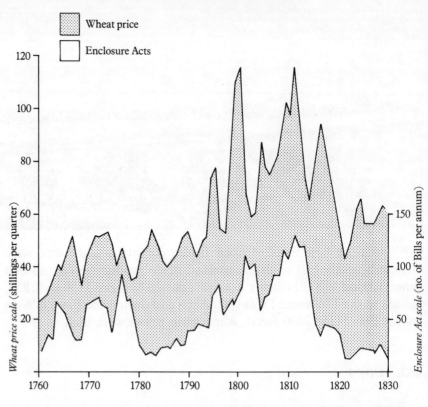

2 These graphs link the price of wheat with the number of Enclosure
Acts passed each year from 1760 to 1830:
Using the evidence of the graphs explain the rise in Enclosure Acts
in the 1770s, and from 1793 to 1812.

Using the evidence: the effects of enclosure

As you read through the sources complete this table:

Benefits of enclosure	Disadvantages of enclosure

Look at source A, opposite. It shows Aston Blank before enclosure.
Notice the commons and the open fields divided into strips. There is
already one enclosed farm in the village. Over half the land (940 acres)
belonged to the Bishop of Waterford. He gave it to his son-in-law the
Rev. M. Noble on his marriage to his daughter. Unfortunately the
Bishop wanted a rent of £276 a year but the estate only made £275 a
year. Noble hoped enclosure would solve his problem. The Act was
passed in 1795.

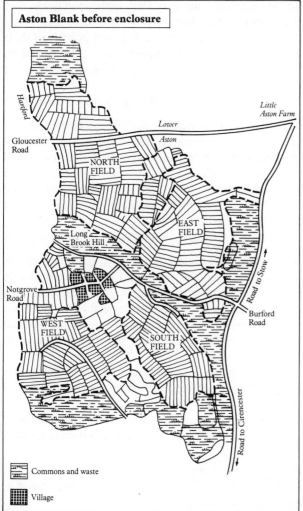

Aston Blank before enclosure

Hartford
Lower
Aston
Little
Aston Farm
Gloucester
Road
NORTH
FIELD
EAST
FIELD
Long
Brook Hill
Notgrove
Road
WEST
FIELD
SOUTH
FIELD
Road to Stow
Burford
Road
Road to Cirencester

Commons and waste

Village

A *Aston Blank, Gloucestershire in 1752*

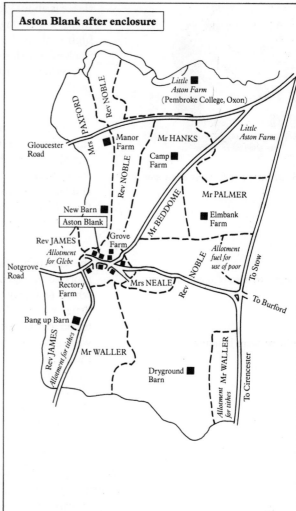

Aston Blank after enclosure

Rev NOBLE
Mrs PAXFORD
Little
Aston Farm
(Pembroke College, Oxon)
Manor
Farm
Mr HANKS
Camp
Farm
Little
Aston Farm
Gloucester
Road
Rev NOBLE
Mr PALMER
Mr BEDDOME
New Barn
Elmbank
Farm
Aston Blank
Rev JAMES
Grove
Farm
Allotment
for Glebe
Allotment
fuel for
use of poor
Notgrove
Road
Rectory
Farm
Mrs NEALE
Rev NOBLE
To Stow
To Burford
Bang up Barn
Rev JAMES
Allotment for tithes
Mr WALLER
Dryground
Barn
Mr WALLER
Allotment for tithes
To Cirencester

B *The land allocated to each landowner by the Enclosure*
Commissioners is shown on the map

From: Agriculture 1730–1872 by J. R. S. Whiting

Notice the change in source B. The total cost of enclosure –
commissioners' fees, fencing and general improvements – to Noble was
£5800. He reduced the number of farms on his land from ten to three
but increased his rent roll to £852 8s. 3d. Find the land allocated to the
poor. The right to collect fuel on the common and waste was lost with
enclosure. Here a small area of land was provided for that purpose
under the Enclosure Act. How else has the village been changed?

C *The agricultural effects of enclosure*

(i)   I must take notice of one circumstance . . . of particular importance,
      which is the amazing superiority of wool and profit in enclosed districts to
      open ones. . . . About Bendsworth, in the Vale of Evesham, the average

A labourer's wife earns extra money

range: an area of open country

offices: farm buildings

fleece is about 9lb in the enclosures, but only 3½lb in the open fields. Can there be a stronger argument for enclosing? . . . Enclosures raise rents; high rents make men industrious, they put a thousand pounds in their pockets to go hire a farm, which open would have taken only £300 or £400. Everything must be turned to good advantage when high rents are paid. . . .

Arthur Young, Northern Tour, 1770

(ii) . . . in the central counties of the kingdom, particularly Northamptonshire, Leicestershire, and parts of Warwick, Huntingdon, and Buckinghamshire, there have been within thirty years large tracts of the open field arable under that vile course: 1. fallow, 2. wheat, 3. spring corn, enclosed and laid down to grass, being much more suited to the wetness of the soil than corn; and yields in beef, mutton, hide, and wool beyond comparison a greater neat produce than when under corn. . . .

Arthur Young, Political Arithmetic, 1774

(iii) the vast benefit of enclosing can, upon inferior soils, be rarely seen in more advantageous light than upon Lincoln-heath. I found a large range which formerly was covered with heath, gorse, etc., and yielding in fact little or no produce, converted by enclosure into profitable arable farms; let on average of 10s. an acre; and a very extensive country, all studded with new farmhouses, barns, offices, and every appearance of thriving industry. . . .

. . . rents have risen on the heath . . . the farmers are in much better circumstances, a great produce is created, cattle and sheep increased, and the poor employed. . . .

Arthur Young, General View of the Agriculture of the County of Lincoln, 2nd edition, 1813

D *The effect of enclosure on agricultural labour*
Some opponents of enclosure claimed that it created unemployment in the countryside. Here is Young's reply:

Respecting open-field lands, the quantity of labour in them is not comparable to that of enclosures; for, not to speak of the great numbers of men . . . constantly employed in winter in hedging and ditching, what comparison can there be between the open field system of one half or a third of the lands being fallow, receiving only three ploughings, and the same proportion now tilled four, five, or six times by midsummer, then sown with turnips, then handhoed twice, and then drawn by hand and carted to stalls for beasts, or else hurdled out in portions for fattening sheep . . . Vast tracts of land uncultivated in the last century . . . have been enclosed and converted into new farms. . . . All this is the effect of enclosures, and consequently they also have yielded a great increase of employment. . . .

Political Arithmetic, 1774

E *Enclosure – the attitude of the poor*

(i) On Tuesday evening a great number of farmers were observed going along Pall Mall with cockades in their hats. On enquiring the reason, it appeared they all lived in or near the parish of Stanwell in the County of Middlesex, and they were returning to their wives and families to carry them the

The cottager's meal-time

agreeable news of a Bill being rejected for inclosing the said common, which if being carried into execution might have been the ruin of a great number of families.

Annual Register, 1 March 1767

(ii) A letter sent to Oliver Cromwell of Cheshunt Park in 1799:
Whe right these lines to you who are the Combin'd of the Parish of Cheshunt in the Defence of our Parish rights which you unlawfully are about to disinherit us of the Same Resolutions is maid by the aforesaid Combind that if you intend of incloseing Our Commond Commond fields Lammas Meads Marches &c. resolve before you shall say & the rest of the heads of that bloudy and unlawful act is finished to have your hearts bloud if you proceede in the aforesaid bloudy act. . . .

F *What the poor lost*
(i) A comment on Mauldeen in Bedfordshire. When the enclosure took place troops had to be called in to quell the riot.

The common was very extensive. I conversed with a farmer and several cottagers. One of them said, enclosing would ruin England; it was worse than ten wars. Why, my friend, what have you lost by it? 'I kept four cows before the parish was enclosed, and now I don't keep so much as a goose; and you ask me what I lose by it!'

Board of Agriculture Report on Bedfordshire, 1808

(ii) In passing through a village near Swaffham . . . I beheld the houses tumbling into ruins, and the common fields all enclosed. . . . I was informed that a gentleman of Lynn had brought that township and the next adjourning to it: that he had thrown the one into three, and the other into four farms; which before the enclosure were in about twenty farms: and upon my further enquiring what was becoming to the farmers who were turned out, the answer was that some of them were dead and the rest were become labourers.

F. Moore, *Considerations on the Exhorbitant Price of Proprietors*, 1773

In the alehouse

(iii) Riding to St. Neots, Arthur Young heard this opinion of the local enclosure from 'a gentleman of the town.'

. . . the poor were ill-treated by having about half a rood given them in lieu of a cowkeep, the inclosure of which land costing more than they could afford, they sold the lots at £5; the money was drank out at the alehouse, and the men . . . came, with their families to the parish; by which means poor rates had risen from 2s. 6d [12½p] to 3s [15p] and 3s. 6d [17½p]. . . .

A Month's Tour of Northamptonshire, Leicestershire etc.

rood: quarter of an acre
cowkeep: the right to graze a cow on the common

poor rates: paid by property-owners to support the parish poor

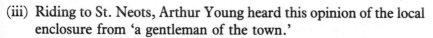

1 Arthur Young warned landowners of the high cost of enclosure, and by the end of the century he was agreeing that the poor usually suffered but he still supported the enclosure movement. Why? (Sources C and D)

2 After the enclosure of Wigston Magna in Leicestershire open-field arable land was converted into pasture. This meant a drop of about 75 per cent in the numbers of labourers needed. Does this information make the evidence in source D worthless? Explain your answer.

3 What appears to be the main reason why the enclosures of Stanwell and Cheshunt were opposed? (Source E)
To what extent does the evidence in source F explain that opposition?

4 It was a fact that poor rates rose at the end of the eighteenth century in rural areas, and that newly-enclosed villages were amongst those affected. At the time rising poor rates were blamed on enclosure.

(a) Is there sufficient evidence in sources D and F to support this claim? Explain your answer.

(b) From your knowledge of these years what other reasons could there be for a rise in poor rates?

5 'The poor always suffered when a village was enclosed.' Is it possible to make this statement after studying all these sources? Give reasons for your opinion.

Arthur Young's remedy

Enclosure Commissioners admitted to Arthur Young that the interests of the poor were often neglected when an enclosure took place.

> . . . Numbers in the practice of feeding the commons cannot prove their right; and many, indeed most who have allotments, have no more than an acre, which being insufficient for the man's cow, both cow and land are ususally sold. . . .
> *An Inquiry into the Propriety of Applying Wastes to the better Maintenance and Support of the Poor*, 1801

Those who could prove their right to graze animals on the common were usually granted allotments under an enclosure scheme. The problem for many was that they did not possess the right or had lost the proof. It was recognised that the right to collect fuel on common or waste was a vital matter for the poor and in many Acts, as at Aston Blank, land was set aside for this purpose. It was either left waste or managed by the parish with the income being used to purchase fuel.

If the cottager lost his common, the squatter on common or waste could lose his cottage and land. He had no legal rights. Many Enclosure Acts, however, gave compensation to those who had occupied such properties for more than twenty years.

In 1801 Arthur Young proposed that where an enclosure was enacted, a small amount of wasteland should be given to the poor to enable the cottagers to keep a cow. He believed that ownership of land would make them independent and self-sufficient, keeping them off the poor rates. It would be cheaper to provide land and a cow than for the parish to maintain a man and his family on the rates. Young accepted that enclosure caused increasing poor rates and he painted this dismal picture of the rural labourers in the village alehouse:

Go to an alehouse kitchen of an old enclosed country, and there you will see the origin of poverty and poor rates. For whom are they to be sober? For whom are they to save? . . . For the parish? If I am diligent, shall I have leave to build a cottage? If I am sober, shall I have land for a cow? If I am frugal, shall I have half an acre of potatoes? You offer no motives; you have nothing but a parish officer and a workhouse! – Bring me another pot!

What point is Young making about the attitudes of the poor in rural areas? Does he sympathise with them?

Enclosure and the small farmer

Agricultural improvers favoured large farms since the tenant would have the capital to adopt new methods. Nevertheless there were still many small farms at the end of the eighteenth century. Small freeholders – men with perhaps 30 to 40 acres – had owned land in the open-field villages. Enclosure, it has been suggested, harmed them. Faced with a bill for perhaps £50 – £100 as the cost of an enclosure they had not wanted, many had to sell out to the richer landowners.

At Wigston Magna there were 47 owner-occupiers in 1766 when the land was enclosed, about half the landowners. This number had fallen to 34 thirty years later, but the typical freeholder now farmed a larger acreage.

Elsewhere the effect was not so dramatic. As at Wigston most free-holders managed to raise the money needed to enclose and improve their land and they prospered during the war years (1793–1815), as Young found in Essex in 1813.

. . . there never was a greater proportion of small and moderate-sized farms, the property of mere farmers, who retain them in their own immediate occupation than at present. . . .

Arthur Young: *General View of the Agriculture of Essex*, 1813

The decline of the small owner-occupier was a gradual process and they suffered more from the agricultural depression after 1815 than from the effects of enclosure.

Questions

1 In the whole of this section the writings of Arthur Young have been extensively used. Do you think they can be relied on to give an accurate account of what was happening in the countryside in the fifty years after 1760? Explain your answer.

2 A strong case *for* enclosure was made at the end of the eighteenth century, and a strong case could be made *against* it. Use the evidence and the material in this chapter to

(a) write a letter to a fellow-landowner explaining why you believe he should support your plan to enclose the open fields, common and waste of a village in which you are both major landowners.

(b) write an introduction to a petition against the enclosure of the commons and waste around the village in which you, a small farmer with a few acres, live.

2

Prosperity and depression: agriculture 1815–1914

Look at the wheat price chart on page 36

quarter: a measure of weight used by corn merchants and farmers.

William Cobbett (1763–1835) was a journalist and politician. He disapproved of the changes he observed in the countryside

Depression and the Corn Laws, 1815–46

During the Napoleonic Wars farmers were prosperous. Grain imports from Europe were reduced by wartime restrictions and the price of home-grown wheat increased. This meant higher profits. Landowners renegotiated leases and raised rents. Investment in new farming methods and in the enclosure of land was encouraged but wartime interest rates on borrowed money were high. When the wars ended in 1815 there was a dramatic fall in corn prices. Farmers and landowners were badly affected.

Speaking in a Commons debate in 1816, Henry Brougham explained the problem arable farmers faced. Too much land was under cultivation, and too much corn was being grown.

Not only have wastes disappeared for miles and miles, giving place to houses, fences and crops; not only have even the most inconsiderable commons, the very village green . . . been . . . cut up into cornfields in the rage for farming; not only have stubborn soils been forced to bear crops . . . by sinking money in the earth . . . but the land that formerly grew something has been fatigued with labour, and loaded with capital, until it yielded much more. . . . New skill has been applied. . . . It may be safely said, not perhaps that two blades of grass now grow where only one grew before, but I am sure that five grow where four used to be!

Fearing competition from imported foreign grain when the war ended, Parliament protected farmers and landowners. The Corn Law of 1815 prevented the import of grain until the home price had reached 80 shillings (£4) a quarter. It did not have the desired effect. More land was being cultivated more productively and in good years low prices were inevitable. Only in the poor summers of 1817 and 1818 did the price consistently rise above 80 shillings. In other years it sank below 50 shillings (250p) a quarter and never rose above 65 shillings (325p). The high-price war years were never to return.

William Cobbett heard farmers' complaints in 1821 when he was in Hampshire.

I have seen a farmer here who can get (or could a few days ago) 28s [140p] . . . for a lot of fat South-Down wethers, which cost him just that money, when they were lambs, *two years ago*! It is impossible that they can have cost him less than 24s each during the two years, having to be fed on turnips or hay in winter, and to be fattened on good grass. . . . A correspondent informs me that one hundred and fifty Welsh sheep were, on the 18th October, offered for 4s. 6d [22½p] a head and they went away unsold!. . . Last week, at Northampton Fair, Mr Thomas Cooper, of Bow, purchased three milch cows and forty sheep for £18 16s. 6d! [£18.82½] The skins, four years ago, would have sold for more . . . Nothing can be clearer than that the present race of farmers . . . must be swept away by bankruptcy. . . .

Rural Rides

A year later he was at the great sheep fair on Weyhill.

. . . About £300 000 used, some years ago, to be carried home by the sheep-sellers. Today, less, perhaps, than £70 000, and yet, the *rents* of these sheep-sellers are, perhaps, as high, on an average, as they were then. The countenances of the farmers were descriptive of their ruinous state. . . . Met a farmer who said he must be ruined, unless another 'good war' should come!. . . .

Rural Rides

Farmers complained about rents, interest rates, poor rates, tithes and wages.

Wages were cut immediately from an average of 12s (60p) to 15s (75p) a week in 1814 to an average of about 9s (45p) in 1822. One consequence of this was a rise in parish poor rates. Landlords had to give rent rebates and when leases were renegotiated, permanent reductions had to be made. Some farmers gave up their tenancies. In the spring of 1816 seventy-six farms were advertised to let in Northumberland and Durham, whilst in 1821 even Thomas Coke was forced to appeal to his bankers for a loan since he could not get his rents in. On his estates rent arrears mounted and there was a great turnover in farms and tenants.

Nothing was done to reduce the burden of poor rates and tithes until the 1830s. Hard-pressed farmers benefited from the rate reduction when the 1834 Poor Law Amendment Act was enforced and in 1836 tithe payment was rationalised.

Small freeholders suffered severely from the fall in prices. One witness told the Select Committee on Agriculture in 1833 that farmers had developed extravagant and expensive habits during the war years which they were reluctant to give up. Those who had borrowed money faced disaster.

. . . . A great many farmers got a considerable sum of money, and were made to lay it out in land. . . . They purchased at very high prices . . . and borrowed probably half the money, and soon after the produce sold for so much less than it had done; they had the interest to pay upon the money they had borrowed, and were in such difficulties they were obliged to sell the properties for what they could get.

tithe: an annual payment by farmers to the Church

The Poor Law Amendment Act of 1834 abolished the payment of allowances to the low-paid agricultural labourers out of the poor rates. These payments contributed to a rapid increase in the poor rate needed in the South

freeholder: a man who owned his farm

Using the evidence: farmers and labourers

A In 1825 Cobbett attended a farm sale in Surrey. He deplored the changes that wartime prosperity had brought about.

. . . there was a *parlour*! Aye, and a *carpet* and *bell-pull* too! One end of the front of this once plain and substantial house had been moulded into a '*parlour*'; and there was a mahogany table, and the fine chairs, and the fine glass . . . there were the decanters, the glasses, the 'dinner-set' of crockery ware. . . And I dare say it has been *Squire* Charington and the *Miss* Charingtons; and not plain Master Charington, and his son Hodge, and his daughter Betty Charington. . .

Rural Rides

James Gilray pokes fun at the farmers made rich by high wartime prices. The cartoon was published in 1809

C William Clift of Bramley, Hampshire, paints a different picture. His father farmed 190 acres and William began working on the family farm in the 1840s.

Our time for rising was 4.30 in the summer, and shortly after 5 in winter. Before breakfast we had all the cattle to feed; and after breakfast . . . we started, with the carters, to our work for the day. . . .

Out early in the field, we set to work till luncheon time. . . . We used to stop from twenty minutes to half-an-hour for lunch. . . .

D Labourers' conditions varied across the country. Cobbett lamented the decay of the old system whereby the farmer provided his workers with board and lodging.

. . . . Why do not farmers now *feed* and *lodge* their work-people, as they did formerly? Because they cannot keep them *upon so little* as they give them in wages. . . .

Rural Rides

E In Worcestershire in 1826 he observed that the labourers and their families seemed more prosperous than elsewhere.

. . . one cause of which, is, I dare say, that *glove-manufacturing*, which cannot be carried on by *fire* or by *wind* or by *water*, and which is therefore carried on by the hands of human beings. It gives work to women and children as well as to men; and that work is, by a great part of the women and children, done in *their cottages*. . . .

Rural Rides

F Things were not much better for many agricultural labourers in the 1850s. When James Caird was in Wiltshire in 1851 he asked a labourer earning just 6s. a week (30p) what he ate. For his breakfast he had

James Caird (1816–92) was an agricultural journalist

. . . flour with a little butter, and water 'from the tea-kettle' poured over it. He takes with him to the field a piece of bread and . . . cheese. . . . He returns in the afternoon to a few pound of potatoes, and possibly a little bacon, though only those who are better off can afford this. The supper very commonly consists of bread and water. The appearance of the labourers showed, as might be expected from such meagre diet, a want of that vigour and activity which mark the well-fed ploughman of the northern and midland counties. . . .

In contrast Caird described the treatment of living-in farm servants in north Derbyshire:

For breakfast they have porridge, then bread and cheese. They take with them to the field each man his pint of ale, and as much bread and cheese as he likes. At one o'clock they have dinner, which is either brawn, beef, or mutton and pudding. . . . At seven o'clock they have supper of milk porridge, then bread and cheese. . . .

English Agriculture 1850/1, 1852

G James Caird divided the country into the areas shown on this map after his tour of agricultural districts in 1851.

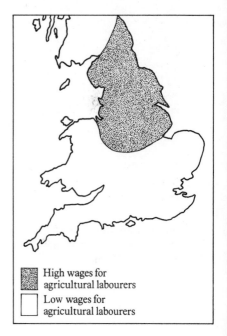

High wages for agricultural labourers

Low wages for agricultural labourers

1 Look at source A and the cartoon (source B).
   (a) How does Gilray make fun of the farmer and his family? List all the things you can find in the cartoon.
   (b) Read source A. Do you think Cobbett would agree or disagree with Gilray? Explain your answer.
2 Now read source C. Does Clift's evidence make Cobbett's comments worthless? Explain your answer very carefully.
3 Read source D. How, according to Cobbett, has the treatment of their labourers by farmers changed? Why does he believe this has happened?
4 William Cobbett always referred to London as the 'wen' and described factories as 'Hell-Holes'. He wrote his *Rural Rides* as records of what he saw in England on tours he made in the 1820s.
   (a) Using sources A, D and E, list the things that Cobbett approved and disapproved of. How does he show his prejudices? Refer to the sources.
   (b) Are his writings more useful to the historian as evidence about William Cobbett or about conditions in the countryside in the 1820s? Explain your answer.
5 Compare the evidence in source F.
   (a) How does it support and how does it contradict Cobbett?
   (b) Study Caird's map (source G). How does it explain the different conditions described in source F?

wen: a disfiguring wart

The prosperous years of 'high farming', 1846–75

When the Corn Laws were repealed in 1846, arable farmers feared a flood of cheap imported grain. Yet, apart from a short depression, 1848–53, the thirty years after repeal were good for farmers. A growing population ensured an expanding market for foodstuffs which absorbed both imported and home-produced grains. More was imported from Russia and North Germany than ever before, but the price for home-produced wheat remained steady. Producers of meat and dairy products benefited from steadily increasing prices for their products.

An expanding railway network contributed to this prosperity. As early as 1846 a railway director informed a parliamentary Select Committee that

. . . so far from the Graziers having anything with driving Cattle 100 or 150 Miles, they will not do it at all, but they will get them upon the Railway and convey them to Market, and come back again; we allow always a Man to go in charge of Two Waggons for the safety of the Cattle themselves, and to return free.

Dairy farmers and market gardeners, able to supply distant urban markets, profited most from this development. Consumers were able to purchase food at lower prices, whilst the farmer's transport expenses for fertilisers, feed, seed and implements were greatly reduced. These were the years of 'high farming'. Improving landowners and farmers invested to obtain the maximum output from their land.

New ideas and techniques were publicised at the annual shows held by the Royal Agricultural Society after 1838. Sir John Lawes advanced soil science at the Rothamsted research station. Guano was being imported from Peru in the 1830s and the import of nitrates from Chile increased. The first commercially-produced artificial fertilisers, super-

guano: bird droppings of sea birds collected from islands off the coast of Peru

The farmer's wife supervised the work of the dairy. What is being made here?

```
┌─────────────────────┐
│ use of artificial   │
│ fertilisers –       │
│ superphosphates     │
└─────────────────────┘

┌──────────────────┐                    ┌──────────────────────┐
│ expenditure on   │                    │ use of guano and     │
│ drainage schemes │                    │ nitrates as fertilisers │
└──────────────────┘                    └──────────────────────┘

┌──────────────────────┐               ┌──────────────────────┐
│ Cirencester Agriculture │            │ steampower and new   │
│ College founded 1845  │              │ implements on the farm │
└──────────────────────┘               └──────────────────────┘

                    ┌─────────────────┐
                    │ 'HIGH FARMING'  │
                    └─────────────────┘

┌──────────────────────┐               ┌──────────────────────┐
│ scientific research at │             │ cheap and fast rail  │
│ Rothamsted by Sir     │              │ transport to markets │
│ John Lawes from 1843  │              └──────────────────────┘
└──────────────────────┘

┌──────────────────────┐
│ Royal Agricultural   │
│ Society formed 1838  │
└──────────────────────┘

                    ┌─────────────────┐
                    │ increased output to │
                    │ meet growing demand │
                    └─────────────────┘
```

phosphates, began to appear in the 1840s. Using these fertilisers farmers could increase the yield from their land and compensate for the shortage of farmyard manure.

Land was improved by new drainage methods using hollow field drains or tiles. One of the wonders of the Great Exhibition in 1851 was Fowler's pipelaying machine, which could place pipes in the ground without breaking the surface. Drainage schemes were expensive and low-interest government loans were made available from 1846 to encourage them. On the Vernon estate at Poynton, Cheshire, the drainage tiles were manufactured on the estate and the tenants laid them at their own expense. The Duke of Northumberland invested nearly £1 000 000 on his estates in drainage and other improvement schemes. It has been estimated that in the thirty years after 1846 landowners spent about £24 000 000.

More machinery was used on the land. Bell patented his reaping machine in 1826 and the McCormick reaper from the United States was on display at the Great Exhibition. Mechanical reapers saved time and reduced labour costs and there were perhaps 40 000 in use by the mid-1870s.

Steam-power on the farm

After 1850 it was possible for farmers to hire steam engines, and contractors made good money at harvest-time. Traction engines rumbled through the country lanes towing mechanical threshing machines from farm to farm and some farmers even employed steam-ploughing teams.

Many farmers were reluctant to use the new implements, which were expensive and often broke down. Steam ploughing was quicker and more efficient but fields had to be enlarged and hedges grubbed up to make its use possible. This account of farming in Staffordshire in the 1870s suggests that the traditional methods were still widely used:

There was little farm machinery used in those days. 'Hand work is best work', my master used to say, and he did not like to have even a horse in the field. Corn was cut with a short 'badging' hook and hay was cut with the scythe. . . .

How country folk laughed when the first machines appeared. A few mowing-machines had already reached Staffordshire. Some had reaping gear fixed to them and were used as reapers, with a dozen men following behind binding. There were a few threshing machines also, but corn was mostly threshed by flail. . . . We tried ploughing using a long wire and two stationary steam engines; it made a rough job but was quicker.

Little artificial manure was used. Cow's water was collected in tanks and carted into the fields in barrels, where it was spread with a long handle ladle. Contractors used to collect night-soil from the towns and sell it to the farmers. . . .

night-soil: human sewage

The end of the 'golden age'

Writing in 1850 James Caird warned English farmers and landowners of the need for change:

With the great mass of consumers, bread still forms the chief article of

Steam ploughing. Why would it be difficult for most farmers to use this equipment?

consumption. But in the manufacturing districts where wages are good, the use of butcher's meat and cheese is enormously on the increase; and even in the agricultural districts the labourer does now occasionally indulge himself in a meat dinner, or seasons his dry bread with a morsel of cheese. . . . It is reasonable to conclude that the great mass of the consumers, as their circumstances improve, will follow the same rule. . . .

Every intelligent farmer ought to keep this steadily in view. Let him produce as much as he can of the articles which have shown a gradual tendency to increase in value.

Livestock farming did increase during the 'golden age' but too many farmers and landowners remained dependent on cereal production. Wheat was the largest single crop.

The 1870s were bad years. Livestock farmers were hit by outbreaks of sheep-rot in 1874 and of cattle plague in 1877. Arable farmers suffered from a series of bad harvests. 1879 was one of the worst ever recorded. They were not compensated by a rise in price. Imports were now large enough and cheap enough to maintain low prices even when home farmers had a bad year. Throughout the 1880s the price of wheat fell steadily, reaching a low of 22s.10d (114p) in 1894.

Cheap grain was now being grown on the North American prairies. The building of the trans-continental railways in the USA meant that grain could be carried cheaply and swiftly to the east coast ports. Steamships completed the journey to Britain at low cost. On the prairies farmers were using machines to farm their rich soils efficiently and profitably.

Free trade in corn had not harmed the British producer for thirty years because there had been no low-price competition. High international transport costs, wars and technical problems had protected British arable farmers. Now that these problems had been removed they faced a bleak future.

The old and the new – a mechanical reaper in the background but the labourers are using sickles

Question

Copy this chart into your book. Complete the 'Causes' boxes. As you read the next section fill in the 'Effects'.

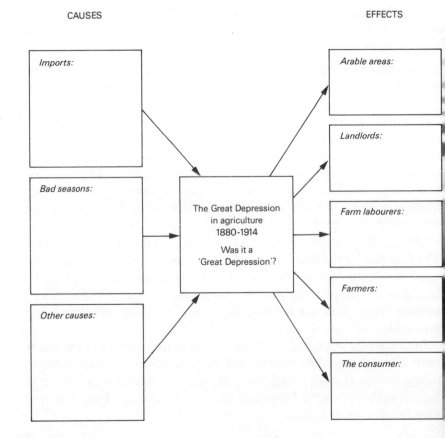

CAUSES

EFFECTS

Imports:

Bad seasons:

Other causes:

The Great Depression
in agriculture
1880-1914

Was it a
'Great Depression'?

Arable areas:

Landlords:

Farm labourers:

Farmers:

The consumer:

The 'Great Depression' in agriculture

Sheep farmers were also facing competition from wool imported from Australia. Refrigerated ships conveying frozen meat from New Zealand and Argentina in the 1880s threatened beef and lamb producers. Cereal

Frozen meat being unloaded at London in 1897. Notice the refrigerated railway wagon

growers, however, were the hardest-hit. James Caird advised them what to do:

Bakers' shops are diminishing, and butchers' shops increasing. Vegetables fresh from our own fields, or brought by fast steamers from the ports of the neighbouring continent, are more and more displacing bread. That proportion which thirty years ago the richer classes in this country alone could afford to spend on other articles of household consumption than bread, is being rapidly reached by the working class. Our agriculture must adapt itself to the change, freely accepting the good it brings, and skilfully using the advantages which greater proximity to the best market must always command.

The pie charts on page 52 show how the acreage under wheat dropped sharply after 1879 with a corresponding increase in pasture.

The Royal Commission on Agriculture's Report of 1897 clearly showed that the arable farming districts in the East and South suffered most in the depression.

Essex: . . . Between 1880 and 1884 the number of farms given up either in despair or for reasons over which the occupiers had no control was stated to have been enormous. . . . On poor estates no attempt was made to bring the land round; it was left alone, and gradually 'tumbled down' to such coarse and inferior herbage as nature produced . . . rents were reduced. . . . Only those who kept a considerable head of stock . . . still continue in occupation.

Suffolk: . . . It is universally stated that the condition of the land has gone back since 1879. . . . On the clay and very light soils the land is frequently very foul, being choked with charlock, weeds and thistles. . . .

charlock: a cornfield weed

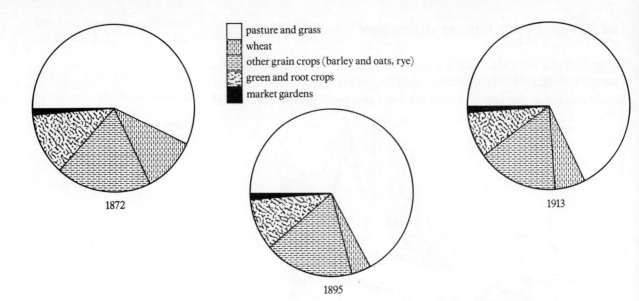

Legend:

- pasture and grass
- wheat
- other grain crops (barley and oats, rye)
- green and root crops
- market gardens

1872

1895

1913

The Impact of the 'Great Depression' – the change in the acreage of land under different crops

Norfolk: . . . The majority of farmers whom I met spoke in a very despondent and frequently almost despairing way of their financial position. . . . I was told of many instances of farmers who had been ruined. . . .

Lincolnshire: . . . [Landlords were hard-hit.] Their rentals have been greatly reduced, the freehold value of their properties has been largely decreased . . . the condition of their land has in many cases deteriorated, and they have . . . been called upon to spend increasingly large sums of money on buildings and repairs. . . .

Although arable farmers in the North and West were experiencing difficulties and sheep breeders were hit by the falling price of wool, livestock farmers were not badly affected.

Gloucestershire: . . . In the hill country between Cirencester and Northleach there is a large amount of land untenanted. . . . This is essentially a sheep district, though corn is also grown to a large extent. . . . In the dairying and grazing districts of the Vale of Gloucester there is, however, no land unlet. . . .

Shropshire, Herefordshire and Worcestershire: . . . Dairying and grazing are the chief branches of farming in these counties. In Herefordshire and Worcestershire fruit and hops are largely grown . . . market gardening is carried on with some success. There are few farms unlet . . . rents have in many instances been maintained, and reductions have . . . seldom exceeded 15 per cent. . . .

Livestock and dairy farmers benefited from the falling price of imported feeding stuffs whilst cheap bread meant that customers had more to spend on meat, dairy produce, vegetables or fruit. Rents in the arable areas fell by an average of 41 per cent but in the pasture areas of the country the fall was only 12 per cent.

Farmers went bankrupt. Landowners who could not stand these rent reductions made economies or tried to sell their estates. Land values fell but even with low prices there was no demand from buyers. Land had ceased to be a good investment.

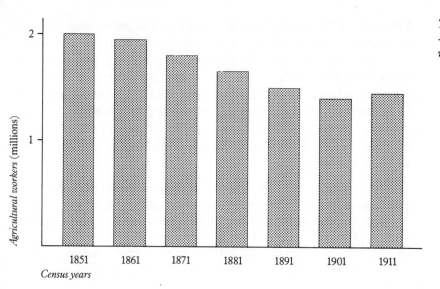

*The drift from the land, 1851–1911
– the reduction in agricultural
workers*

The 'flight from the land'

During the 'golden age' labourers' wages began to rise. Landowners built improved cottages for their workers. Allotments became more common. Rising prices, however, eroded wage increases and farm labourers remained discontented.

The coming of the railway brought alternative better-paid employment and the opportunity to escape. Farmers had to pay higher wages to keep their men. The adoption of machines is evidence that the size of the workforce was declining.

This poster compares the value of farm labourers with the prizes given for animals at agricultural shows.
1 *Which has the greatest value?*
2 *What, according to the poster, can the labourer expect in his life?*
3 *How far does this evidence help to explain the 'drift from the land'?*

Compulsory education played its part in the move from the land. Labourers did not want their sons to follow them onto the farms, while farmers regretted the spread of elementary education. Of the boy who had been in a schoolroom it was said: 'when he comes out he does not like a cold north-easter with sleet and rain, and mud over his boot tops.'

In Somerset in 1902 a farmer lamented that it was impossible to get a boy to stay on the land. He blamed an education system which kept them at school until thirteen and made them 'more fit to drive a pen than to follow the plough.'

From his neighbourhood they nearly all went to the Welsh coalfields, where during three of four days they earned good wages, and employed the remainder of the week in spending them. A boy who was perhaps taking 6s. [30p] a week at farm work would be enticed to the mines, where he receives 15s. [75p] a week or more . . . and on his first holiday returns home with glowing tales of the money that is to be had for the asking by those who are willing to follow his example. . . .

R. Haggard, *Rural England*, 1902

Sub-standard housing, low wages and long hours of work all helped to drive men and their families into the towns. The 'Great Depression' accelerated the trend. Farms that changed from arable to pasture required fewer workers.

For those who stayed, wages did increase and the fall in food prices at the end of the nineteenth century meant that spending power was greater. Despite this, however, the farm labourer's wage remained below the poverty level drawn by both Charles Booth and Seebohm Rowntree in their surveys of poverty in London and York in the 1890s.

Booth's and Rowntree's surveys are described in Volume 8, Chapter 2

The
industrial
revolution

3

Textiles in the industrial revolution

Using the evidence: the textile revolution

A This graph shows the value of cotton and woollen exports from Britain in the eighteenth and early nineteenth centuries.

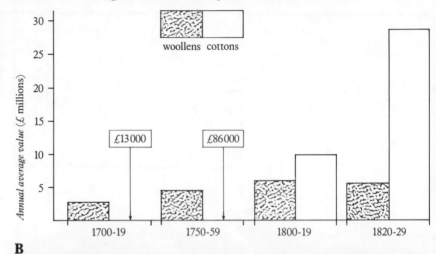

The home as the workplace. The woman is spinning

B

The machines are spinning mules (see p. 62). What are the differences between this workplace and source B?

C

D A description of the Lancashire cotton industry in the second half of the eighteenth century:

In the year 1770, the land in our township was occupied by between fifty to sixty farmers. . . . There were only six or seven who raised their rents directly from the produce of their farms; all the rest got their rent partly in some branch of trade, such as spinning and weaving woollen, linen, or cotton. The cottagers were employed entirely in this manner, except for a few weeks in the harvest. . . . The father of a family would earn from eight shillings [40p] to half-a-guinea [52½p] at his loom, and his sons . . . alongside of him, six [30p] or eight [40p] shillings each per week: but the great sheet anchor of all cottages and small farms, was the labour attached to the hand-wheel. . . . It required six to eight hands to prepare and spin yarn . . . sufficient for the consumption of one weaver.

William Radcliffe, *Origin of the New System of Manufacture commonly called 'Power-Loom Weaving'*, 1828

E The Lancashire cotton industry in 1830:

It is by iron fingers, teeth, and wheels . . . that the cotton is opened, cleaned, spread, carded, drawn, roved, spun, wound, warped, dressed, and woven. . . . All derive their motion from the mighty engine, which, firmly seated in the lower part of the building, and constantly fed with water and fuel, toils through the day. . . . Men . . . have merely to attend on this wonderful series of mechanisms, to supply it with work, to oil its joints, and to check its slight and infrequent irregularities; each workman performing . . . as much work as could have been done by two or three hundred men sixty years ago. At the approach of darkness, the building is illuminated by jets of flame, whose brilliance mimics the light of day. . . .

Edward Baines, *History of the Cotton Manufacture*, 1835

1 Using all the sources make a list of the changes that had occurred in the cotton and textile industries between the middle of the eighteenth century and the 1830s.
2 What can you deduce about the development of the cotton and woollen industries from source A? Explain your answer.
3 What changes in other industries made possible the scene described by Baines in source E?

Textiles in the early eighteenth century

England's main export since the Middle Ages had been woollen cloth. This was manufactured in all parts of the country, but there were three major centres of production – East Anglia, the West Country and the West Riding of Yorkshire.

Woollen manufacturers feared competition from cottons. They were more comfortable to wear and the printed calicoes were more attractive. In 1700 high duties were placed on imported Indian printed cotton fabrics and in 1721 the manufacture of cotton fabrics for sale in Britain was forbidden by Parliament. Fustian, the main product in Lancashire, was excluded from this ban.

Fustian was a fabric with a cotton weft yarn and a linen warp. Raw cotton was, therefore, still imported, and cottons were still produced, especially for export to Africa. There was also an increasing demand for cotton yarn from the East Midland hosiery industry. Cotton stockings were being made after 1732.

All these branches of the textile industry were organised on the domestic system. Travelling in the West Riding in the early eighteenth century Daniel Defoe was impressed by the busy activity he saw. The clothier together with his sons and workers wove the cloth in workshops attached to the cottages whilst the womenfolk and the younger children prepared the wool for the weavers.

weft: the yarn that is woven under and over the alternate warps

warp: the fixed yarn on the loom

THE PRODUCTION OF CLOTH IN 1750

Processes — Wool / Cotton	Special equipment	The worker
Cleaning and washing (Wool) / 'Batting' or cleaning – picking out seeds (Cotton)		Women and children in wool industry. Mainly women in cotton.
Carding – straightening out the fibres and laying them parallel.	Carding combs	Women and children working at home.
Cotton fibres are made into rovings.		
Spinning the fibres into yarn by twisting them together.	Spinning wheel	Women working at home.
Weaving the yarn into cloth.	Handloom	Men working at home.
Finish processes, e.g. dyeing / (Cottons) fulling / bleaching cropping / printing		Men in workshops owned by the merchant. Expensive equipment was needed.

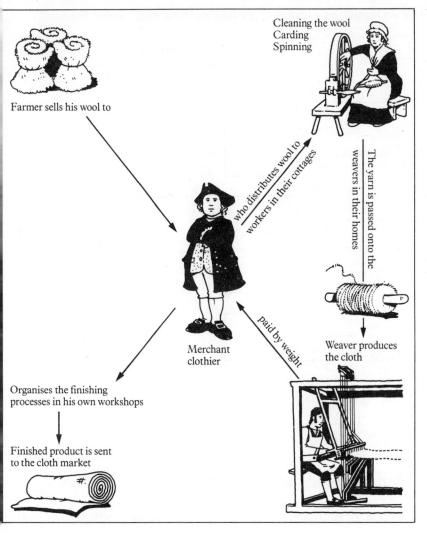

Farmer sells his wool to

Cleaning the wool
Carding
Spinning

who distributes wool to workers in their cottages

The yarn is passed onto the weavers in their homes

Merchant clothier

paid by weight

Weaver produces the cloth

Organises the finishing processes in his own workshops

Finished product is sent to the cloth market

cottons/fustians

woollens

hosiery

silk

Kendal

Liverpool

Manchester

Macclesfield

Derby

Norwich

Coventry

London

Bristol

Exeter

Main textile-making areas in 1750

The 'domestic' or 'putting out' system in the eighteenth-century woollen industry

Weekly or fortnightly the clothiers loaded their packhorses and trudged to the cloth markets in the nearby towns of Leeds or Halifax where the cloth merchants purchased their product.

Lancashire's fustian industry, like the woollen industry in the West Country, was controlled by wealthy merchants. Based in Manchester or Bolton, they purchased the raw materials (linen and cotton) in London and distributed them to spinners and weavers working in their own homes. For the first half of the century much of the cloth was then sent to London for bleaching and printing.

Silk was an exception. In 1717 the Lombe brothers took over a water-powered silk mill in Derby and installed the latest silk-throwing machines from Italy. This was to be the first successful textile factory and soon other silk mills were built in Stockport, Congleton and Macclesfield. Although the silk manufacturers pioneered the factory system of working the decisive changes were to come in the cotton industry.

As you read this section, complete the flow chart which follows.

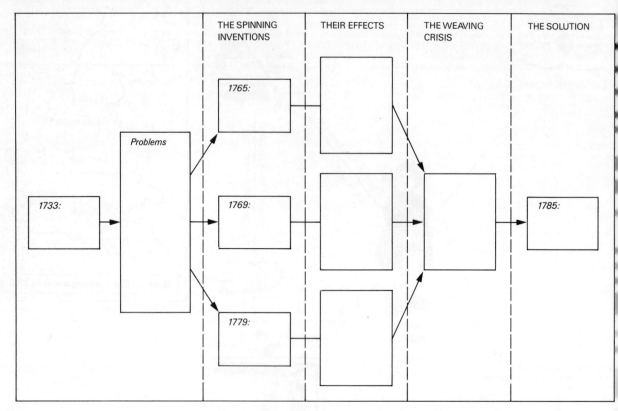

| | THE SPINNING INVENTIONS | THEIR EFFECTS | THE WEAVING CRISIS | THE SOLUTION |

Changes in the cotton industry: (1) the technology

Technological changes made possible the mass production of cotton yarn.

An increasing home demand for cottons and an expanding export market provided the incentive entrepreneurs needed to invest in new ideas and new methods. As output increased, prices fell and demand grew. The 1721 ban was ignored.

1 The flying shuttle

John Kay, a Bury weaver, patented his flying shuttle in 1733. The width of the cloth woven on the handloom was restricted by the stretch of the weaver's arms. Broad cloth had to be woven by two men who threw the shuttle to each other. Kay hoped to overcome this problem with his invention. By pulling a string the weaver activated hammers which knocked the shuttle back and forth, enabling him to produce a wider piece.

Kay's invention was easily copied and it began to be used in Lancashire to speed up the weaving of narrow cloth. In 1760 his son, Robert Kay, invented the drop box. The weaver could now interchange

shuttles containing different coloured yarns to weave checked fabrics using the flying shuttle. Its use became more widespread.

Weaving was speeded up to such an extent that there was now a severe shortage of yarn, particularly of the cotton weft needed for fustians. This shortage coincided with an increasing demand for Lancashire cottons from merchants trading with Africa, and with Jedediah Strutt's modification of the stocking frame. His invention allowed the stocking knitter to produce the fashionable ribbed stockings. The Nottingham hosiers were soon buying more and more cotton yarn from the Lancashire spinners as the demand for the new stockings grew.

2 The spinning jenny

The first successful spinning machine was built in 1765 by James Hargreaves, a Blackburn weaver. He did not patent his spinning jenny until 1770 by which time it was too late to protect his invention from others. With up to sixteen spindles it needed a skilled operator to coordinate its complex movements. Nevertheless, because machines were simple to make and small enough to fit into the workers' cottages, Hargreaves design was quickly copied.

These were first used by the country people . . . twelve spindles being thought a great matter; while the awkward posture required to spin on them was discouraging to grown-up people, who saw with surprise children from nine to twelve years of age manage them with dexterity, whereby plenty was brought into families formerly overburthened with children, and the poor weavers were delivered from the bondage to which they had lain from the insolence of spinners. . . .

      J. Aiken, *Description of the Country round Manchester*, 1795

John Kay escapes from angry handloom weavers who are attacking his house. The flying-shuttle attachment for the loom is on the floor. They feared it would take away their jobs

These later jennies were much simpler to operate

A reconstructon of the spinning jenny

The jenny provided the cotton weft yarn the fustian weavers needed. Gradually it was improved and larger versions with eighty spindles soon appeared. During the depression of 1779 rioters broke up all jennies which had more than twenty spindles. Many of these would have been installed in small factories and workshops. Meanwhile Hargreaves, alarmed by an earlier attack on his house and the destruction of the machines he was making, had moved to Nottingham. Here he became a partner in a small spinning factory manufacturing yarn for the hosiers.

3 The water frame

Richard Arkwright was a barber and wigmaker at Preston. He patented his spinning machine, the water frame, in 1769. It produced a coarser yarn than the jenny but one that was much stronger. More importantly it was too large for cottages and needed power to operate it. The water frame had to be installed in factories.

Arkwright took his invention to Nottingham. His strong, coarse yarn was what the hosiery manufacturers needed. In partnership with Samuel Need, a Nottingham hosier, and Jedediah Strutt, he built a horse-powered factory in Nottingham. By 1771 he had chosen Cromford in Derbyshire as the site for his first water-powered mill.

Because the water frame was similar to earlier unsuccessful machines, Arkwright was accused of stealing other men's ideas, and in 1785 his patent rights were withdrawn.

4 The spinning mule

By combining the strong water frame warp yarn with a jenny weft yarn, the cotton masters could produce British cotton cloth cheaply and in large quantities. In 1774 they successfully campaigned for the removal of all the old restrictions on the manufacture of cotton cloth for sale in Britain. Their cloth, however, was still too coarse to compete with fine imported Indian muslins.

Samuel Crompton's spinning mule provided the answer. Crompton was a Bolton spinner who began working with a jenny at the age of 16 in 1769. Three years later he began to improve the jenny, working in secret in the attics of his house. In 1779 he began spinning yarn on his new machine, amazing the local manufacturers with its strength and quality. Eventually they persuaded him to reveal his secret, and not to take out patents. The subscription they promised him did not materialise and it was 1812 before Crompton was granted £10 000 by Parliament for an invention that had made fortunes for others.

Combining features of the jenny and the waterframe, the mule enabled manufacturers to produce fine quality British cotton cloth equal to the finest muslins imported from India. As the price of yarn fell, so home demand rose and exports grew. Output of cloth increased to satisfy both these markets.

The first mules were small machines, mainly made of wood, for use in the spinner's cottage. Gradually the number of spindles increased and mules were installed in factories. In 1790 William Kelly managed to adapt the mule for water-power operation. His self-acting mule, patented in 1792, ended the need for supervision by a skilled spinner. Like the water frame it could now be minded by children.

Using the evidence: the growth of the cotton industry

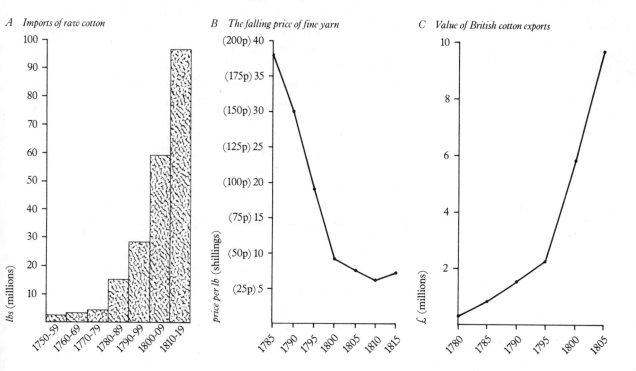

A Imports of raw cotton

B The falling price of fine yarn

C Value of British cotton exports

Tables A, B, and C show the effects of the spinning inventions. Two key dates are 1779 when the mule became available and 1785 when Arkwright's patent rights were ended. Manufacturers could then freely use the water frame.

(a) What is the connection between B and the spinning inventions?
(b) How does B help to explain A and C? Give reasons for your answer.
(c) Briefly explain what these graphs tell us about the growth of the cotton industry.
(d) Why does the growth of exports help to explain the expansion of the cotton industry?

5 The power loom

The rapidly increasing output of cotton yarn and the growing popularity of the cotton fabrics created a new bottleneck. Even with the flying shuttle, weaving remained a handcraft and the handloom weavers could not cope with these new demands. William Radcliffe describes what happened.

loom shops: workrooms housing
handlooms

. . . The fabrics made from wool or linen vanished, while the old loom shops being insufficient, every lumber-room, even old barns, cart-houses and out-buildings of every description, were repaired, windows broke through the old blank walls, and all fitted up for loom shops. . . . New weavers cottages . . . rose up in every direction. . . . The price of labour rose to five times the amount ever before experienced in this district, every family bringing home weekly 40, 60, 80, 100, or even 120 shillings per week!. . . .

These were very high wages. 120
shillings is £6. Compare them
with Source D, on page 57

Weaving had to be speeded up to satisfy the demand for cotton cloth.

Edmund Cartwright was a clergyman from Oxfordshire who had never seen a handloom. On a visit to Matlock he heard cotton manufacturers lamenting the slowness of handloom weaving. These Manchester men were convinced that a complex process like weaving could never be mechanised. Cartwright took up the challenge and in 1785 he patented his first power loom. After further improvements he opened a weaving factory in 1787 in Doncaster.

Few followed his example. Trade was bad and, in 1791, a new weaving mill in Manchester was burnt down by angry handloom weavers. Cartwright lost the money he had invested in the Manchester scheme, and in 1793 he was forced to close his Doncaster factory.

The early power looms were difficult to operate and not always mechanically sound. Considerable improvement was necessary before they were widely adopted, and other inventors were to play an important part in their development. Cartwright managed to get a £10 000 grant from Parliament in 1809 because the new power looms still owed much to his original patents.

No. of power looms in cotton industry	
1813	2 400
1820	14 000
1829	69 000
1833	100 000
1850	247 000

Power looms in the 1830s. What are the advantages over the handloom? How does the power reach the machines?

Changes in the cotton industry: (2) organisation

The mill-owner needed large sums of money.

Mill construction improved. This mill was fire-proof with cast iron pillars and brick arches and floors.

All the processes of cotton production took place in one building. At Belper the cotton was prepared for spinning on the upper floors and spun on the lower floors. Weaving sheds might be added later.

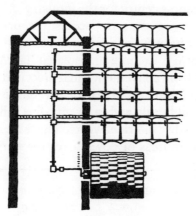

Close supervision by the mill-owner was possible. Quality improved.

Belper North Mill was built for the Strutts in 1803/4. Notice how the power is transmitted from the water-wheel to all parts of the mill.

Workers had to learn a new routine and discipline. The Strutts enforced it by fines deducted from wages.

Specialised machinery was installed for all processes – cleaning, carding, drawing, reeling, spinning and eventually weaving.

There was a source of power. At Belper it was water, elsewhere it might be steam.

Changes in the cotton industry: (3) power and location

Early mills were water-powered but by the 1790s most of the best water-power sites had been taken. In Lancashire, Cheshire, Derbyshire, Nottinghamshire and in Central Scotland suitable streams and rivers were lined by mills.

By 1800, only ninety-two Boulton and Watt steam engines had been installed in cotton mills, although other engine-makers were selling to mill-owners. Water remained the main power source well into the nineteenth century. Mill-owners were discouraged by the high cost of a Boulton and Watt engine and many preferred something that they understood. Water power systems – digging the headrace and tailrace, weirs and mill ponds – were often expensive and complicated to install, but they were cheap to maintain and operate. Steam-engine running costs were high and frequent maintenance was needed. Thirty-five years later steam engines provided the bulk of the power.

With the coming of steam mills, some water-powered mills closed. They tended to be small and isolated ones. The mill towns on or close to the Lancashire coalfield expanded. They had the added advantage of being close to Liverpool, which had always been the main port of entry for North American cotton, and to Manchester, which became the business centre for the industry. Although the more distant water mills were closed down successful concerns like the Gregs at Styal and the Strutts at Belper depended on water-power throughout the nineteenth century. Remote and isolated East Midland mills suffered severely. Cut off from convenient canal links and backward in their techniques, they went into a rapid decline. In contrast there were about one hundred and twenty mills within twenty-five miles of Glasgow by 1812, an increase of eighty in fifteen years. The table below shows the changes in location and sources of power over the period 1838–50:

County	Change in number of mills	% decline in water-power	% increase in steam-power
Cheshire	−21	35	16
Derbyshire	−21	21	65
Lancashire	+49	5	57
Yorkshire	+54	11	143
	+61	16	56

Questions

1 What do these figures tell you about the location of the cotton industry?
2 What do they tell you about changes in power sources?
3 What extra information do you need to get a fuller picture of what was happening?

The meaning of the changes

By 1820 the cotton industry had surged ahead of the woollen industry. Machinery and factories came later in the woollen areas, and only the West Riding had the natural resources of fast-flowing water and coal to benefit from them. Water-powered woollen mills were built in the West Country but the West Riding rapidly became the major area of woollen production. Output increased but at a much slower rate than cotton.

A developing cotton industry contributed to transport changes and improvements. Increasing traffic between Liverpool and Manchester encouraged the Duke of Bridgewater to build a canal to compete with the Mersey and Irwell Navigation. The needs of the cotton industry

Calico printing old-style, using wooden blocks

were also foremost in the minds of the promotors of the Liverpool to Manchester Railway. Cotton mills were amongst the first iron-framed buildings. Specialist engineering and machine-making firms grew up to service the textile industry. Other processes were mechanised – for example, calico printing.

Change in the chemical industry was both a consequence and an accelerator of expansion. Cloth had always been bleached by a soaking in sour milk followed by exposure to the sun. It took a long time. After 1749 it was possible to produce sulphuric acid cheaply and in large quantities. That replaced sour milk but exposure to sunlight was still needed. In 1799 Charles Tennant improved the chlorine bleaching process of Bertollet, a French chemist. A rapid and cheap chemical bleaching technique was now available.

Mechanised calico printing using rollers

The mill town – this is Bradford about 1869

Changes in the cotton industry affected every industry and every person. In 1783 the *London Magazine* reported that 'every servant girl has her cotton gown and her cotton stockings'. Cheap and hygienic cottons replaced woollens. Fashionable muslins and other fine cloths were worn by the better-off. In Lancashire, and in the West Riding, the mill towns became a feature of the new age with their grimy mills, smoky atmosphere and squalid working-class housing. Despite the wealth they produced, the textile industries created many of the problems the nineteenth century had to solve.

Using the evidence: Richard Arkwright, inventor and businessman (1732–92)

Unlike Crompton and Hargreaves, Arkwright became a wealthy man. He built factories and a great mansion; he rose to be High Sheriff of Derbyshire; he was knighted; he left £800 000 to his heirs, and he founded a new family of landed gentry. His was a success story but he made many enemies. What sort of person do you think he was?

Read these contemporary opinions and sources about Arkwright. Here is a list of statements that could be made about him.

Statement	Source(s)	Statement	Source(s)
He was ambitious		He was inventive	
He was arrogant		He was a good employer	
He was quick-tempered		He was a social climber	
He was a good companion		He exploited his workers	
He was avaricious		He was secretive	

Sir Richard Arkwright sits proudly beside a model of his water frame

Copy the chart and note which sources support the different opinions.

A This account of Arkwright as a young man, at Bolton in the 1750s, was written by Thomas Ridgeway in 1799. Arkwright's son had asked for the information.

. . . He . . . married your Mother, and began business for himself. . . . He had a decent House, a cleaner one could not be and his friends and acquaintances always found in it a cordial reception from him. . . . His genius for Mechanics was observed. . . . I well remember we had often great fun with a Clock he put up in his shop, which had all the appearance of being worked by the smoke of the chimney and we have caused a many to believe it was so; I have often seen him cut pasteboard into different shapes such as forming squares from oblongs without adding or diminishing, and a Hundred curious knackey things that one cannot find words to explain. He was always thought clever in his peruke making business and very capital in Bleeding and   peruke: wig
toothdrawing and allowed by all his acquaintances to be a very ingenious man.

B Arkwright was never a great letter-writer, but he wrote this letter to his partner Jedediah Strutt in 1772 to report progress at the new Cromford mill.

. . . one person will spin a Thousand Hanks a Day so that wee shall not want ⅕ of the hands I First Expected. I see Greate Improvement Every day. . . . I have made trial to twist it for Velverets and find what they do with five operations I can do with one. . . . I am sertain I can make the first fraim, I have hands to make three frames in a fortnet. . . . Richd has hit upon a method to spin woostid with Roulers, it is quite sertain, and only altering the shape – that is Round on one side and flat on the other so that the twist gets under or betwixt   worsted, velvet, whipcord were
them at sertain time. It will ansuar, I am sertain. Query, will not Cotton make   all types of cloth
whipcord as good as silk, properly Twisted. . . . Desire ward to send those
other Locks and allso Some sort of Hangins for the sashes . . . and some good   sashes: windows
Latches and Catches for the outdoors and a few for the inner ans allso and a Large Knocker or a Bell to the First door. I am Determined for the feuter to Let no person in to look at the works. . . .

C In 1779 a mill at Chorley in Lancashire in which Arkwright had an interest was destroyed by rioters. On 12 October 1779 the *Manchester Mercury* described Arkwright's reaction at Cromford.

All the Gentlemen in this Neighbourhood being determined to support Mr Arkwright, in the defence of his Works. . . . Fifteen hundred stand of small Arms are already collected from Derby and the Neighbouring Towns, and a great Battery of Cannon raised of 9 and 12 Pounders with great plenty of Powder and Grape Shot, besides which, upwards of 500 Spears are fixt in Poles of between 2 and 3 Yards long. The Spears and Battery are always to be kept in Repair for the Defence of the Works and Protection of the Village, and 5000 or 6000 Men, Miners, etc. can . . . be assembled in less than an Hour . . . determined to defend to the very last Extremity, the Works, by which many Hundreds of their Wives and Children get a decent and comfortable Livelihood.

A visitor in 1781 noted that Arkwright

. . . by his conduct appears to be a man of great understanding and to know the way of making his people do their best. He not only distributes pecuniary   pecuniary: money
rewards, but gives distinguishing dresses to the most deserving of both sexes,

which excites great emulation. He also gives two Balls at the Greyhound to the workmen and their wives and families with a weeks jubilee at the time of each ball. This makes them industrious and sober all the rest of the year.

D The evidence of Thomas Highs, the Lancashire inventor, at the 1785 enquiry into Arkwright's patents:

Q Did you ever see rollers like those before 1775, before Mr Arkwright's patent?
A I have seen rollers, I made rollers in 1767.
Q Have you looked at them; you see one is fluted, the other covered with Leather?
A I see it is.

The water frame. The disputed rollers are at the top

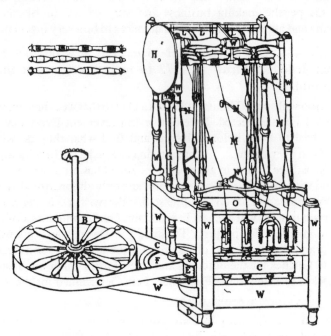

Q Was yours the same way?
A Yes mine was, two years after, but not then.
Q Not at first?
A No.
Q In 1769 yours were like it?
A They were, mine had fluted work, fluted wood, upon an iron axis; but the other roller was the same, only it was covered with shoe leather instead of that leather; . . . .
Q Who did you employ when you first conceived this invention, who did you employ to make it for you?
A I employed one Kay who came from Warrington.
Q What trade was he?
A He followed Clock-making at that time.
Q You employed him to make it?
A Yes, I employed him to make a small model. . . .

John Kay, a clock-maker from Warrington, worked with Arkwright in 1768 when he made his first models of the water frame.

E Arkwright was a difficult man to work with. In 1773 Strutt had to try to make peace between him and John Smalley. Smalley had been Arkwright's original partner in Preston and was manager of the Cromford mill. Relations with his employer were not easy.

. . . am sorry to find matters betwixt you and Mr Arkwright have come to such extremities and wonder he he shoud persist in giving you fresh provocations. I said what I coud to persuade him to oblige you in any thing that was reasonable and to endeavour to live on good terms. . . . We cannot prevent him saying Ill-natured things nor can we regulate his actions. . . .

F *What others thought of Arkwright*

(i) [Arkwright] within the small space of ten years, from being a poor man not worth £5, now keeps his carriage and servants, is become a Lord of a Manor, and has purchased an estate of £20,000; while thousands of women, when they can get work, must make a long day to card, spin and reel 5040 yards of cotton and for this they have *four-pence or five-pence and no more.*

An Impartial Representation of the Case of the Poor Cotton Spinners in Lancashire, 1780

(ii) Matthew Boulton wrote to James Watt in December 1780 when Arkwright's parents were being challenged in the courts for the first time. Other manufacturers took this step because Arkwright claimed large payments if they used water frames.

. . . he has already built a great building for Cotton Works (at Manchester), yet he swears it shall never be worked and will sooner let it for Barricks for Soldiers, swears he will take the Cotton Spinning abroad, and that he will ruin those Manchester rascals whom he has been the making of. It is agreed by all who know him that he is a Tyrant . . . . and 'tis thought that his disappointment will kill him. If he had been a man of sense and reason he would not have lost his patent. . . . Surely you cannot think it just that any tyrant should tyrannise over so large a manufactory by false pretences.

manufactory: industry

(iii) James Watt writing to Matthew Boulton in 1785 after Arkwright had finally lost his patents:

As to Mr Arkwright, he is, to say no worse, one of the most self-sufficient ignorant men I have ever met with, yet . . . he is certainly . . . one to whom Britain is much indebted, and whom she should honour and reward, for whoever invented the spinning machine, Arkwright certainly had the merit of performing the most difficult part, which was the making it useful.

(iv) We all look up to him and have imitated his mode of building.

Sir Robert Peel, *Select Committee Report on Children in Manufactories*, 1816

1 (a) What impression does the picture, on page 68 give of Arkwright?
(b) Do you think that a portrait like this is of much value to the historian? Explain your answer.
2 Source A appears to be contradicted by some of the other evidence.
(a) How do sources E and F differ from Ridgeway in their assessment of Arkwright's character?
(b) Source A claims that Arkwright had a 'genius for Mechanics'. Which pieces of evidence support this claim, and which pieces of evidence appear to contradict it? Explain your answer.
(c) Do these contradictions make Ridgeway's evidence worthless? Explain your answer, making reference to the sources.
3 Consult sources C and F.
(a) How do these sources differ in the impression they give us of Arkwright as an employer?
(b) How do you explain the differences? Which piece of evidence is of most value to the historian? Explain your answer.
4 (a) What conclusion can you draw about Arkwright the inventor from source D and the comments of James Watt in source F?
(b) To what extent do you agree with Watt's comments that 'Arkwright certainly had the merit of performing the most difficult part'?

Now read these opinions of modern historians on Arkwright's achievements.

H . . . it seems that the Arkwright 'water frame' owed its conception to Highs and Kay as well as Arkwright, although most people agree that, without the perseverance and business acumen of Arkwright, it would never have become a commercial proposition.

R.L. Hills, *Power in the Industrial Revolution*, 1970

I . . . Cromford proved a poor site for water power and Arkwright would have forseen this if he had any real understanding of watermills. . . . The only possible attraction of Cromford was its isolation which could have made it a good location for developing new techniques in secret, and relatively safe from rioting spinners and knitters . . . This advantage seems small . . . compared with the very real handicaps which transport costs and isolation from the centre of the cotton textile industry imposed. . . .

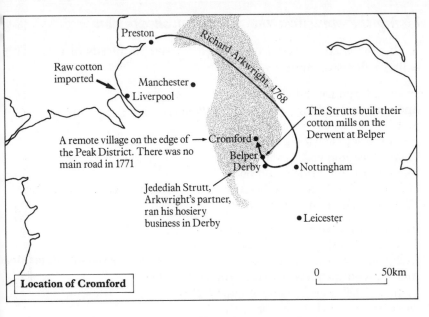

Location of Cromford

Map features:
- Preston
- Richard Arkwright, 1768
- Raw cotton imported
- Manchester
- Liverpool
- A remote village on the edge of → Cromford the Peak District. There was no main road in 1771
- The Strutts built their cotton mills on the Derwent at Belper
- Belper
- Derby
- Nottingham
- Jedediah Strutt, Arkwright's partner, ran his hosiery business in Derby
- Leicester
- 0 ___ 50km

. . . He demonstrated the profitability of warp-spinning by power. . . . His genius . . . was that of the successful innovating entrepreneur; for while there are several witnesses to his mechanical ability, he could lay small claims to the title of inventor and, indeed, showed little originality as a mechanic. Certainly he did not originate or develop the idea of roller-spinning. . . . Arkwright's achievement was to translate Paul's mechanical success into the factory system of organisation, and into commercial success.

S.D. Chapman, *The Early Factory Masters*, 1967

entrepreneur: businessman

Lewis Paul was the first inventor to try roller spinning, in the 1730s

1 (a) In what ways do these two historians question Arkwright's reputation as an inventor and a good businessman?
(b) How fair do you think their assessments of Arkwright are? Use the evidence from the other sources and elsewhere in this chapter in your answer.
2 Using the evidence and the facts you have been given, write your own assessment of the character and achievement of Richard Arkwright. Explain why you think he succeeded and Hargreaves and Crompton failed.

4 The iron industry: entrepreneurs in action

Using the evidence: the impact of cheap iron

In the 1820s cheap cast iron seemed to have hundreds of uses. This ballad tells us of some.

Since cast iron has got all the rage,
And scarcely anything's now made without it;
As I live in this cast-iron age,
I mean to say something about it.
There's cast-iron coffins and carts,
There's cast-iron bridges and boats,
Corn-factors with cast-iron hearts,   corn-factor: a corn merchant
That I'd hang up in cast-iron coats.

Iron bedsteads have long been in use;
With cast-iron they now pave our streets;
Each tailor has a cast-iron goose,   a tailor's goose was his pressing
And we soon shall have cast-iron sheets.   iron
Tommy Whalebone has grown quite a blade,
So dextrous and clever his hand is,
Swears he now shall have excellent trade
Making cast-iron stays for the dandies.   stays: corsets

We have cast-iron gates and lamp-posts,
We have cast-iron mortars and mills, too,
And our enemies know to their cost
We have plenty of cast-iron pills, too.   What are 'cast-iron pills'?
We have cast-iron fenders and grates,
We have cast-iron pokers and tongs, sir;
And we soon shall have cast-iron plates,
And cast-iron small-clothes, ere long, sir. small-clothes: knee-breeches

Cast iron for every purpose

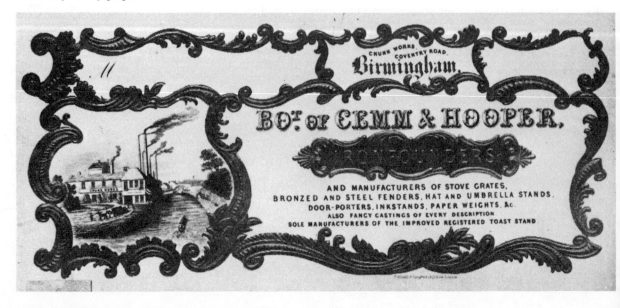

1 How many actual uses of cast iron are mentioned in the song? List them.
2 There are other less serious and more amusing references to cast iron. Find them. Can you explain the reference to 'Corn-factors with cast-iron hearts'?
3 What can we really learn from this source about the use of cast iron in the early nineteenth century?

Cheap and plentiful iron made the changes in industry and transport possible. In 1740 British blast furnaces produced only about 20 000 tons of pig iron, whilst 30 000–40 000 tons were imported from Sweden and Russia. By 1850 the output from British blast furnaces exceeded 2 000 000 tons. A ruthless exploitation of new methods and techniques by hard-headed ironmasters made this dramatic increase possible.

The crisis of the charcoal iron industry

Charcoal burners supplied the iron industry with its blast furnace fuel. Dwindling supplies of suitable timber caused a crisis in the industry at the beginning of the eighteenth century

In 1720 there were fifty-nine charcoal blast furnaces scattered through the Sussex Weald, the Forest of Dean, South Wales, North Wales, Shropshire, the West Midlands, South Yorkshire and Derbyshire. Sussex, an old iron-making area, was in decline, barely kept alive by government armament contracts which lasted until after 1750.

At the beginning of the eighteenth century there were few uses for cast iron, which was brittle. Most pig iron was reheated and hammered to remove the impurities and make it into wrought or bar iron. This contained less carbon than cast iron and could be worked by the smiths and nailmakers at their forges.

Pig iron from Shropshire and the Forest of Dean was taken to the nail and chainmakers of the West Midlands by barge and packhorse. The

1 Sussex Weald
2 Forest of Dean
3 South Wales
4 West Midlands including Shropshire
5 North Wales
6 North Staffordshire and Cheshire
7 Derbyshire and South Yorkshire
8 Furness

Charcoal blast-furnace sites at the beginning of the eighteenth century

West Midlands was the main ironworking district, despite lacking the plentiful timber and fast flowing streams that were needed to exploit the area's own rich iron ore reserves. High-quality imported wrought iron from Sweden and Russia was also worked around Sheffield.

The siting of a blast furnace, where the iron ore was smelted, was determined by the availability of water-power to operate the bellows to provide the blast. Transport was also important. The ironmasters of the Forest of Dean and Shropshire depended on the River Severn to distribute their products.

The iron industry's development was hampered by the exhaustion of timber resources and by its dependence on water-power. Unless these problems could be overcome, rich deposits of iron ore could not be exploited and the industry's slow decline would continue.

Coke-smelting: the contribution of the Darby family

In January 1709, Abraham Darby begun smelting iron at Coalbrookdale in Shropshire. Born in 1678, Darby, a Quaker, was apprenticed to a maker of malt mills in Birmingham. Moving to Bristol in 1699, he eventually became a partner in a brass foundry and in 1707 took out a patent for a new method of casting iron pots in sand moulds. He rented the disused Coalbrookdale furnace to profit from this invention.

Coalbrookdale, with plentiful supplies of local iron ore, limestone to hand and the River Severn providing transport to Bristol and the sea, was an ideal location. Even Coalbrookdale's remoteness was an advantage if Darby was to keep his new techniques secret for as long as possible. At Coalbrookdale he made the crucial discovery which made the Industrial Revolution possible.

There had been experiments using coal to smelt iron in the seventeenth century, but the sulphur content of coal made the iron brittle and useless. Now read Abiah Darby's account of her father-in-law's breakthrough.

About the year 1709 he came into Shropshire in Coalbrookdale. . . . He here cast Iron Goods in sand out of the Blast Furnace that blow'd with wood charcoal. . . . Sometime after he suggested the thought, that it might be practicable to smelt the Iron . . . with Pit Coal: Upon this he first try'd with raw coal as it came out of the Mines, but it did not answer. He not discouraged, had the coal coak'd into Cynder, as is done for drying Malt, and it then succeeded to his satisfaction. . . .

Darby's account books for 1708 and 1709 contain entries which suggest that coal was being purchased rather than charcoal. Amongst the payments made for the period up to 30 April 1709 is one

. . . to coals reserved by Roger Cock from Darrall's pit – 9 stack 7 loads. . . .

Other payments were for 'Charking coles'.

Questions

1 What does Abiah Darby's evidence tell us of the reasons why Darby went to Coalbrookdale, and of the way in which he made his discovery?
2 To what extent did Darby's previous experience help him?
3 It has been suggested that there was a shortage of charcoal in Coalbrookdale. How might this explain Darby's experiments?

Coke-smelted iron was suitable for casting iron domestic utensils – pots, grates, etc. – direct from the furnace in sand moulds. Knowledge of the new process spread slowly. The relative isolation of Coalbrookdale and the reticence of the Darby family partially explained this. More important, perhaps, charcoal-produced iron remained cheaper until after the 1750s, and its quality was far superior. Coke-smelted pigs were too impure to make good wrought iron. Hence the forgemasters would not buy them.

Abraham Darby I died in 1717 when his son, Abraham Darby II, was only six. Until he became a full partner in the business in 1738 little changed, although cast-iron cylinders for steam engines were added to the company's products. Once he was in control Abraham Darby II began a time of renewed innovation.

Blast furnaces were dependent on water-power to operate the bellows that provided the blast. Consequently furnaces were often unused for perhaps four months in a year when a continuous supply of water was not available. In 1742 Darby installed a Newcomen steam engine at Coalbrookdale to pump water back into the feeder pond after it had passed over the water wheel.

Ironmaking in the eighteenth century – the processes

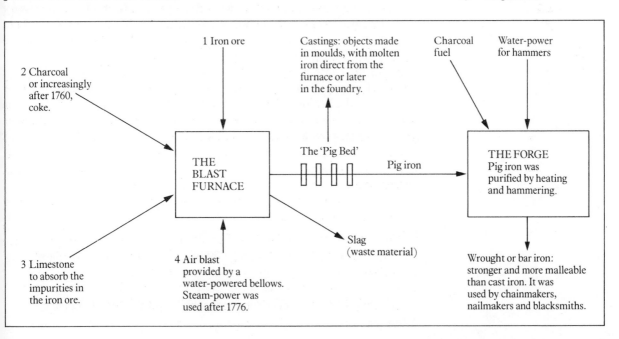

Coalbrookdale in 1758. The furnace is in the centre of the group of buildings on the left. Coke is being made in the heaps. Note the size of the cast-iron cylinder on the cart. Why is there a large pool?

He was also determined to improve the quality of coke-smelted iron. His father's success had been assisted by the low sulphur content of the local Shropshire coal. The son experimented with coking techniques, the blast-furnace mixture and the strength of the blast, at one crucial point spending six days and nights without rest at the furnace, being carried home exhausted and asleep when the work was completed. In 1755 the Coalbrookdale Company put a new furnace in blast, selling its pig iron to forgemasters. Falling costs meant that coke-smelted iron could compete with the charcoal product.

In 1760 there were only seventeen coke furnaces in blast; thirty years later there were over eighty with only twenty-five charcoal furnaces left in production. Some were undoubtedly converted for coke operation as this letter, dated 6 October 1779, suggests. Francis Dorset was proposing to lease a furnace near Sheffield.

. . . I will endeavour to point out what Repairs . . . are absolutely necessary . . . . I want to work with it upon the principle Mr Walker's of Rotherham work theirs, that is with Pit coal instead of charcoal . . . on account of the Scarcity and Dearness of Cordwood. . . . When Furnaces are worked on this Plan they are constantly going Winter and Summer; on account of the great scarcity of water in Summer it will be necessary to build a Fire Engine to lift the Water from the Bottom of the Wheel into the Pond, to work it over and over again . . . there is at present a great Demand for Cannon Balls and I should wish to get to work as soon as possible. . . .

cordwood: branches of trees prepared for making charcoal

Questions

1 What is a 'fire engine'?
2 Dorset estimated that the improvements would cost £744, of which £400 would purchase the 'fire engine'. Why was this expenditure worthwhile?
3 To what extent does this letter point to the problems faced by the iron industry and the contribution of the Darby family in solving them?

The furnace is being tapped. The molten iron is running into the pig bed

Cheap wrought iron – the contribution of Henry Cort

Henry Cort owned a forge at Fontley near Portsmouth where he worked on Admiralty contracts using imported Swedish wrought iron.

Wrought iron was in short supply despite the increasing output of pig iron from the new coke furnaces. The purification of the pigs by alternate heating and hammering was a slow and expensive process whilst the forgemasters still depended on charcoal.

Several unsuccessful and unsatisfactory attempts to speed up the process had been made before Cort patented his puddling and rolling process in 1784. Cort's use of a reverberatory furnace ended the need for charcoal since the coal with all its impurities was not in direct contact with the molten pig iron which lay on the other side of the fire bridge. As the heat bounced down from the roof of the furnace the puddler stirred the molten mixture with his rabble until the impurities in the iron had been burnt off. Removed in balls, the metal was hammered to remove cinders and to shape it ready for rolling. Rolling

Henry Cort's puddling furnace

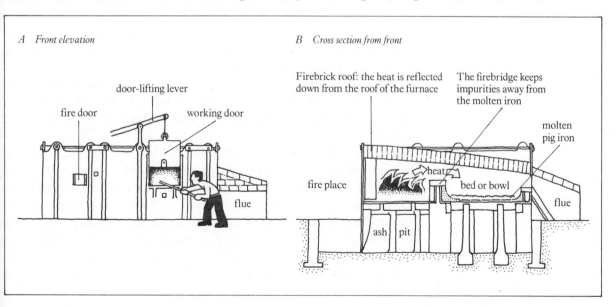

A Front elevation

fire door

door-lifting lever

working door

flue

B Cross section from front

Firebrick roof: the heat is reflected down from the roof of the furnace

The firebridge keeps impurities away from the molten iron

molten pig iron

fire place

heat

bed or bowl

flue

ash   pit

Puddling furnaces are in the background. In the foreground the iron worker holds a ball of molten wrought iron before it goes under the hammer. Wrought iron plates and rods are being rolled

was not new but Cort devised grooved rollers so that bars in a variety of shapes could be produced.

The new technique was adopted slowly. Under the terms of the patent, payment had to be made to Cort, and technical problems remained to be solved. In 1787 Richard Crawshay took Cort's process to his Cyfarthfa Ironworks, perfected it and made it a commercial success. By the mid-1790s every large ironmaking concern had its puddling furnaces.

Iron technology in the nineteenth century

By 1800 the main changes had taken place. Although blast-furnace design was improved and the puddling process made more efficient, the basic techniques remained the same. Large integrated ironworks with two or more blast furnaces surrounded by cupola furnaces (for remelting pigs), puddling furnaces and rolling mills, were to be found on all the ironworking coalfields.

James Neilson's hot blast (1829) was the only major innovation in iron technology during the nineteenth century. By preheating the blast of air in an oven before it entered the furnace, great savings in fuel could be achieved.

Adopted only slowly in England, the hot blast laid the foundations of the iron industry in Scotland. Scotland's first coke furnace had come into blast at Carron in 1759, but there were no more than thirty in 1830. Twenty years later 144 furnaces produced 775 000 tons to make Central Scotland one of the three leading ironmaking districts in Britain. The higher temperatures the hot blast gave enabled the Scottish ironmasters to use the local low grade coal, which coked badly, as furnace fuel. Central Scotland's blackband ironstone could be effectively and cheaply exploited.

New uses for iron

Mass-produced iron became the basic material of industrial change. Cast-iron cylinders for the Newcomen engine were amongst the first industrial uses pioneered at Coalbrookdale where, in 1767, iron rails for tramways were laid for the first time. The most spectacular use of cast iron was the construction of the Iron Bridge across the River Severn to link the ironworks, coalmines and limestone quarries which lined both banks of the river. Abraham Darby III was amongst the scheme's leading promotors, the iron for the structure being smelted and possibly cast at Coalbrookdale. Certainly the original Coalbrookdale blast furnace was enlarged to cope with the needs of the project and Darby seems to have lost money when costs exceeded the original estimates.

Completed in 1779, the bridge soon became a tourist attraction, but it also demonstrated how cast iron could be used and the first iron bridge was soon followed by others. Cast-iron pillars and beams replaced timber and brick in the new textile mills and in 1796 Thomas Telford designed the first cast-iron canal aqueduct. All kinds of industrial and agricultural machinery had cast-iron parts. The song at the beginning of this chapter accurately reflects the revolution in materials that was taking place. Cheap, durable wrought iron was snapped up by industrialists and engineers. The railway revolution of the 1830s and 1840s created an insatiable demand for the iron industry's products.

The Iron Bridge

Cheap and plentiful supplies of wrought and cast iron were the raw materials which made the Industrial Revolution possible. Steel was only produced in small quantities, at great expense and for specialist purposes. Not until after 1860 did mass-produced steel begin to replace wrought iron.

The Pavilion, Buxton, Derbyshire. Cheap iron and cheap glass made buildings like this possible

Using the evidence: British pig iron production, 1720–1860

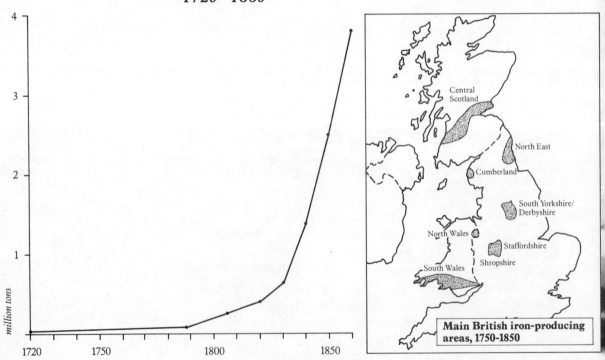

Table 1   Pig iron output, 1720–1860

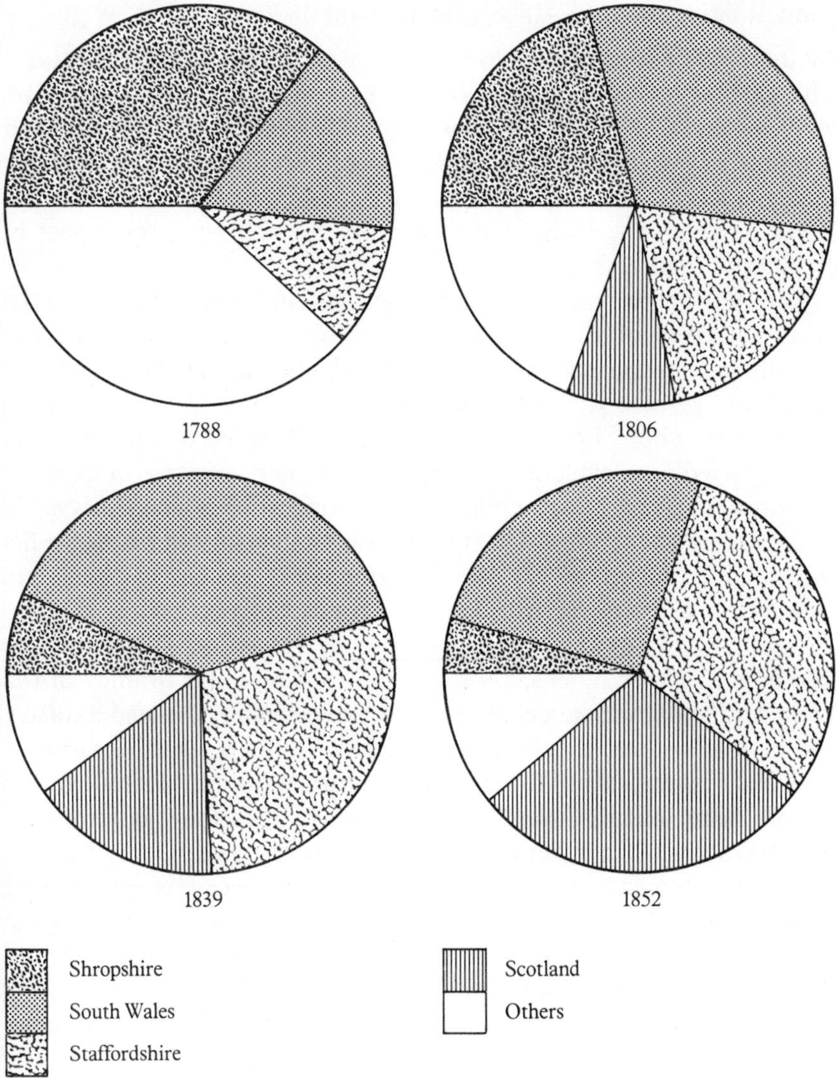

Table 2 The changing importance of the main iron producing areas. The charts show their percentage share of the total amount of pig iron produced

1788

1806

1839

1852

Shropshire

South Wales

Staffordshire

Scotland

Others

1 Here is a series of dates, events and names which help to explain Table 1: 'Railway mania', Abraham Darby I, John Wilkinson, 1784, the Iron Bridge, James Neilson.
   (a) Put them into the correct chronological sequence;
   (b) Explain how each contributed to the rise in output or demand for pig iron.
2 Study Table 2. What can you learn from it about the iron-producing areas?
   (a) What happened to Shropshire as a centre of iron production?
   (b) What happened to Scotland as a centre of iron production?
   (c) How do you explain the late rise of Scotland to prominence as an ironmaking area?
   (d) What is there to remember about total pig-iron production throughout this period?

John Wilkinson (1728–1808), Ironmaster

By the 1760s developments in Shropshire were pointing to the future. The Coalbrookdale Company owned several furnaces, it worked its own coal and iron ore mines, took limestone from its own quarries and operated its own forges. A network of wagonways linked the company's mines, quarries and works with each other and with the wharves on the River Severn. The integrated ironworks controlling every aspect of production had emerged.

John Wilkinson was a more dramatic and flamboyant figure than the sober Quakers of Coalbrookdale. Ruthless and unscrupulous, not hesitating to ruin members of his own family, he was hated by many and feared but respected by his workers.

The man whom Lord Dundonald believed 'to be one of the most hard-hearted, malevolent Old Scoundrels now existing in Britain' legitimised his illegitimate children, the youngest born when he was 77, to disinherit his nephew. On the seventh anniversary of his death his workmen gathered at his Bradley ironworks expecting their late employer's ghost to ride through on a tour of inspection.

Wilkinson's interests were widespread. He owned ironworks at Bersham in North Wales, Broseley in Shropshire and Bradley in the West Midlands, was involved in the copper industry, the lead industry and in at least three canal projects. Arthur Young praised his farms as excellent examples of 'the new agriculture'. Joseph Priestley, the Birmingham scientist, was his brother-in-law. Matthew Boulton and James Watt benefited from his expertise and Abraham Darby III from his encouragement when planning the Iron Bridge. His active mind never rested. Never an inventor, although he devised the cupola furnace for remelting iron in the 1780s, Wilkinson exploited and developed other men's ideas.

At Brosley in the 1770s he unsuccessfully tried to adapt a Newcomen engine to operate the bellows for his furnaces. Encountering Boulton and Watt in 1774 he realised that their improved steam engine could solve his problem. In return, his cannon boring lathe could provide the accurately made iron cylinders the steam engine manufacturers needed. They sold him their second engine in 1776 to operate his bellows at Broseley.

Steam-power had arrived, freeing the iron industry from its dependence on water-power. Rotary steam engines were quickly adapted to drive rolling mills and steam-power replaced water-power in the forges where hammers were used. The ironmaster's profits were no longer restricted by the weather, and sites by fast-flowing streams were no longer essential. Staffordshire, long hampered by a shortage of water-power sources developed as a major iron-making district. Since British iron ore reserves were found close to coal the industry located itself on the coalfields of the West Midlands, South Wales and Scotland.

Wilkinson's enthusiasm helped to extend the use of iron. He launched the first iron boat on the Severn in 1787, exported cast-iron

John Wilkinson's head on one of the wage tokens paid to his employees

pipes to carry water for Parisians and built himself an iron coffin although he no longer fitted it when he died.

His virtual monopoly as the maker of Boulton and Watt's steam engine cylinders added to his fame but his partners eventually discovered that whilst making parts officially he was also selling pirate engines on his own behalf which did not pay the patent royalties. They forced him to pay compensation, and set up a foundry at their Soho works where they manufactured their own cylinders.

Using the evidence: the ironmaster and his workers

The South Wales iron industry developed because of coke-smelting. Dynasties of ironmasters were founded at the end of the eighteenth century when the great works at Dowlais, Cyfarthfa and Penydarren were established. By 1810 there were four major ironworks and seventeen blast furnaces within a two-mile radius of Merthyr, a town where the ironmaster ruled supreme. All the following sources refer to the Cyfarthfa works of the Crawshay family or to the Dowlais works of the Guest family.

A Richard Crawshay had first taken the lease on the Cyfarthfa ironworks in 1786 and his fortune rested on the success with which he had exploited Cort's puddling process. In 1797 the Duke of Bedford visited Merthyr and toured Cyfarthfa meeting Crawshay. This is his description:

. . . He told us, that when he originally came to the place, about 10 years ago, there was only one furnace . . . . There could not be fewer than 1000 able-bodied men employed. . . .

By the mid-nineteenth century ironworks were immense concerns. Blast furnaces, puddling furnaces, rolling mills and forges were worked on the same site and companies usually owned coal-mines and limestome quarries

We first saw, and entered one or two of the workmen's houses, which he had himself built for them at the rate of 30 guineas per house; they are extremely neat and clean. . . .

Very fortunately, iron ore, coal and limestone, are all found in the same hills, so that Mr Crawshay has every requisite for his works close at home. He pointed out to us one shaft of coal, which would yield daily 200 tons. . . .

The active . . . mind of Mr C. is continually engaged in some new piece of machinery . . . . He talked of having spent £20 000 in improving some parts of his machinery. . . .

When we were there, three furnaces were at work, but there are five, all of which this single wheel is sufficient to blow, iron tubes connecting the whole and joining them. . . .

He has cultivated the country around him, which on his arrival at the place was as barren as the bare rock. . . .

Mr C. showed us a turnpike he was going to make and a canal is finished from the works as far as Cardiff, which is to communicate with the sea. . . .

Journal of a Tour through North and South Wales, London, 1805

B These pieces of evidence are about relations between the Guests and their workforce at Dowlais. The extracts all come from letters.

(i) Richard Crawshay to Robert Thompson, Manager at Dowlais, 13 May 1797.

For some time back it has been in Contemplation to regulate a very few Individuals Labourers Wages at this place (Cyfarthfa) . . . . They have stood out for more, finding a ready Assylum under Mr Thompson they say; by giveing them 14/- a Week each with house and fire . . . a Wage as far as we know never given for such sort of Labourers. If when any of our Men or yours insist upon Wages incompatible the other will Countenance them by immediate employ, we shall injure all our Works and make resistance to all reasonable remonstrance with the Workmen in vain. . . .

remonstrance: dispute

(ii) William Taitt (partner at Dowlais) to Thomas Guest, 17 January 1799.

guineas to the foundry: a bonus payment

I have had some Conversation with Mr Homfray and Mr Richard Hill about the Guineas to the Foundry. The former says he will immediately Stop the payment of them to his Men and the latter says that as soon as the existing Agreements are out with their Founders he also will refuse to continue it. . . .

One thing I must insist on, that we pay our Men only once a Month in future which will save us 3 broken days in the Month. . . .

(iii) The men refused to accept the ending of the payment, with this result:

John Davis to Thomas Guest, Cowbridge Bridewell, 28 February 1799.

I ham sorry that I abuesed your Honer in taking so much Upon me to speak for Others. I hope you will Get me out of this whole of a place so soon as your Honer shall think fitt as I shall be starved a Live for my money is all spent – and I have nuthing But the bear 3 alpence of bread in four & 20 ouers and a drop of Caen water. I hope you will Let me Com back to your work again – and I hope the Rest will take warning by me as I ham in such a Place at Present.

I have but one ours Liberty out of 24 to walk in the Yard.

(iv) William Lewis to Thomas Guest, 27 September 1800.

. . . I hope by this time the misguided People are come to their senses, and are returned to their several occupations. As far as the Dowlais Company are concerned the Workmen ought to be told and satisfied that our opening a Warehouse was intended to accomodate them, and not with a view of profit to ourselves. If our good intention fails of it's good effect, for my own part I am ready to give it up and to let them have their Money to lay out where they please. . . . I understood we were only to supply our own Workmen with Flour, Cheeses etc., if they think the price too high pay them their Money and let them buy where they please. . . .

(v) William Taitt to Josiah John Guest, 4 March 1814.

You do right in dismissing all the Men who enter'd into the Combination.   combination: a trade union

1 Consult source A.
   (a) Cyfarthfa was one of the most extensive ironworks of its time. List as many points as you can find in the Duke's description which would support this.
   (b) How do you explain Crawshay's interest in the turnpike road and the canal to Cardiff? What might this tell you about Merthyr?
2 Consult the extracts in source B.
   (a) Why do you think William Taitt only wanted to pay the men once a month?
   (b) What problem is worrying Richard Crawshay in his letter of 13 May 1797? What does this suggest about the labour situation in the Merthyr area?
   (c) There is a contradiction in these sources between the attitude of the ironmasters to combination or unions amongst the men, and to agreements between themselves. Find the contradiction and explain it.
3 The Merthyr ironmasters could be described as paternalistic employers, caring for their workers like a family.
   (a) List all the pieces of evidence in sources A and B which could be used to support this claim.
   (b) The workmen would probably have disagreed. Write a report from one of the workmen to a local newspaper, giving their version of the events described in sources B(ii), B(iii) and B(iv).
4 Using all the sources write your own assessment of the ironmasters' treatment of their workmen. Refer to the sources in your answer.

Using the evidence: the Davy Safety Lamp, 1815

Coal mining was always a hazardous occupation and the coal-owners were not always concerned with safety. Underground accidents were frequent and injuries or death were accepted risks. The great explosion had most impact on the mining community because of the high loss of life and because its effects could be seen on the surface. Here is a description of the Felling explosion in 1812.

The deep caverns, where the explosion first vented its fury, confined the eruption too much for its upmost noise to be heard on the surface; but for half a mile round the trembling vibration of the earth proclaimed the occurence before the sound escaped, and for four or five miles an alarm was created by the slow and hollow rumblings in the air. Immense quantities of coal, pieces of wood, and dust, drove high into the atmosphere, and the lacerated remains of several bodies were thrown up the shaft. . . . The roads and paths were covered in all directions with pieces of coal and coal dust; . . . machinery about the shafts was . . . blown to pieces or set on fire; and . . . Heworth, situated near the mine, was enveloped in darkness.

> J.H.H. Holmes, *A Treatise on the Coal Mines of Durham and Northumberland*, 1816

A The following extract is from a late nineteenth-century newspaper article on colliery disasters in the North East. The extract refers to the eighteenth century and early nineteenth century.

procurable: available

. . . Until comparatively recent days great pressure was put upon newspapers to prevent the publication of details, and, except when the tragedy was independently notorious, the very fact of an accident . . . small mischances involving only two or three lives were ignored. . . . Coal-owners, being naturally anxious to conceal their own negligence, exerted all the influence they could command to stifle both inquiry and publicity. More generally . . . their motive . . . was the fear of so alarming industrous men that a sufficient number of miners would not be procurable. . . . Their best course was to hush up all accidents as much and as soon as they could. Their disinclination for inquiry was . . . to some extent shared in by the authorities, and perhaps also . . . by newspaper editors. . . .

B 'Regulations in the Whitehaven Collieries relative to the use of Sir Humphrey Davy's Safety Lamp' (Whitehaven 13 November 1819).

hewer: the coalface worker

If any Hewer, or other Workman, employed in the Whitehaven Coalpits where any danger can exist from Fire Damp, shall neglect to approach his Work with the SAFETY LAMP or shall use CANDLES in doing so, he shall (for every Offence) forfeit the Sum of Five Shillings [25p] And when Orders are given to continue the Use of the Lamp, during the whole Time of Working, any person who shall remove the SAFETY CYLINDER or use Candles in the Workings, shall also forfeit Five Shillings.

John Buddle was the leading mining engineer on the north-east coalfield

C From a letter from John Buddle to Davy on 1 January 1824.

Its importance in a material point of view is enabling the miner to produce coal to the community, which without its aid, *never could have seen the light of day.*

D From Buddle's evidence to the committee of the House of Lords on the Coal Trade, 1830.

. . . almost all the collieries below the bridge on the Tyne could have been at this time extinct, but for the Safety Lamp.

We are working mines from having the advantage of the safety lamp, which we could not have possibly worked without it, and of course they are in a more dangerous situation and the risk is increased in a very great degree.

1 Consult source A. How do you explain the reluctance of mine owners, the authorities and newspaper editors to give publicity to accidents?
2 What does source B suggest to you about the attitude of the miners to the new lamp? (For most men a five shilling (25p) fine was more than a day's pay.)
3 From Buddle's evidence (sources C and D) explain why the mine owners would welcome the safety lamp.
4 Buddle is very enthusiastic about the lamp. From his evidence do you think his enthusiasm would have been shared by the pitmen? Explain your answer.
5 The Safety Lamp was designed to save lives. What additional evidence would you need if you were to assess its success? Given Extract A, what difficulties might the historian face?

Over 200 lives were lost in the explosion at Haydock Colliery in 1878

A Davy lamp – the fine wire mesh diffused the heat. It could not ignite the fire damp

The eighteenth-century background

By 1700 some coal was being mined in all Britain's present-day coalfields with the exception of the Kent field. Demand was low since there were few industrial uses for coal, the main market being for domestic heating. Production was limited by more serious problems.

During the eighteenth century the last of the shallow, easily-worked seams were exhausted. Mining deeper seams presented many technical problems, and was very expensive.

The most developed coalfield in the early eighteenth century was the North East. It was on the coast and the inland mines had ready access to water transport. The high transport costs of coal meant that it was uneconomic to move it overland for more than about ten miles. This restricted the development of all inland coalfields, but the North East was able to expand because access to the sea and cheap transport gave it the monopoly of the largest market in the country, London.

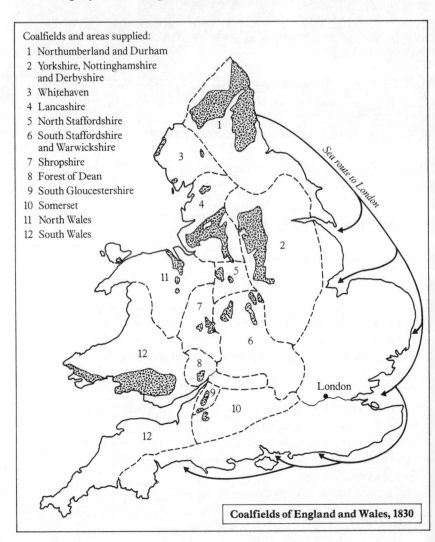

Coalfields and areas supplied:
1 Northumberland and Durham
2 Yorkshire, Nottinghamshire and Derbyshire
3 Whitehaven
4 Lancashire
5 North Staffordshire
6 South Staffordshire and Warwickshire
7 Shropshire
8 Forest of Dean
9 South Gloucestershire
10 Somerset
11 North Wales
12 South Wales

Sea route to London

London

Coalfields of England and Wales, 1830

The map shows the area each coalfield supplied. By 1830 the inland coalfields were benefiting from the canal network

A growing demand

Population growth and urbanisation affected the demand for coal in two ways. Firstly it meant that more was needed for domestic heating. Secondly it increased the production of industries like brickmaking and brewing, which had already begun to use coal by the beginning of the eighteenth century. Technical developments in other industries were, however, the main reason for increasing demand.

Changes in the iron industry played a major part in this. It took eight tons of coal to smelt one ton of iron in the new coke furnaces after 1750. See Chapter 4 To produce one ton of bar iron using Cort's puddling process the ironmasters needed between four and eight tons of coal. Certain coalfields benefited immensely. In the West Midlands coal production soared as the iron industry expanded; the development of the eastern valleys of the South Wales coalfield was closely linked to the iron industry. After 1830 the extensive use of Neilson's hot blast contributed to a rapidly growing output from the Scottish pits.

Equally important was the growing use of steam power by industry. Coalfields which directly benefited included Lancashire, as the cotton industry changed to steam power; and Yorkshire, as the wollen industry followed. To some extent all coalfields were affected by this development. By the 1830s the application of steam power to transport, in railways and steamships, had opened the way to even larger demands on the coalfields. Railway construction in its turn, consumed huge quantities of iron and therefore indirectly added to the growing market for coal, the basic raw material of the Industrial Revolution.

By 1830 the conversion of coal into gas for lighting purposes was creating a new source of demand. The London Gas Light and Coke Company had been formed in 1812. Within twenty years most growing towns had a gas works and gas lighting in their main streets.

Using the evidence: growing demand and output

COAL OUTPUT, 1700–1850	
	(million tons)
1700	2.9
1750	5.2
1775	8.8
1800	15.0
1815	22.2
1830	30.3
1854★	64.7
★First official figures available	

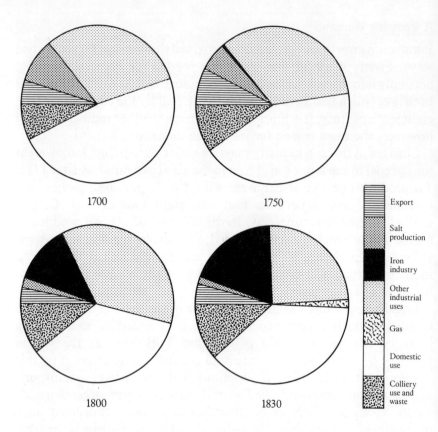

1700   1750   1800   1830

Export

Salt production

Iron industry

Other industrial uses

Gas

Domestic use

Colliery use and waste

1 What do the pie charts tell you about the changing use of coal? Remember that output was increasing all the time.
2 Which industry played the largest part in stimulating demand for coal? What technical changes were important here?
3 Coal output had almost doubled again by 1854. What transport development contributed to this, and how?
4 The figures on which these charts are based are only estimates. What are the difficulties in using them?

Problems and solutions

1 Working methods

The miner's tools, the pick and shovel, did not change but the technique of winning the coal did. In the North East the pillar-and-chamber method of working was used. Pillars of uncut coal were left to support the roof as the coal was extracted. When the seams were exhausted the pillars were removed as the miners worked back to the shaft bottom. The Longwall system, pioneered in the Midlands, spread rapidly to the other coalfields because more of the coal could be dug out. Miners worked on a broad front extracting the coal from the seam, packing waste into the spaces behind them to support the roof, and using pit props where necessary.

Pillar and chamber   *The Longwall system*

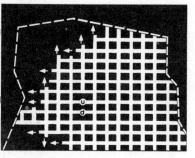
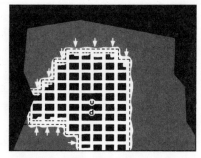
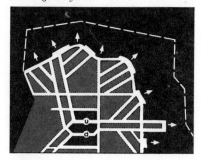

A Working out from the shafts,
  pillars of coal are left.

B Working back to the shafts,
  removing the pillars.

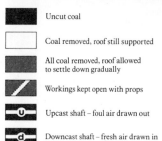

Based on Neil Cossons, *The BP
Book of Industrial Archaeology*,
p. 128

2 Drainage

Mine owners had to use new technology to solve the problems they
encountered as deep mining became more common in the eighteenth
century. The King Pit at the Whitehaven Hogwill Colliery was 993 feet
in 1793, the Gosforth and Jarrow pits were more than 1000 feet deep in
the 1820s, and coal was struck at 1578 feet when the Monkwearmouth
shaft was completed in 1834. Drainage was the most serious difficulty.
Early mines above the water table, and drift mines, had been drained by
soughs or adits. It was no hard task to keep the mine clear of water
although these drainage tunnels were long and expensive to construct.

In deep mines the drainage shaft had to run to the deepest point
where all the water would collect. Buckets on ropes or continuous
chains were used to raise the water to the surface. Occasionally
windmills provided the power to operate this system, and water wheels
were also used. In most mines, however, water was raised to the surface
by horse-power. These methods were costly and inefficient.

Newcomen's steam engine was first installed as a pumping engine at a
colliery in Staffordshire in 1712. The early engines were clumsy, badly-
made, and wasteful of coal, but their operating costs were less than
horse gins. A reduction in costs meant it was now possible to exploit the
deeper seams.

There were 78 steam engines on the coalfields when the Newcomen
patent expired in 1733. By 1775 there were 399, 159 of these being in
the North East. A steam pump had become a normal feature of all but
the shallowest or smallest collieries.

Boulton and Watt engines were more efficient at lifting water from
greater depths. The first began work in a West Midlands colliery in
1776 and one was in operation at Byker in the North East by 1778. By
1800 the battle against water had been won.

3 Ventilation

As mines got deeper, effective ventilation became an urgent necessity.
The most dangerous gas was fire damp (methane gas) which exploded if
it came into contact with a naked flame. The explosion could be

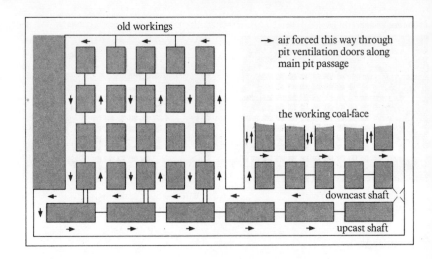

old workings

→ air forced this way through pit ventilation doors along main pit passage

the working coal-face

downcast shaft

upcast shaft

A colliery ventilation system. The arrows indicate the route the air was forced to take through the pit. There are three ventilation doors along the main passage. Barriers prevent the fresh air from taking a more direct route. This is to prevent the build-up of gas in the little-used parts of the mine. It was essential to maintain a good flow of air through the old workings

devastating. Ripping through the mine, destroying everything in its path, the blast would seriously damage the shaft and winding gear, making rescue doubly difficult. The explosion was followed by after-damp, which suffocated the survivors. John Buddle stated in 1814 that the actual blast only caused about a quarter of the deaths from a fire-damp explosion.

Fresh air circulating through the workings would prevent the accumulation of pockets of fire damp and of other suffocating gases.

By the middle of the eighteenth century convection currents were being exploited. Two shafts were sunk, or one shaft with a partition dividing it into two. A furnace was placed at the foot or at the top of the upcast shaft. This set up the convection currents. Fresh air drawn down the downcast shaft passed through the mine before escaping up the ventilation (upcast) shaft. This ended in a brick funnel capped by a large windvane. Explosions caused by the furnace igniting methane that had been drawn through the mine were not infrequent.

Another serious problem was to ensure that the fresh air passed

Harrington Mill Pitt Colliery, an early nineteenth-century pithead scene in the North East. There is a horse gin and steam winding engine. In the centre is the tube from the ventilation furnace. How are the men descending the shaft?

through all parts of the mine. From about 1760 the coursing system began to be used. The ventilation diagram opposite explains this. Fresh air was forced to follow a set route. Disused passages were blocked up and airdoors were placed on main roadways. Trappers, young boys from the age of six, were employed to open and shut these doors as coal was moved along.

Experiments with safer steam fans and suction bellows began about 1800. It was 1827 before the first successful steam-driven fan was installed in a pit at Paisley. Prints of collieries from the 1840s show that the old and risky furnace method was still widely used.

4 Lighting

For centuries miners had used candles underground but in the gassy North East pits this means of lighting was becoming increasingly hazardous. About 1730 the steel mill was invented. A wheel striking a flint sent a shower of sparks scattering over the working area but explosions still occurred. Public concern was focused on the problem in 1812 after the Felling Colliery disaster in which 92 lives were lost.

The Society for the Prevention of Accidents in Coal Mines invited Sir Humphrey Davy to investigate. In 1815 he demonstrated his safety lamp. Since fire damp could not be ignited through very small openings the flame was surrounded by a fine wire mesh. To improve the dim light the new lamp produced he added a metallic reflector. Simultaneously George Stephenson announced his own invention of a safety lamp. The 'Geordie lamp' was used exclusively by some North East collieries but the Davy lamp was the most widely adopted.

Nevertheless, despite its cheapness, accidents still happened. The wire mesh was fragile and easily damaged. It gave a very poor light compared to candles and many men preferred them despite the risks.

5 Haulage and winding

Underground putters or hurriers (terms differed from coalfield to coalfield) moved the full corves (containers of coal) from the coalface to the main passageways or the foot of the shaft. Boys and, in some coalfields, women and girls did this work. Before the end of the eighteenth century wheeled trollies were replacing the wooden sledges

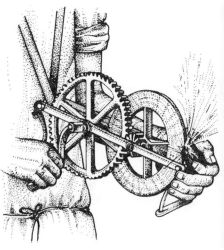

A steel mill in use

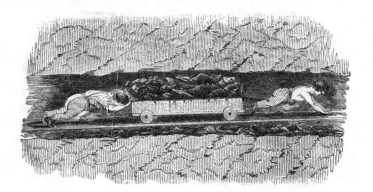

Boys 'hurrying' coal in a Lancashire pit in 1842

Underground in a Staffordshire colliery. The hewers are working the ten-foot seam so conditions are good. Pit ponies provide transport. Was this a gassy pit?

used to move the corves and rails were being laid to make movement easier. Pit ponies or donkeys were being used in the main passageways by the nineteenth century.

Mine owners valued these ponies far more highly than their human workers. In this song from the North East the pony is killed in an accident, its driver only injured.

galloway – a type of pony

> I had a little galloway
> His name was Little Chance
> He used to make the full uns fly
> And make the tyum-uns dance

tyum-uns – the empties

After the accident

Why did the 'owerman' 'twist his face'?

> The boss he called the owerman in
> The happening to relate
> And when he heard that Chance was dead
> It made him twist his face.
> I knew the lad was badly hurt,
> He was a stretcher case,
> But galloways like Little Chance
> Are harder to replace.

Winding coal to the surface could have been a serious bottleneck preventing the expansion of output to meet demand. For much of the eighteenth century mines relied on horse-power, horse gins being found at most pitheads. A horse gin, however, could raise no more than 100 tons of coal in 24 hours.

Where it was available, water-power was used but the real breakthrough came after 1782 with the development of rotary steam engines. At least 130 steam winding engines had been installed in collieries by 1800, about a third supplied by Boulton and Watt. The 'whimsey', a small steam winding engine, became a common coalfield sight.

Corves and miners were hauled up and down the shaft at the end of twisting hemp ropes. They weakened with time and needed constant checking. In 1798 John Curr devised a flat rope; elsewhere flat winding chains were being developed, particularly in the Black Country. They

were cheaper and lasted longer than ropes. In the 1830s wire ropes began to be used and in 1835 effective shaft guide rails and the pit cage were invented.

The effects of these changes on output were dramatic. At one north-east colliery it increased from 300 tons a day in the mid-1830s to 800 tons a day in 1850. Miners benefited from a safer, smoother ride in the cages.

6 Surface transport

Coal was expensive to transport. When coal was carried by a packhorse, sales ceased to be profitable outside a radius of about ten miles from the pithead. Coal-owners, therefore, played a leading part in promoting transport improvements. When the Liverpool to Prescot turnpike was completed in 1725 it was expected to reduce the cost of coal in Liverpool and increase the sales of the Lancashire mine owners. A horse pulling a wagon on a good road could haul more coal than several packhorses could carry.

Wooden rails, or wagonways, were first used at Wollaton near Nottingham in 1604. These dramatically reduced costs. An estimate of

A north-east wagonway at the end of the eighteenth century. The driver is braking the wagon on a downhill section. The horse gets a rest. A keel or river barge is being loaded on the river

1711 from the Tanfield Moor Colliery showed that transport to the River Tyne by road gave £1. 17s. 6d (187½p) per ton profit, whilst use of a wagonway gave £5. 5s. 9d (529p) per ton. During the eighteenth century, the north-east coalfield was criss-crossed by wagonways linking the collieries with the rivers Tyne and Wear. This pattern was to be repeated on other coalfields as the canal network was extended. Routes were generally short and full advantage was taken of downhill sections to exploit gravity. The main motive power, however, remained the horse.

The Duke of Bridgewater said that 'Every canal must have coals at the heel of it', and until the growth of the national railway network water transport was essential for the movement of coal.

As early as 1711 there were canals connecting the Griff Colliery in Warwickshire with nearby tramways. In 1757 the Sankey Brook Canal linked the coalfield around St Helens with the River Mersey. It was financed by Liverpool coal consumers who wanted cheaper fuel and by coal-owners wishing to supply the Cheshire saltmakers with the coal they needed.

This was followed by the Duke of Bridgewater's canal from his pits at Worsley to Manchester, begun in 1759 and completed in 1763. The coal was brought out from the workings via underground drainage soughs – effectively, therefore, the canal went into the mine.

These successful ventures encouraged similar developments on other coalfields, particularly in the East and West Midlands. Wherever canals were built coal-owners benefited. Costs were reduced, markets widened and the exploitation of previously uneconomic sites was made possible.

The application of steam power to transport was pioneered on the coalfields as a cheap and efficient means of moving coal. John Blenkinsop, William Hedley and George Stephenson were all designers of colliery locomotives. Blenkinsop's line at Leeds in 1812 was probably the first successful example. In 1813 John Watson, viewer or manager at Kenton Colliery in the North East, was able to write enthusiastically to John Bailey, agent for the Duke of Portland, who was considering using steam locomotives at his Scottish collieries.

Richard Trevithick built the first working railway locomotive in 1804

The Engine which is used is considered of Four Horse Power of Trevithick's Invention, and is made by Messrs Fenton, Murray and Wood of Leeds . . . and costs £380. . . .

chaldron – wagon used in the North East

It is supposed . . . with a tolerable degree of Correctness that ⅚ of the Expence of Leading the Coals by Horses will be saved by the invention, as I find it has cost us at Kenton 2s [10p]. per Chaldron Leading our coals to the River by Horses (a distance of 5½ Miles) while I am satisfied so sooner we get our Way completed to the River it will not cost us more than 4d [1½p] per Chaldron conveying them by Mr Blenkinsop's Mode; Consequently as our Leading from that Colliery are about 36 000 Chaldrons a year we presume we shall save at least £3000 p. annum at the Concern.

. . . The Number of Men necessary to be employed in both instances has been two, yet they frequently have only one at Leeds. . . .

In Regard to the Expence of making the Railway suitable for the Conveying the Coals by the Steam Engine, as the Engine is of the greatest Weight that will bear at any one time upon each Rail, it will be necessary to have the Rail of such a Strength, as will resist *its Weight* without Risque of breaking. . . .

With Respect to the Formation of the Rail-Way it is not absolutely necessary that it should be a right line, yet as many Turns as possible should be avoided.

. . . I consider it of more Consequence in forming the Way to endeavour to keep it Level. . . .

Questions

1 (a) Watson is very enthusiastic about his steam locomotive. From the evidence he gives, and referring to the illustration of the wagonway on page 97 give as many reasons as you can for his enthusiasm.
(b) Elsewhere he estimated it will cost £352 per mile more to lay a track for a steam locomotive than for horses. Why does he suggest that the track will have to be relaid?
(c) Why do you think he considers it 'of more Consequence in forming the Way to endeavour to keep it Level?'
2 Now study the print of George Stephenson's Hetton Colliery Railway opened in 1822. It used a mixture of locomotives, stationary steam engines winding trains of wagons along and gravity inclines. Using Watson's evidence and the picture, explain why all these methods were used.

The main reason for constructing the Stockton and Darlington Railway, opened in 1825, was to carry coal from West Durham to Stockton on the river Tees for export to London and other coastal markets.

Advances in inland transport were the most important explanation for the expansion of the industry. Railways also added to the growing demand for its product.

Coal was the essential raw material of the Industrial Revolution and of Britain's nineteenth-century economic predominance. The technical developments were not as dramatic as those in the cotton industry but without them the output of the coalmines would not have satisfied an ever increasing demand.

Using the evidence: Poynton Collieries and the railways

Production at the Poynton Collieries in Cheshire expanded rapidly in the 1830s and 1840s. Here are two facts, sales figures, and extracts from the agent's annual report.

A In 1831 the Macclesfield Canal to the east of the collieries was opened.

In 1845 the Macclesfield branch railway from the Manchester to Crewe main line was opened. It passed through Poynton.

To what extent is this notice evidence of the changes that had taken place in pit safety by 1853?

Instructions and Cautions to be observed by the Managers and Workmen employed at the POYNTON AND WORTH COLLIERIES, for the Prevention of Accidents, 1853.

1st.—The Engine Driver is carefully to examine his Engine and Ropes every morning, and is to run the empty cages up and down the shaft once, before any of the Workmen descend.

2nd.—The Banksman is to be on duty at the Pit's mouth at the time the Workmen descend, and he shall not allow more than Four Men and Two Boys to ascend or descend any Pit in double cages; and not more than Three Men in single cages, at the same time; and in Pits where Gas is known to exist, he shall see that the Colliers and other Workmen have their Lamps with the tops on, and shall not allow any Man or Boy to descend with a naked light.

3rd.—In any Pit in which Gas is known to exist, the Manager or his Deputy, shall see that the Workmen have every possible protection and assistance; and no Collier or Workman will be allowed to take the top off his Lamp, to Smoke, to use Candles or Lucifer Matches, in any place in any Pit where Gas exists.

4th.—In case any Air Door shall be found open that ought to have been closed, or any Air Door be found shut that ought to have been left open, or any dirt or impediment be found or placed in any Air Road, by any person (thereby to impede the ventilation); or if any Workman shall observe any part of the under-ground works out of order, or any thing out of its place, whereby an accident might ensue, it is expected that he will without delay give such information and requisite assistance to the Manager, as may lead to the prevention of injury or accident arising therefrom, to any person.

5th.—If any Workman shall be found wilfully or carelessly doing any act whereby an accident or an explosion of Gas may occur, he shall immediately be dismissed.—And if there should arise any defect or deficiency in the ventilation of any part of any Pit, from any cause whatever, information of the same is to be immediately given to the Manager of such Pit, who is required to undertake and apply the requisite remedies without delay, and with the utmost skill and caution of which he is capable.

6th.—The Fireman of the Air Furnace is required to regulate his Fire, so as to supply the requisite quantity of Air for the proper ventilation of each Pit.

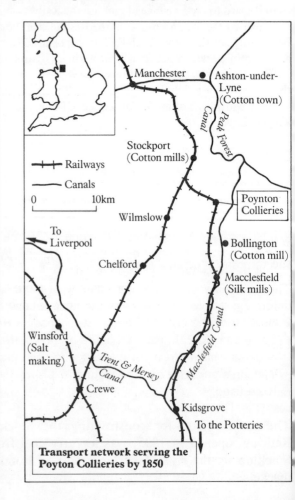

— Railways
— Canals
0   10km

Manchester
Ashton-under-Lyne (Cotton town)
Stockport (Cotton mills)
Peak Forest
Poynton Collieries
Wilmslow
To Liverpool
Bollington (Cotton mill)
Chelford
Macclesfield (Silk mills)
Winsford (Salt making)
Trent & Mersey Canal
Macclesfield Canal
Crewe
Kidsgrove
To the Potteries

Transport network serving the Poynton Collieries by 1850

B Sales figures for selected years:

Year	Coal sold (tons)	Income £	Profit £
1831	86514		
1836	170581	46048	21998
1842	129074	41243	11317
1844	150792	51746	16969
1845	206700	82076	27466
1846	237000	90773	30637
1849	235078	81788	27625
1850	234387	78036	22894
1851	235951	73598	16505

C In 1846 Thomas Ashworth, the agent, informed Lord Vernon of the price advantage the railway had brought to Poynton. The cost of sending coal to Stockport by road was 2 shillings 9d (14p) to 3 shillings (15p) a ton. The coast by rail was 6d (2½p) to 6¾d per ton.

D Coal sales in different towns and markets in 1847:

Town	Transport used	Tons sold
Stockport	Railway	57382
Manchester	Railway	35919
Macclesfield	Railway and canal	32453
Bollington	Canal	7610
Ashton	Canal	26642
At the Pit		26179
Wilmslow	Railway	9270
Chelford	Railway	11530
Crewe	Railway	7026
Winsford	Railway	14528

E In 1849 and in 1851 Ashworth was complaining about the effects of the rapidly expanding railway network.

The coal trade in Lancashire and especially Manchester has been very depressed due to the completion of new railways and therefore severe competition has occurred [1849].

I have never seen in 30 years in the trade such unscrupulous competition and consequent depression in the prices. This has risen mainly from the determination on the part of proprietors of remote collieries to sell, and from railway companies competing for carriage of coals from remote areas at lower cost [1851].

Using the evidence given, write an account of the effects transport developments had on the Poynton Collieries between 1831 and 1851.

6 Power: the impact of steam

Water-power

Water was the main source of power for the mills, factories and ironworks of the Industrial Revolution.

After 1750 the design of water-wheels improved, and they became more efficient. After 1769 cast-iron shafts appeared and larger wheels of greater horse-power could be constructed. By 1800 the complete wheel was being made from iron. The largest transmitted up to 100 horse-power. At that time no steam engine could produce that amount of power.

A water-powered forge at Tintern in Monmouthshire. Water-wheels built for the new textile mills were larger and more powerful. What would this wheel operate?

Water-power at Quarry Bank Mill, Styal, Cheshire

The Greg's mill at Styal always depended on water-power. It opened in 1784 with one wheel, and in 1792 a second was added. A new weir was built in 1799 at a cost of £456 to provide a storage lake capable of holding sufficient water for a full day's work.

Between 1818 and 1821 over £21 000 was spent on extending the mill and increasing the power available. A new water-wheel was installed. It was a breast wheel, 32 feet in diameter, 21 feet wide and producing 100 horse-power. The bottom of the new wheelpit was fifteen feet below the level of the river Bollin as it passed the mill. A tunnel, nearly three quarters of a mile long, had to be dug to carry the water in the tailrace to a point where it could rejoin the river. The wheel, the new headrace and the tunnel cost over £7500.

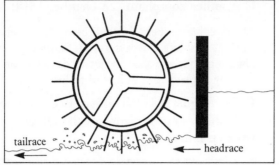

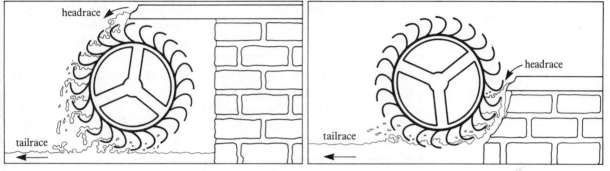

1 The undershot wheel was inefficient. The wheel was turned by the flow of the stream. Only about 25 per cent of the energy available was used. →

2 In an overshot wheel about 55 per cent of the available energy was exploited. Engineers now used gravity to turn the wheel. The paddles had become large, bucket-like containers.

3 The breastshot wheel was the most efficient type. It used up to 80 per cent of the energy available. A large wheel could produce up to 100hp.

tailrace

headrace

headrace

tailrace

tailrace

headrace

Using the evidence: the problems of water-power

A In 1810 Peter Ewart, Samuel Greg's partner at Styal, was negotiating the purchase of a steam engine from the Boulton and Watt Company. These extracts come from letters he wrote at that time. The company was not very good at sticking to its delivery dates.

. . . . The month of March is generally the time when our water falls short and it will be an important object to us to have it here in the course of this month.
(4 February 1810)

Had not this month (March 1810) been unusually moist we should have been short of water ere now, and you will conceive how anxious we are to have the engine set up.

(2 April 1810)

On the very day we got it to work we had a plentiful fall of rain, and we have not since been short of water – had the dry weather continued, however, we should have derived much benefit from the engine.

(29 May 1810)

The steam engine was only 10 h.p. It was not powerful enough to drive the mill machinery on its own.

B A letter to Samuel Greg from a solicitor writing on behalf of a mill-owner downstream from Styal, 12 June 1815:

It is quite impossible that Mr Greg could be in perfect ignorance of this complaint. Mr Greg has for years past so impounded the water that in dry seasons Mr Nield's mill has stopped every day until noon. . . .

Impounded: held up

C Another complaint, 28 October 1818:

The river having been fordable before the erection of your weir which rendered a bridge absolutely necessary, Mr Worral . . . is . . . entitled to insist on your lowering your weir, so as not to dam the water upon the ancient ford and thereby deprive him of a road to his estate.

D In August 1819 Thomas Eccles, a weaver living in Bingley in Yorkshire, kept a record of the effect of water shortage on the local woollen mills:

Yorkshire Woollen Mills	Daily hours worked		Daily hours lost		Time started
	hrs	m	hrs	m	
Illingworth at Grove Mill	8	57	5	00	0600
Roper's Mill at Dam Ems	7	40	6	03	0600
Greenwood's Mill at Spring Head	5	11	7	41	1033
Newsholme's Mill at Mytholroyd	6	30	6	14	1000
Craven's Mill at Eller Carr	5	30	8	20	0715
Knight's Mill at Morton	9	00	5	00	0600

1 List the problems a mill-owner might encounter if he depended on water-power.
2 According to source A why was a steam engine installed at Styal?
3 (a) How does source B help to explain the short hours at Greenwood's Mill and Newsholme's Mill in source D?
(b) Other mills in source D were able to start at the correct time. How do you explain the short hours they worked?
(c) To what extent was Greg responsible for the late start at Nield's Mill? What could Nield do to ease the problem? What do you think he wanted Greg to do?
4 From this evidence, what advantages did the owners of steam-powered mills have over their water-powered rivals?

Steam-power: the work of Savery and Newcomen

In 1698 Thomas Savery (c. 1650–1717) took out his patent for 'Raising water by the impellent force of fire.' This pump was the first practical working steam engine. Savery knew of the drainage problems facing Cornish tin miners and he hoped to provide them with a solution.

This advertisement appeared in a London newspaper in 1702:

'incumbred' (encumbered) with: hampered by

Captain Savery's Engines which raise Water by the force of Fire in any reasonable quantities and to any height being now brought to perfection and ready for publick use, These are to give notice to all Proprietors of Mines and Collieries which are incumbred with Water, that they may be furnished with Engines to drain the same, at his Workhouse in Salisbury Court, London, . . . where it may be seen working on Wednesdays and Saturdays . . . from 3 to 6 in the afternoon. . . .

Savery's engine was not a success. Since it could only raise water about seventeen metres it could not solve the drainage problems of the deeper mines that were being sunk.

Thomas Newcomen (1663–1729) was an ironmonger at Dartmouth in Devon. Maufacturing many of the articles he sold, he was also a skilled metal-worker. On his sales trips into Cornwall he learnt of the drainage crisis hampering the tin mines.

His search for a solution took about ten years. It is possible that he installed a pumping engine in a Cornish tin mine in 1710 but it was not a success. In 1712, however, a Newcomen engine began to operate successfully at a coal mine in Staffordshire. It pumped water from a depth of about 50 metres. Other colliery-owners bought the engine. Its high fuel consumption was no great disadvantage to them.

This description of the Newcomen engine at a colliery in White-haven, was written in 1725:

At last the famous fire-engine discharges the water, which is a notable piece of machinery working itself entirely; it creates a *vacuum* by first rarefying the air with hot steam, then condenses it suddenly by cold water; whence a piston is drawn up and down alternatively, at one end of the beam: this activates a pump at the other end, which let down into the works draws the water out: it makes about fourteen strokes a minute, so that it empties 140 hogsheads in an hour with moderate working.

hogshead: a large barrel holding just over 50 gallons

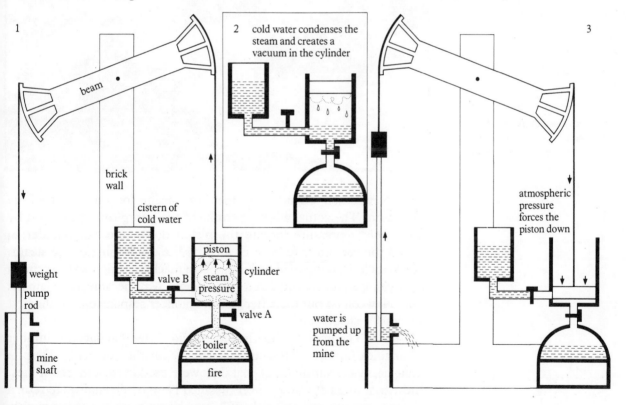

How the Newcomen engine worked. Compare this with the description above and the illustration of the Newcomen engine on page 106

A Newcomen engine working at a coal mine. Can you identify its parts from the diagram on page 105?

The Newcomen engine depended on steam for only part of its operation. The actual working stroke of the pump rod was caused by atmospheric pressure forcing the piston down into the cylinder in which the vacuum had been created by the condensing of the steam. Nevertheless Newcomen had designed a machine which was to remain little changed for two hundred years. James Watt became more famous than Newcomen but the latter was the pioneer responsible for the first successful steam engine.

Until 1733 patent royalties had to be paid. After that date the number of engines rapidly increased, particularly on the coalfields. Despite their heavy consumption of coal they were used in tin and lead mines. Industrial users of water-power installed Newcomen engines to return water to storage reservoirs. In 1726 one began work as a water supply pump in London. It was abandoned five years later.

There is a famous machine in York Buildings, which was erected to force water by means of fire, thro' pipes laid for that purpose into several parts of the town, and it was carry'd on for some time to effect; but the charge of working it . . . made its proprietors, . . . lay aside the design; and no doubt but the inhabitants in its neighbourhood are very glad of it, for its working, which was by sea-coal, was attended with so much smoke, that it not only must pollute the air thereabouts, but spoil the furniture.

Alive and Merry; or the London Daily Post, 18 April 1741

The contribution of James Watt

James Watt (1736–1819) is best known for his improvements to the steam engine. He was a fine craftsman but he was also a capable mathematician and practical chemist. As an engineer he was willing to work with his men and to solve problems on site. At Kinneil where he built his experimental engine after 1769 he

had a suit of pit cloaths made in which (he) went down the shaft and like any of the other workmen changed the buckets of the pumps, and overhauled the engine, and continued to do so, till (he) was completely master of the practical workings of it.

James Watt's improvements to the steam engine

1769   Separate condenser patented. It made the engine more efficient.

1782   The sun and planet gearing enabled the engine to give rotary motion and drive machinery.
The double acting engine patented. Steam drove both strokes of the piston. This gave the smoother motion needed for the efficient operation of machinery.

1784   Parallel motion devised as a means of transmitting the simple up-and-down motion of the piston rod to the beam.

1788   The Governor was a device to regulate the speed of the engine.

As scientific instrument-maker for Glasgow University Watt was asked to repair an unsatisfactory model of a Newcomen engine in 1763. He quickly realised that the reason for its inefficiency and poor working was the alternate heating and cooling of the cylinder. If the cylinder could be kept hot, fuel would be saved and the engine would work more effectively. It took months of thought before Watt discovered the answer. Later he described how he had the inspiration whilst walking on Glasgow Green one Sunday. The cylinder could be kept hot if the steam was drawn out to be condensed elsewhere. The separate condenser was patented in 1769. He also proposed to line the cylinder with a steam jacket as additional insulation and to close the top of the cylinder.

The saving in fuel and the increased efficiency were an advance on the Newcomen engine but it was 1776 before the first two engines were in operation.

There were two reasons for this. When the engineer John Smeaton read Watt's 1769 patent he commented that

neither tools nor workmen existed that could manufacture so complex a machine with sufficient precision.

The second difficulty was money. Watt's first partner was John Roebuck. Roebuck wanted a pumping engine more powerful than the existing Newcomen engines to drain his deep mines at Kinneil. Unfortunately, as Smeaton foretold, it proved impossible to manufacture the accurate parts required and then, in 1773, Roebuck went bankrupt.

Matthew Boulton saved James Watt from this disaster. Boulton, a Birmingham metalwork manufacturer, had opened his Soho works in 1762. It was powered by a water-wheel, but Boulton was concerned by summer water shortages and was looking for a steam engine. He first met Watt in 1768 and was impressed by the inventor and his ideas. As Roebuck's financial positioned worsened Boulton offered to buy out his share of the partnership with Watt and in 1773 this was done.

The Soho works of Boulton and Watt. When Boulton met Watt he wanted a reliable engine to pump the water back into the mill pond after it had turned his water-wheel

Boulton provided the business expertise that Watt lacked and his factory contained many of the skilled workers the inventor needed. John Wilkinson, the ironmaster, patented his cannon boring lathe in 1774 and this was used to manufacture the precise and accurate cylinders the Boulton and Watt engines required.

The first two Boulton and Watt engines left the Soho works in 1776, one for colliery drainage and the other to be a blowing engine at Wilkinson's Broseley ironworks. Most of the pumping engines sold in the next six years went to Cornwall, where the fuel economy of the Boulton and Watt machines was appreciated by the tin-mine owners.

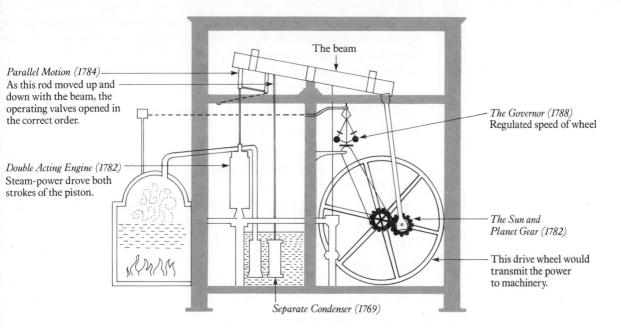

The beam

Parallel Motion (1784)
As this rod moved up and
down with the beam, the
operating valves opened in
the correct order.

Double Acting Engine (1782)
Steam-power drove both
strokes of the piston.

The Governor (1788)
Regulated speed of wheel

*The Sun and
Planet Gear (1782)*

This drive wheel would
transmit the power
to machinery.

Separate Condenser (1769)

By 1780 the possibility of adapting the steam engine to drive machinery was being considered. Boulton, the businessman, pressed the reluctant Watt into action, writing on 21 July 1781:

. . . as the people in London, Manchester, and Birmingham, are Steam Mill Mad . . . therefore let us be wise and take the advantage. I don't mean to hurry you into any determination, but I think . . . we should determine to take out a patent for certain methods of producing Rotative Motions from the vibrating or reciprocating Motion of the Fire Engine. . . . There is no other Cornwall to be found and the most likely line for the consumption of our engines is the application of them to mills which is certainly an extensive field.

Joseph Pickard, a Birmingham man, had already taken out a patent for using the crank to convert the up-and-down movement of the steam engine into rotary motion. Although it was alleged that he had stolen this idea from the Soho works, Boulton and Watt did not challenge him in the courts. Instead Watt took out patents for several means of providing rotary motion. The most successful of these was the sun-and-planet gearing. By making the engine double-acting, Watt provided the smooth regular motion needed to drive machinery.

*James Watt's main improvements to
the steam engine*

reciprocating: to and fro

The use and importance of steam-power

Refer back to the chapters on textiles, coal and iron. Find and list all the references to the use of steam-power in those industries.

Steam-power freed the manufacturer from all the problems associated with natural sources of power. It was reliable and could be controlled. Factories could be built in more convenient locations provided there was a supply of cheap coal available.

Before the introduction of the steam engine, water-power was invaluable, but we now see that it cannot at all times be depended upon, and that in most cases where a large amount of power is required the chief source from which it must be derived is steam.

W. Fairburn, *Treatise on Mills and Millwork*, London, 1861

In 1830 a Parliamentary Select Committee was informed that the woollen industry

has in great measure migrated from Essex, Suffolk, and other southern counties to the northern districts, where coal for the use of the steam-engine is much cheaper.

Between 1775 and 1800, when their patents expired, the Boulton and Watt Company sold 496 steam engines of which 308 were rotary engines. The four largest users of rotary engines were:

Textile mills	114
Ironworks	37
Collieries	33
Tin and copper mines	22

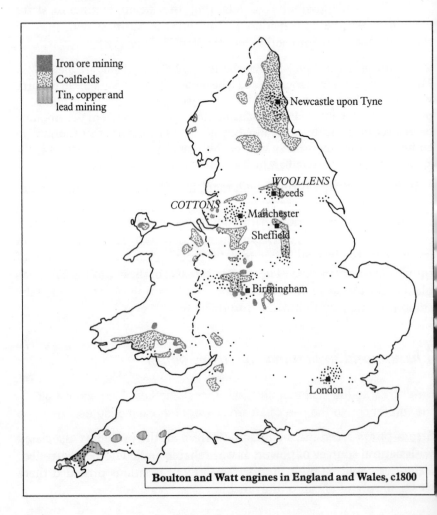

Boulton and Watt engines in England and Wales, c1800

Based on D. Gregory, *Regional Transformation and Industrial Revolution*, p. 209

West Riding woollen mills using steam-power by 1800

Boulton and Watt were not the only steam engine manufacturers. The company erected nine engines in the West Riding woollen districts before 1800 but, as the map indicates, there were about 80 in use in the area by that date.

Fifty-five engines were sold to Lancashire cotton mills, but although the double-acting Watt engine was most suitable for the cotton masters it had other disadvantages. James Watt, Jnr wrote to his father from Manchester on 30 September 1790 about Joseph Young, a local steam engine manufacturer who

has already constructed some engines upon the old plan, and . . . undertakes to erect engines of the power of 4 horses, at little more than £200, including the waterwheel which they are to put in motion. . . . the gross sum which your engines cost at first, startles all the lesser manufacturers here, and it is scarcely possible to make them comprehend the advantage . . . from a regular motion, from a machine liable to few repairs, and from an annual saving of fuel, when weighed against two or three hundred pounds more of ready cash.

Delivery dates were rarely kept, for all sorts of reasons.

It is extremely unpleasant to Messrs Boulton & Watt thus to solicit your patience. . . . The great demand for engines, the great scarcity of men, and their rebellion in some of the foundrys about us can only be brought in to plead for the delay. . . .

The most important Manchester steam engine manufacturers at the end of the eighteenth century were Bateman and Sherratt who had a large foundry in Salford.

. . . Mr Sherratt is a very ingenious and able engineer, who has improved upon and brought the steam engine to great perfection. Most of those that are used and set up in and about Manchester are of their make and fitting up. They are now used in cotton mills . . . and for winding up coals. . . .
J. Aikin, *A Description of the Country from Thirty to Forty Miles round Manchester*, 1795

It has been estimated that about 1200 steam engines were at work by 1800. Steam-power was the key invention of the Industrial Revolution. It enabled the cotton industry to expand its mass-production techniques. The output of iron increased once steam hammers, blowing engines and rolling mills speeded up production. This increased the demand for coal and steam-winding brought it to the surface more efficiently and in larger quantities.

Although the advantages of steam-power had been recognised, water-power remained the main power source long after 1800. By the 1838 there were still 236 water-wheels in Yorkshire woollen mills but by then there were 373 steam engines. The nineteenth century was the age of steam.

James Nasmyth's steam hammer, 1839, another use for steam-power

JOHN DAWES & SONS.

BROMFORD IRON WORKS, WEST BROMWICH.
STAFFORDSHIRE.

Questions

1 Compare the advantages and disadvantages of water-power and steam-power. This could be a poster or chart.
2 After Boulton and Watt had erected a steam engine the purchaser had to pay an annual sum to them. This was calculated at ⅓ of the money saved by using an efficient Watt engine instead of a Newcomen engine.
   (a) From the evidence you have seen, why do you think industrialists were reluctant to purchase from Boulton and Watt?
   (b) Why could local firms like Bateman and Sherratt sell them inferior machines in preference to Watt engines?
3 What were the contributions of Thomas Newcomen; James Watt; Matthew Boulton, to the development of steam-power?
4 Why could the invention of the steam engine be described as 'the most important development of the Industrial Revolution'? Explain your answer.

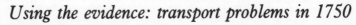

7 Revolution in transport: roads and canals to 1830

Using the evidence: transport problems in 1750

A The River Severn was busy with traffic.

This river . . . is of great importance on account of its trade, being navigated by vessels of large burden more than 160 miles from the sea. . . . Upwards of 100 000 tons of coals are annually shipped from the collieries about Broseley and Madeley to the towns situate on its banks, and from thence into the adjacent countries: also great quantities of grain, pig and bar iron, iron manufactures, and earthenwares; as well as wool, hops, cyder and provisions, are constantly exported to Bristol and other places, from whence merchants' goods are brought in return. The freight from Shrewsbury to Bristol is about 10s. (50p) per ton, and from Bristol to Shrewsbury 15s. [75p], the rates to the intermediate towns being in proportion. . . .

Gentleman's Magazine, 1758

B This is an account of road traffic passing through the Potteries in 1760:

There are three pot waggons go from Newcastle and Burslem weekly . . . to Bridgnorth and carry about eight tons of potware every week, at £3 per ton. The same waggons load back with ten tons of close goods, consisting of white clay, grocery and iron. . . . Large quantities of potware are conveyed on horses' backs . . . to Bridgnorth and Bewdley, for exportation, about one hundred tons yearly, at £2.10 [250p] per ton. Two broad-wheel waggons (exclusive of 150 pack-horses) go from Manchester through Stafford weekly, and may be computed to carry 312 tons of cloth and Manchester wares in the year, at £3.10s [350p] per ton. . . .

1 How did the industries and communities along its banks benefit from the River Severn?
2 What evidence is there in the sources to explain why industrialists preferred water transport to land transport?
3 What difficulties would dependence on these forms of transport create for coal owners and ironmasters in particular? Explain your answer from this evidence.

Roads in the early eighteenth century

Since the sixteenth century local people had had the responsibility of maintaining roads that passed through their parish. Six days' work on road repair was required from all parishioners every year, the parish providing tools, carts and materials. Reluctantly and without any skill the work was done, and usually done badly. At best the worst ruts and potholes were filled up with stones which were soon scattered by the traffic. Throughout the country the roads were in an appalling state, impassable in winter and dangerous in summer.

As traffic grew, particularly in the developing industrial areas, the local people increasingly resented the task and expense imposed on them. In 1706 the people of Droitwich in Worcestershire complained to Parliament that the increased movement of salt, iron, coal and other

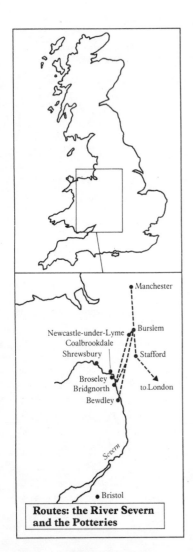

Routes: the River Severn and the Potteries

goods had made the local roads 'almost impassable'. Since they had not caused the damage, they asked, why should they have to remedy it?

In the North, where many roads were unsuitable for wheeled traffic, all goods were carried on packhorses. Most roads were, therefore, packhorse routes, narrow causeways only wide enough for a single horse. It was 1760 before wagons could cover the whole journey from Liverpool to Manchester. Large stage wagons rumbling along the country roads at two or three miles an hour with the wagoner ambling along beside it were common sights in the South. They contributed to the poor road surface, crushing it to dust in dry weather and churning it into mud when it was wet.

1 What is the poster trying to prevent?
2 How serious a problem was it? Explain your answer from this piece of evidence

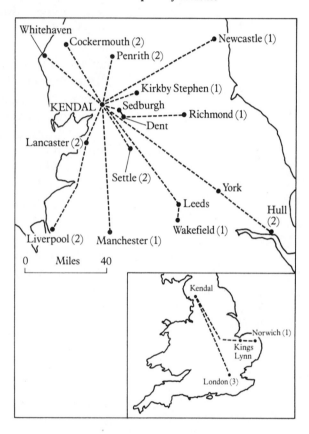

Caution to Waggoners.

WHEREAS great INJURY has of late been done to the TURNPIKE-ROADS, owing to Waggons and other Carriages, with Narrow Wheels, being drawn by a greater Number of Horses than the Law allows:

Notice is hereby given,

That from and after the 1st Day of April next, Informations will be laid, and the Penalties be levied on the Owner and Driver of every Waggon, Wain, Cart, or other heavy Carriage, which shall be found passing on any Turnpike-Road having the Wheels of less Breadth, and being drawn by a greater Number of Horses than under-mentioned, or having a Middle Tire or Binding round the Wheels, contrary to Act of Parliament.

By the General Turnpike Act, 13 G. 3d, C. 84, No Waggon, Wain, Cart, or other Carriage, (except Coaches, &c.) shall pass on any Turnpike-Road but with Wheels of such a Breadth, and with such a Number of Horses drawing the same, as follows:

Breadth of Wheels.		No. of Horses.
Four-Wheel Carriages	9 Inches	8 Horses and no more.
	6	6
Less than	6	4
Two-Wheel Carriages	9	5
	6	4
Less than	6	3

And the Wheels to roll on a *Flat* Surface.

On Pain that the Owner of every such Carriage shall forfeit 5l. and the Driver 20s.

Dated March 20th, 1800.

Despite the poor roads many towns had several carriers working from them. This map shows the network centred on Kendal in 1698 and the number of packhorse trains that left each week for the various destinations

Water transport in the eighteenth century

Road transport was unsuitable for heavy, low-value bulky commodities such as coal or iron. Fortunately the country had an extensive network of navigable rivers and the coastal trade employed more ships than foreign trade. Iron from Coalbrookdale Company's Horsehay Works was sent down the Severn to Bristol and then by sea to Chester, the direct and much shorter overland route being ignored. Staffordshire potters moved their goods to river ports like Bridgnorth and Bewdley on the Severn for national distribution by water. The north-east coalfield is a good example of a successful industrial region that benefited from access to cheap and easy water transport to a major market, London. Whilst it cost 12s (60p) a ton to send goods from Liverpool to Manchester by river in the 1750s, it cost £2 a ton by road.

Although rivers could be improved they were unsatisfactory in many ways. In summer low water-levels meant that barges which could carry up to eighty tons had to sail with a reduced cargo, whilst winter conditions could close a waterway completely. Millers, and others whose livelihood depended on the level of the river, opposed improvement schemes which threatened to deprive them of their supply. Barges could be held up for days at weirs until the miller was prepared to allow them through. Most river barges had sails but frequently they had to be towed either by horses or, more often, by gangs of men wading through the shallows. Towpaths were opposed by landowners who feared damage to their property.

Improvement to existing waterways had extended the navigable river system to its maximum by 1750. Locks could raise water levels and lessen the resistance of mill-owners, cuts might shorten routes and towpaths improved haulage, but the basic shortcomings remained. Journey distances were always greater than the more direct overland routes, and if a watershed had to be crossed then roads had to be used. Rivers could not provide cross-country routes.

Finally, although much of the country was no more than fifteen miles from a navigable river, important industries and industrial areas were remote from suitable waterways. Further growth of the pottery industry of Staffordshire and of the West Midlands ironworking area around Birmingham was likely to be hampered by poor communications.

The road solution

Improving the roads – turnpike trusts

In 1663 Hertfordshire magistrates obtained an Act of Parliament setting up the first turnpike road. Concerned at the expense of maintaining the Great North Road through the county they proposed that road-users should contribute by paying a toll. This solution to the problem was increasingly adopted, and by 1750, 143 turnpike trusts had had their Acts of Parliament.

	No. of turnpike trusts	Mileage of turnpike roads
1750	143	3 400
1770	500	15 000
1836	1 000	22 000

The growth of the turnpike system is clear from these figures. In 1836 the network was at its peak before the effects of railway competition were felt.

A turnpike trust was set up by Act of Parliament to maintain a specified section of road. It was empowered to set up toll gates and to use the revenue received for repairs and road-building. In country districts local landowners and farmers often formed themselves into a trust to improve their access to local markets but in the developing industrial areas the local cottonmasters, coal-owners or ironmasters were prominent. Josiah Wedgwood played a leading part in the promotion of turnpikes in Staffordshire and the neighbouring counties.

On 1st February 1765 he wrote to his brother:

> . . we have another Turnpike broke out . . . here betwixt Leek and Newcastle. They have mounted me upon my hobbyhorse again. . . . He carried me yesterday to Leek from whence I am just returned, much satisfied with our reception there. . . . We pray to have the Burslem and Uttoxeter Turnpikes joined and the road made Turnpike from Buxton and Bakewell to Leek and from Leek to Newcastle. . . .

Whilst the potters built up their regional network, John Wilkinson and Abraham Darby III were leading members of the trustees who managed the turnpike systems covering Shropshire. Turnpike routes radiated out from London and the developing Lancashire and Yorkshire industrial districts were linked by roads across the Pennines.

Josiah Wedgwood (1730–95), potter and founder of the Wedgwood company. He produced a distinctive style of pottery. At his factory he pioneered mass-production methods. He was a keen supporter of improved communications for the Potteries

A

LIST OF
TOLLS
PAYABLE AT THE
Trafford Gates,
AND THE
NETHERTON GATE:

	S.	D.
For every Horse or other Beast drawing any Coach, Chaise, Gig, &c. the sum of	0	6
For the same passing through a Second Gate	0	3
For every Horse or other Beast drawing any Waggon, Wain, Cart, or other such Carriage, with the Fellies of the Wheels of the Breadth of Six Inches or more	0	5
If the Fellies of the Wheels are of less Breadth than Six Inches and not less than Four and a Half Inches	0	7½
If the Fellies are of less Breadth than Four and a Half Inches	0	9
For every Horse, Mule, or Ass, Laden or Unladen, and not drawing	0	2
For the same passing through a Second Gate	0	1
For every Score of Oxen or neat Cattle	1	0
For every Score of Pigs, Sheep, Lambs, &c.	0	10
For every Waggon, Cart, or such like Carriage, having the Nails of the Tires of the Wheels projecting more than One Quarter of an Inch from the surface of such Tires for each time of passing through any of the above Gates	10	0

Toll to be taken at One Gate only on the Ashton Lane Road.

No exemption from Toll allowed for Manure, Dung, Compost, or Implements of Husbandry, if the Nails of the Wheels project more than a Quarter of an Inch above the Tire or Tires of the Wheels.

Tolls charged on the Chester and Frodsham Road, 1828

B Turnpikes were not always welcomed by local people, as this description of events at Bristol in 1749 indicates:

Bristol 29 July – On Monday 24th at night great numbers of Somerset people, having demolished the turnpike gates near Bedminster on the Ashton road, the commissioners offered a reward of £100 to the discovery of any persons concerned therein. On the 25th at night, a body of Gloucestershire people destroyed a second time the turnpike gates and house at Don John's cross, about a mile from this city. . . . [The gates were re-erected].

. . . On the 26th between ten and eleven at night a prodigious body of

Somersetshire people came with drum beating and loud shouts, armed with cutting instruments . . . some disguised in women's apparel and demolished the turnpike erection newly fixed. . . . On 29th the turnpike gate was again erected on the Ashton road. . . .

. . . On Tuesday the 1st . . . about 400 Somersetshire people cut down a third time the turnpikes on the Ashton road and burnt the timber. . . .

Gentleman's Magazine, 1749

C A turnpike trust's purpose was to improve a road. Arthur Young was a regular traveller in the late eighteenth century and he made frequent comments on the roads he used. On his tours of the South of England in 1768 and of the North in 1771 he found a wide range of conditions. Here are some examples:

. . . that from Salisbury, to four miles the other side of Romsey . . . is, without exception, the finest I ever saw. The trustees of that road, highly deserve all the praise that can be given, by everyone who travels it, for their excellent management . . . It is everywhere broad enough for 3 carriages to pass each other; and lying in straight lines, with an even edge of grass the whole way, it has more the appearance of an elegant gravel walk, than of an high-road. (1768)

. . . the execrable muddy road from Bury to Sudbury in Suffolk, in which I was forced to move as slow as in any unmended lane in Wales . . . Ponds of liquid dirt, and a scattering of loose flints, just sufficient to lame every horse that moves near them, with the addition of vile grips across the road, under the pretence of letting water off, but without the effect, all together render it, at least 12 out of these 16 miles, as infamous a turnpike as ever was travelled. (1768)

grips: drainage channels

From Grimsthorpe to Coltsworth are eight miles, called by the courtesy of the neighbourhood, a turnpike – but in which we were every moment either buried in quagmires of mud, or racked to dislocation over pieces of rock which they term mending. . . . (1771)

From Beverley to Driffield is, I think, by much the best turnpike road I have met with in Yorkshire. (1771)

D

[The Warrington to Altrincham turnpike] If possible this execrable road is worse than that from Preston. It is a heavy sand, which cuts into such prodigious ruts, that a carriage moves with great danger. These sands turn to floods of mud in any season the least wet. (1771)

Nevertheless forty years later Arthur Young was praising the roads of Oxfordshire:

. . . forty years ago . . . they were in a condition formidable to the bones of all who travelled on wheels. . . . A noble changes has taken place. The turnpikes are very good, and, where gravel is to be had, excellent . . . (1809)

The same point was made in the *Gentleman's Magazine* in 1792:

The great improvement which, in the memory of man, has been made in the turnpike roads throughout this kingdom, would be incredible, did we not actually perceive them.

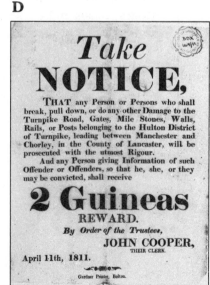

Take NOTICE,

THAT any Person or Persons who shall break, pull down, or do any other Damage to the Turnpike Road, Gates, Mile Stones, Walls, Rails, or Posts belonging to the Hulton District of Turnpike, leading between Manchester and Chorley, in the County of Lancaster, will be prosecuted with the utmost Rigour.

And any Person giving Information of such Offender or Offenders, so that he, she, or they may be convicted, shall receive

2 Guineas REWARD.

By Order of the Trustees,

JOHN COOPER, THEIR CLERK.

April 11th, 1811.

Gardner Printer, Bolton.

1 Look at the list of tolls (Source A).
(a) What kind of traffic used the road?
(b) The 'fellies' are the rims of the wheel. How do you explain the different charges for waggons and carts?
(c) Explain the high charge of 10 shillings (50p) on waggons or carriages with nails projecting from the wheel.
2 Now refer to source B and the reward poster (Source D).
(a) What evidence is there that breaking-up of turnpikes was regarded as a serious offence?
(b) Source B would suggest that such damage only took place when a turnpike was opened. Does the poster confirm this? Explain your answer.
(c) Re-read source A. What can you learn about toll payment which would lessen local opposition to a turnpike road? Does this help explain who might oppose a turnpike? Explain your answer.
3 From the evidence in Source C explain how the condition of roads was affected by the turnpike system during the second half of the eighteenth century. What were the main problems turnpike trusts had to overcome?

Engineer

John Metcalfe
(1717–1780)
He was blind from childhood. Had a varied career as a carrier and contractor.

Thomas Telford – 'the Colossus of Roads')
(1757–1834)
The first civil engineer. He built roads, bridges, canals and docks. First president of the Institution of Civil Engineers in 1818.

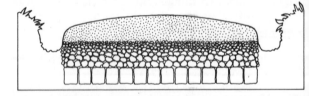

John Loudon McAdam
(1756–1836)

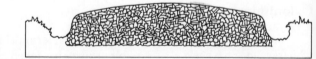

Turnpikes were not a perfect system. Tolls were often misappropriated since there was no provision in a Turnpike Act compelling the trustees to spend money on road repairs. The network was set up in a very haphazard fashion, roads being turnpiked to serve local and regional needs. Most trusts were only responsible for a few miles of road, the average in the 1750s and 1760s being 30 miles. Only Telford's London to Holyhead road and some in Scotland were improved and built under government control. Eventually most main routes were turnpikes but the traveller had to pay tolls to the different trusts whose sections he used. Stagecoach proprietors operating on the London to Edinburgh run in 1830 had to pay tolls at 216 gates.

More seriously, however, few early trusts were able to employ surveyors who had the necessary skills. Where the land was well drained, good roads would be provided, but until a new generation of road engineers trained by Telford, McAdam and their assistants had emerged, little progress could be made. Telford's methods were expensive and best suited to new roads and prestigious government schemes like the improved road to Holyhead whilst the turnpike trusts readily adopted McAdam's techniques. They were cheaper and quicker to implement.

Roadbuilding method	Where employed
1 Stressed importance of firm foundations. 2 Made the road surface convex. 3 Good drainage ditches were dug to take the water.	1755 His first contract on the Boroughbridge to Knaresborough road. Responsible for about 180 miles of turnpike road in Yorkshire, Lancashire and Cheshire.
1 Course of road had to be level and drained. 2 Gradients had to be gentle for coach travel. 3 'Solid pavement' of large stones carefully laid as foundations for the road. 4 Layer of stones the 'size of walnuts' laid on the foundations. Packed firmly together. 5 Gravel laid over the surface. 6 Convex road surface.	Surveyor of roads in Shropshire, 1787–1834. Surveyed roads in the Highlands for the government in 1803 to bring them up to coaching standard. From 1815 engaged in repairing and building the London-Holyhead road. Worked in lowlands of Scotland and on the Carlisle–Glasgow road. Surveyed route of Great North Road in 1820s. Much of his work was on government contracts.
1 Stressed need for good drainage. 2 If subsoil well drained and dry no need for heavy foundation. 3 Road level should be raised above the surrounding land. 4 Road made of angular chippings which bonded together under weight of traffic to make a watertight surface. 5 Recommended a good camber.	A repairer of roads rather than a builder. By 1819 had been responsible for about 700 miles of road, and had been consulted by 34 turnpike trusts. Surveyor to the Bristol Trust. Wanted to bring all roads in the London area under the control of one Trust.

The effects of changes in road transport

The best way to judge the effects of road improvement is to examine their impact on the movement of goods and people.

There never was a more astonishing revolution accomplished in the internal system of any country. The carriage of grain, merchandise, etc. is in general conducted with little more than half the number of horses which it formerly was. . . . The hinge which has guided all these movements, and upon which they turn, is the reformation which has been made in our public roads.
Henry Homer, *Enquiry into the Means of Preserving and Improving the Publick Roads*, 1767

This refers to the coal-mining district of Somerset

Before the turnpike roads were established, coal was carried on horses' backs. . . . Now one horse with a light cart, will draw ten hundredweight, or four times more than a horse could carry. . . .
John Billingsley, Board of Agriculture Report on Somerset, 1798

About half a century ago, the heavy goods passing through Leicester for London . . . and . . . to Leeds and Manchester did not require more than about one daily broad-wheeled waggon each way. . . . One weekly waggon, to and fro, served Coventry, Warwick, Birmingham and on to Bristol and the west of England. . . . At present there are about two waggons, two caravans, and two fly-boats, daily passing or starting from Leicester for London. . . . The same number . . . extend the connection . . . to Leeds and Manchester. . . . There are at least six weekly waggons to Birmingham, independent of those to Bristol three times a week and the same to Stamford, Cambridge, Wisebeach, and the eastern counties; to Nottingham to the same extent . . . and at least two hundred and fifty country carriers to and from the villages. . . .
J. Phillips, *Tour Through the United Kingdom*, 1828

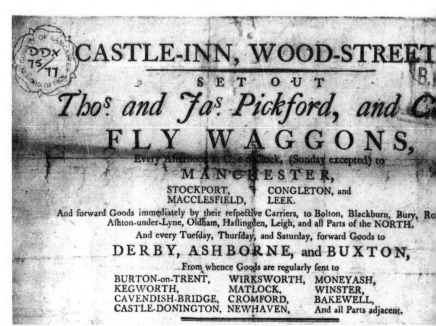

A Pickford's poster advertising their regular carrying service in 1795

Questions

1 What change do Henry Homer and John Billingsley suggest had taken place in the way goods were carried by road? Give an explanation for your answer.
2 Study the poster.
  (a) What forms of transport were Pickfords using?
  (b) What areas of the country were they serving?
  (c) What do you think a 'fly-waggon' was?
  (d) What can you learn from the poster about the way Pickfords organised their carrying business?
  (e) What changes had made possible the existence of firms like Pickfords?
3 Using all these sources, explain what appears to have happened to the carriage of goods by road. Explain whether you think all the problems described in the opening sections of this chapter had been solved.

Stagecoach travel

As you read this section complete a chart comparing the advantages and disadvantages of stagecoach travel.

In 1760 Leicester was merely a stopping-point on the London-to-Manchester, London-to-Leeds and London-to-Sheffield stagecoach routes. By 1828 there were at least 12 daily journeys to London, five to Birmingham, three to Sheffield and Leeds, six to Nottingham, five to Manchester, two to Derby and two to Stamford.

In 1801 seven coaches left Chester daily, thirty years later there were twenty-six. Just before main-line railways reached London in 1835 fifty coaches left London daily for Brighton, 22 to Birmingham, fifteen to Dover, twelve to Exeter, ten to Leeds, eleven to Manchester and sixteen to Portsmouth.

As the following advertisement for the Leicester–Bristol coach (1772) suggests, connections were closely timetabled into cross-country routes.

The Bristol coach

. . . meets the London coaches from Birmingham, Liverpool, Warrington, Lancaster, Chester and Kendal at Coventry; the Worcester at Moreton, and the Gloucester and Oxford at Cirencester – by which Passengers and Parcels will be forwarded to the above places, with utmost Care and Expedition.

Jackson's Oxford Journal, 1 August 1772

As roads were improved, coach design became lighter and better-sprung but a journey could be a hair-raising experience. Read Miss Weeton's description of her journey in 1824. Apart from the rough company there were other problems.

BOLT-IN-TUN

ROYAL MAIL & COACH ESTABLISHMENT,
Sussex Tavern and Family Hotel,
FLEET STREET, LONDON.

Royal Mails.

PORTSMOUTH & ISLE of WIGHT, | HASTINGS & TUNBRIDGE WELLS,
With a Branch to Chichester, Bognor, & Petworth. | With a Branch to Rye and Hawkhurst.
Every Evening | at Half-past Seven o'Clock.

Fast Coaches.

	Morning	Afternoon		Morning	Afternoon
ABERYSTWITH, Kington, Penybont, and Rhayader	7	½ past 5	HEREFORD, Ross, Gloucester, Cheltenham, and Oxford	½ to 7	½ to 6
ALRESFORD, Alton, and Farnham	½ past 8		HASTINGS, Battle, Robertsbridge, Flimwell, and Tunbridge	10	½ past 7
BATH, Melksham, Devizes, Marlborough, and Hungerford	7	½ to 7	MARGATE and Ramsgate	9	½ past 6
BIRMINGHAM and Stratford-on-Avon	7		MONMOUTH, Whitchurch, and Ross	7	½ past 5
BLACKWATER, Sandhurst (Royal Military College,) Egham, and Staines		3	OXFORD	7, 8 & 10	½ to 6
BRISTOL, Clifton, Bath, Devizes, and Newbury	7	½ to 7	PORTSMOUTH, Horndean, Petersfield, Liphook, and Godalming	½ past 11	½ past 7
BRIGHTON, Reigate, and Crawley	½ past 8 ½ past 10		READING, Wokingham, Bracknell, and Virginia Water	½ past 11	4
CHELTENHAM, Witney, and Oxford	7 & ½ to 8	½ to 6	RYE, Northiam, Sandhurst, Hawkhurst, and Lamberhurst	11	½ past 6
CHICHESTER, Midhurst, Hazlemere, Petworth, and Godalming	9	½ past 7	SHREWSBURY, Bridgenorth, and Kidderminster	7	½ past 5
CHIPPING NORTON, Enstone, Woodstock	10		SOUTHAMPTON, Winchester, Alton, Farnham, and Guildford	½ past 8	
CHERTSEY, Shepperton, Halliford, Sunbury, and Hampton		½ past 3	St. LEONARDS and Hastings	10	½ past 7
CAERMARTHEN, Llandilo, Llandovery, Brecon, and Crickowell	7	½ past 5	SEVEN OAKS and Riverhead	10 & 11	½ past 3 ½ past 7
DOVER, Deal, Canterbury, Sittingbourne, and Rochester	9	½ past 6	SWANSEA, Neath, Cowbridge, Cardiff, Newport, and Chepstow	7	½ past 5
ESHER, Claremont, Ditton, and Kingston	8 & 9	½ past 3	TUNBRIDGE WELLS, Tunbridge, and Seven Oaks	10	½ past 2 ½ past 7
EXETER, Collumpton, Wellington, Bridgewater, Taunton, and Wells	7	½ to 7	TROWBRIDGE and Devizes	7	½ to 7
FROME, Trowbridge, and Devizes	7		WEYBRIDGE, Oatlands, Walton, Moulsey, and Hampton Court		4
GLOUCESTER, Cheltenham, Northleach, Burford, Witney, and Oxford	7 & ½ to 8	½ to 6	WINCHESTER and Farnham	½ past 8	
(In direct communication with Coaches for all parts of South Wales.)			WINDSOR, Eton, and Slough (Patronized by Her Majesty.)	½ past 9	½ past 2 4
GODALMING, Guildford, Ripley, Cobham, and Esher	8 & 9	½ past 3	WORCESTER and Tewkesbury	7	½ to 6
HAMPTON COURT, Hampton, Twickenham, and Richmond	8 & ½ p.10	½ past 3 ½ past 5	WANTAGE, Wallingford, and Henley	8	

ROBERT GRAY & CO. Proprietors.

Every information relative to the different STEAM PACKETS from

BRISTOL .... to Cork, Waterford, Swansea, Ilfracomb, Haverfordwest, and Tenby.
PORTSMOUTH .... to the Isle of Wight, Torquay, Plymouth, and Falmouth.
SOUTHAMPTON .... to the Isle of Wight, Guernsey, Jersey, St. Maloes, Havre de Grace, France, and Italy.

☞ NOTICE—No Parcel, or Passenger's Luggage, will be accounted for above the Value of Ten Pounds unless entered as such, and Insurance paid accordingly.

. . . I rode . . . on a very dangerous outside seat behind, backwards. We were four upon it, and it was too short by much for this number; but every seat was equally crowded. It was very necessary to keep my eyes open, for the least drowsiness and I should have dropped headlong. The man on my left kept a constant motion with his head upon my shoulder up and down the night through, being heavy to sleep, the brim of his hat endangering my eyes. . . . The iron rail bruised me sadly, I was so jammed against it.

People did fall off. In winter outside passengers were chilled and frozen stiff. In wet weather they were soaked through. Inside passengers, who paid double the fare, had straw to warm their feet and marginally more comfort. Yet swaying coaches induced sickness and even the new roads caused discomfort, as Miss Weeton noted:

The roads laid on McAdam's plan are better for carriages and easier for draught horses, but for human beings in dry weather, are almost beyond endurance; they are one continuous cloud of dust, blinding to the eyes, filling the nostrils, going down to the mouth and throat by quantities to suffocation and completely ruinous to all decent clothing.

Coach travel was not cheap. The average fare in 1800 worked out between 2d and 3d (1p) a mile, half that for outside passengers. In 1830 'insides' paid £6.15s. (675p) from London to Edinburgh. To this had to be added the tips expected by the coachman and the guard (mail coach guards were only paid 10s.6d (52½p) per week since it was expected that tips would be given) and the meals consumed at the inns *en route*.

In 1784 John Palmer of Bath persuaded the government to transfer the mail from horse-riding post boys to stagecoaches. The first mail coach ran from London to Bristol in sixteen hours. A network of routes soon covered the country. Mail coaches kept to a very tight schedules, passengers taking second place to the mails. Stops were brief, horses were changed quickly, toll gates had to be opened as the mail coach paid no toll, and everything else on the road had to get out of the way. It was an offence to delay the mail.

Speeds increased and journey times decreased. Telford's rebuilding of the Holyhead Road cut the mail coach time from London from 44 hours 50 minutes to 26 hours 55 minutes, an average speed of 10 miles

A busy scene at a London coaching inn as the mail coaches prepare to depart. Notice how all the inn rooms open into the courtyard

On the open road. This heavily-loaded stage coach is approaching the open turnpike gate

an hour. By the end of the eighteenth century winter and summer timetables had been abandoned. There was one all-year timetable – more evidence of improvement in road surfaces.

Some examples of reduced journey times		
London–Edinburgh	1754	10 days
	1836	2 days
London–Manchester	1750	3 days
	1836	18 hours
London–York	1750	4 days
	1836	20 hours
London–Bristol	1750	2 days
	1836	under 12 hours

A cheaper and reliable mail service helped industry. Manufacturers of consumer goods like Josiah Wedgwood took full advantage of the new opportunities. He had showrooms for his pottery in London, Bath,

Liverpool and Dublin, employed three travelling salesmen with catalogues and samples and advertised in local newspapers. Improved communications widened the sale of newspapers and helped to create an active provincial press which could carry Wedgwood's advertisements and up-to-date news.

On the other hand some did not appreciate the changes that progress brought:

I wish with all my heart that half the turnpike roads of the kingdom were plough'd up, which have imported London manners, and depopulated the country – I meet milkmaids on the road, with dress and looks of Strand misses.

Byng, *The Torrington Diaries*

Question

Using the information and sources in this section write a letter describing a stagecoach journey. Study all the sources and illustrations very carefully. Include details of your journey and experiences. What were your feelings about it all?

The canal solution

Using the evidence: the Barton Aqueduct

A The Barton Aqueduct and the Duke's Canal soon become a major tourist attraction.

. . . the ingenious Mr Brindley, has indeed made such improvements in this way as are truly astonishing. At Barton bridge he has erected a navigable canal in the air; for it is as high as the top of the trees. Whilst I was surveying it with a mixture of wonder and delight, four barges passed me in the space of about three minutes, two of them being chained together, and dragged by two horses, who went on the terras of the canal, whereon, I durst hardly venture to walk as I almost trembled to behold the large river Irwell underneath me, across which this navigation is carried by a bridge. . . .

Annual Register, 1763

1 Refer to source A.
   (a) What does the writer find so amazing?
   (b) Who does he state was responsible for this engineering feat?
2 Study the picture (Source B). Why do you think that the Duke of Bridgewater wanted to be painted with the canal aqueduct in the background? What does his gesture suggest?
3 What evidence do these sources provide about attitudes to canal construction and engineering at that time? Give reasons for your answer.

B

The Duke of Bridgewater points to the Barton aqueduct on his canal from Worsley to Manchester. On the River Irwell gangs of men towing river barges can be seen

The Duke, Brindley and the canal system

Improved roads did not solve the problem of moving heavy loads long distances. In industrial areas the purpose of many turnpikes was to improve access to the nearest navigable river. The coal industry was seriously hampered by this difficulty. In 1757 the opening of the Sankey Brook Canal utilising a tributary of the River Mersey had shown the advantages of constructing artificial waterways to move coal.

Manchester suffered from high coal prices. Coals had to be carried to the town overland since the Mersey and Irwell Navigation did not pass close to the pits. Manchester, with its growing population, was a vast market for any colliery-owner who could get his product to the town cheaply.

Three men worked together to solve the problem. The Duke of Bridgewater owned coal mines at Worsley, seven miles from Manchester. In 1759, putting a broken engagement behind him, he retired to his estates and began his career as coal-owner, industrialist and canal-builder. The manager of the Worsley estate was John Gilbert who fully appreciated the possibilities of the vast and growing Manchester market. It was probably Gilbert who had the idea of constructing a canal to Salford using the drainage sough from the mines to supply the water. The next stage in his thinking was to take the canal into the mine workings themselves to further reduce transport costs. Impressed by these proposals the Duke obtained the necessary Act of Parliament in 1759 and work began.

sough: a drainage tunnel

It was at this point that James Brindley became involved in the scheme. A millwright from Leek, already possessing a reputation as a skilful engineer, he was recommended to the Duke as consulting engineer by Gilbert. Brindley's role in the construction of the canal has been much debated, but most contemporaries thought his was the major responsibility.

In 1760 the route was altered to take the waterway into Manchester, and Brindley had to design his masterpiece – the Barton Aqueduct taking the canal over the River Irwell. Brindley was the pioneer who solved many of the basic problems. It is said that he was the first to line a canal with puddled clay to prevent the water leaking away.

The Duke's coal reached Manchester in 1761, and as he had promised, he sold it at half the old price of 7d (3p) a hundredweight (51 kilos). An instant success with its Manchester customers, the canal became an example to other industrialists starved of raw materials or markets because of inadequate transport facilities.

The Duke himself had already decided to extend his canal to Runcorn and the mouth of the Mersey. He intended to cater for the increasing traffic between Manchester and Liverpool in competition with the Mersey and Irwell Navigation. Brindley surveyed the route and at Runcorn had to design and construct his first set of locks to join canal and river. The Bridgewater Canal was completed to Runcorn in 1767.

By now Brindley had become the national canal expert and his services were in great demand. Promoters everywhere wanted him to survey their routes and to be their consultant engineer. His own plan was to link the four main river networks by canal. He surveyed the lines of the Staffordshire and Worcestershire Canal, the Trent and Mersey Canal, the Birmingham Canal, the Coventry Canal and the Oxford Canal. In 1790 when the Oxford Canal was finally completed it was possible to move cargo from the North West or the Midlands to London by water.

Brindley, however, had died in 1772, worn out by the work he undertook and the diabetes from which he suffered. In March 1767 Josiah Wedgwood had written:

Mr Brindley . . . is going to Scotland and Ireland. . . . I am afraid he will do too much and leave us before his vast designs are executed, he is so incessantly harassed on every side, that he hath no rest either for his mind or Body, and will not be prevailed upon to take proper care of his health. . . . I think Mr Brindley – The Great, the fortunate, money-getting Brindley, an object of Pity! and a real sufferer for the good of the Public. He may get a few thousands, but what does he give in exchange? His Health and I fear his Life too, unless he grows wiser, and takes the advice of his friends before it is too late.

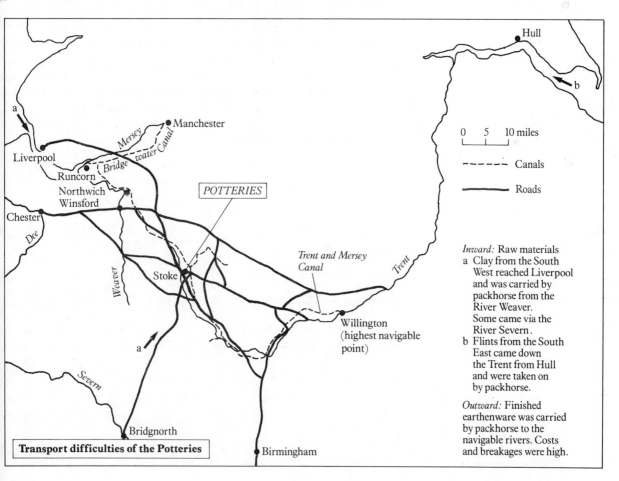

Transport difficulties of the Potteries

Inward: Raw materials
a Clay from the South West reached Liverpool and was carried by packhorse from the River Weaver. Some came via the River Severn.
b Flints from the South East came down the Trent from Hull and were taken on by packhorse.

Outward: Finished earthenware was carried by packhorse to the navigable rivers. Costs and breakages were high.

Using the evidence: promoting a canal

A proposal to build a canal linking the rivers Trent and Mersey along a route surveyed in 1758 by Brindley for Earl Gower was revived in 1765. The Potteries, as the map on page 129 indicates, suffered from serious transport difficulties. The canal scheme's leading promoter was Josiah Wedgwood.

A All these extracts concern the Trent and Mersey Canal and are taken from Wedgwood's letters and documents.

(i) On Friday last I dined with Mr Brindley . . . after which we had a meeting at the Leopard on the subject of a Navigation from Hull or Wilden Ferry to Burslem. . . . Our Gentn. seem very warm in setting this matter on foot again. . . . (11 March 1765)

(ii) The present price of flint, freight and carriage of clay and flint for pottery in Staffordshire which is 15/- [75p] per Ton on average, will be reduced by this new conveyance to 2/- [10p] per Ton on about 4000 Tons, which are sent up annually; and the Carriage and freight of the Earthenware in return, will be reduced from 28/-[140p] to about 12/- [60p] per Ton, which must greatly increase the exportation of that manufacture from this Port. (Liverpool, 16 May 1765)

(iii) . . . have been waiting upon his G—— the D—— of Bridgewater with plans respecting inland navigation. . . . Spent about 8 hours in his . . . compy., and had all the assurances of his concurrence with our design. . . . His G—— gave me an ordr. for the completest Table service of Cream colour that I could make. . . . The next day we waited upon the Cheshire Gentn. at a meeting of the Commissioners for the Weaver Navigation at Northwich, who promised like wise to me their interest in favour of our design provided we fall into their Navigation. . . . (6 July 1765)

fall into: link up with

Plan of the proposed canal linking the rivers Trent and Mersey

B The passage of the Act of Parliament was a time for celebration.

(i) . . . on receiving the agreeable news that His Majesty had been at the House of Peers and signed the Bill for making the Navigable Canal from this Town to Wolverhampton, the Bells were set ringing, which were continued the whole Day.

J.A. Langford, *A Century of Birmingham Life*, 1868, quoting a local newspaper

An Act of Parliament was needed for two reasons. To give the company the compulsory power to purchase the land it needed and to enable it to be set up as a joint-stock company. Canal building was expensive and there had to be many shareholders to provide the capital.

(ii) Since by the canal navigation,
   Of coals we've the best in the nation,
   Around the gay circle your bumpers then put,
   For the cut of all cuts is as Birmingham cut,
   Birmingham cut, fairly wrought,
   For the cut of all cuts is a Birmingham cut.
             (Song to celebrate the opening of the Birmingham Canal)

C The advantages of a canal to an agricultural district.

. . . An object of still greater importance is the likelihood of this canal being the means of promoting the cultivation of the extensive barren grounds . . . thro' a great part of which it must necessarily pass, after having been first conducted through a country full of chalk, from whence that manure is now carried in large quantities, at the expence of one shilling per waggon load per mile; whereas by the canal it will cost but one penny a ton for the same distance, and the boats will return laden with peat and peat-ashes. . . .

   Rev. S. Shaw, *A Journey to the West of England in 1788*, 1789

D Not everyone thought a canal was a good thing.

(i) The Petitioners, being Owners or Occupiers of Houses and Lands near to or through which the said Canal is intended to be cut, apprehended that great Injury will arise to them . . . by the near Approach of the said intended Canal to the Houses and Pleasure Grounds of several of the Petitioners, which they have made at great Expence.

             Journal of the House of Commons, 23 January 1783

(ii) A Mr Curzon objected to the Ashby-de-la-Zouch canal, and was accused by its promotors of declaring

his apprehension that, if the projected canal should take place, Ashby and Measham would become places of as great trade as Manchester and Sheffield.

             The Times, 16 March 1793

1 After studying the map on page 129 and the extracts in source A explain why the potters wanted to build the Trent and Mersey Canal.
2 (a) What evidence is there in source A of the importance of the Duke of Bridgewater? After you have studied the maps explain why it was vital to have his 'concurrence'.

(b) What evidence is there in the extracts in source A of opposition to the canal project? Explain your answer as fully as possible.

(c) Extract A(ii) is taken from a document Wedgwood wrote to counter possible opposition to the plan in Liverpool. How is he trying to convince the Liverpool doubters that the scheme is good for them?

(d) What impression do you get from these letters of the character of Josiah Wedgwood and of his attitude to the canal scheme?

3 (a) Is there sufficient evidence in source A to explain the popular enthusiasm for a new canal shown by the extracts in source B? Explain your answer.

(b) Source C deals with other advantages of canal development. Who does it claim will benefit from canal construction and why?

4 In both sources A and D there is evidence of opposition to canal schemes.

(a) Wedgwood probably regarded canals as progress. What evidence is there in these sources of an opposite opinion?

(b) Is there any evidence in this section which might change the opinion of the landowners who signed the petition in source D? Explain your answer.

Canal mania, 1793–4, and after

The first period of canal construction ended in the 1770s. Twenty years later the economy had revived and for five years there was a hectic flurry of canal schemes placed before the public. Encouraged by the profits made by the first canals and by the benefit to the districts they served, businessmen made plans and investors rushed to hand over their money. Many projects never reached Parliament but in the years 1791–6 fifty-one Canal Acts were passed, thirty of them in the peak years of 1793–4.

Shareholders did not always make money and although canals in industrial areas were highly profitable those built in the south were rarely successful. War with France led to inflation, and construction work frequently came to a halt as estimates were exceeded.

By 1836 there were about 4000 miles of canal but the basic network was completed soon after 1800. The Grand Trunk (or Trent and Mersey) together with Brindley's other canals had made the initial link between the rivers Trent, Mersey, Severn and Thames. Birmingham rapidly developed as the centre of the network with cuts radiating out to all the main inland waterways. The Grand Junction Canal, completed in 1805, shortened the route to London and took canal traffic into the capital, avoiding the Thames. Opened in 1783, the Thames and Severn hoped to provide a profitable route between those two rivers but was superseded by the more prosperous Kennet and Avon Canal in 1810.

Once the Leeds–Liverpool Canal was completed in 1816 there were three trans-Pennine routes. The others were the Rochdale Canal and the Huddersfield Canal. Coast-to-coast waterways were dug in Scotland, the Forth–Clyde Canal and the Caledonian Canal.

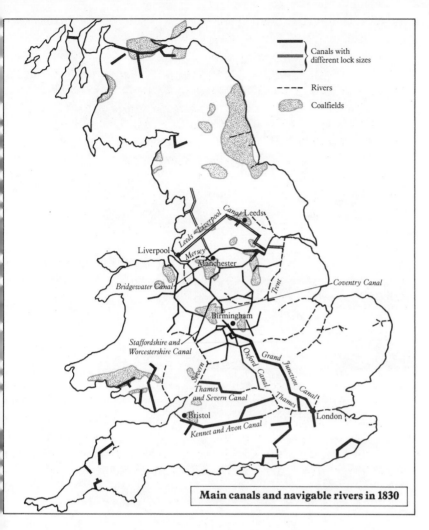

Canals with different lock sizes

- - - - Rivers

Coalfields

Main canals and navigable rivers in 1830

In South Wales the ironmasters and colliery-owners contributed to the construction of canals which could take their products down the valleys to Cardiff, Swansea or Newport for export to other parts of Britain or abroad.

Who gained from canals?

Writing in 1803 John Phillips claimed that 90 of the 165 Canal Acts passed since 1758 had been to serve collieries and that 47 others primarily served iron, lead or copper mines and works. Inland coalfields certainly were able to expand and develop. The building of canals in the East Midlands, for instance, opened new markets to the coal-owners of Derbyshire and Nottinghamshire, and by utilising rivers and canals they were able to reach London markets.

Wherever canals were made, industrialists found transport more convenient and costs lower, whether it was the West Midlands, Lancashire or Staffordshire. Raw materials could be obtained more easily and the finished product dispatched more efficiently.

Locks enabled barges to travel uphill. What are their disadvantages?

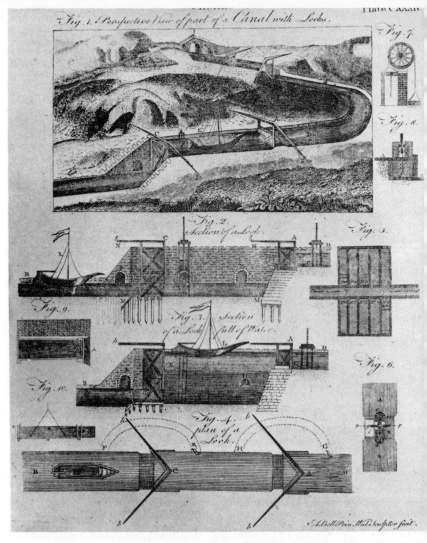

verdure: green grass

Although most rural canals were unprofitable, farmers gained. Lime, manure and marl could be carried cheaply. Lime kilns were a common feature of canal wharves. Produce grown on the improved land could be carried back to distant towns although farmers close to urban areas usually opposed canals that would bring them competition. The consumer benefited from a more dependable supply and lower prices.

The last word can be left with Thomas Pennant who travelled the Trent and Mersey Canal in 1782:

The cottage, instead of being half-covered with miserable thatch, is now secured with a substantial covering of tiles or slates, brought from the distant hills of Wales or Cumberland. The fields, which before were barren, are now drained, and, by the assistance of manure, conveyed . . . toll-free, are clothed with beautiful verdure. Places which rarely knew the use of coal, are plentifully supplied . . . and . . . it affords a conveyance of corn unknown to past ages. . . .

Thomas Pennant, *Journey from Chester to London, 1782*

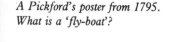

A Pickford's poster from 1795. What is a 'fly-boat'?

Where the slopes were too steep for locks, or where there was insufficient water, other methods had to be used. Can you explain how the mechanism shown here solved the problem?

Cost of carrying goods, 1792	By canal per ton (1000 kilo)	By land per ton (1000 kilo)
	£ s d	£ s d
Manchester to Etruria	15 0 (75p)	2 15 0 (275p)
Manchester to Newark	2 0 0 (200p)	5 6 8 (533p)
Manchester to Birmingham	1 10 0 (150p)	4 0 0 (400p)
Liverpool to Wolverhampton	1 5 0 (125p)	5 0 0 (500p)
Liverpool to Stourport	1 10 0 (150p)	5 0 0 (500p)

How much cheaper was canal transport than land transport? Why did it cost less to move goods by water?

Defects of the system

Canal companies were not directly challenged until the coming of railways. Lack of competition meant that obvious defects were not removed, and the movement of goods could have been cheaper and more efficient.

Thomas Telford, canal and road engineer. He surveyed routes for the Caledonian Canal, for the Ellesmere Canal and the Macclesfield Canal, as well as 'modernising' Brindley's Birmingham Canal. He used embankments and cuttings to keep routes as direct as possible. He pioneered the use of cast-iron water troughs for aqueducts. That enabled him to build the Pont Cysyllte aqueduct 40 metres above the river Dee. Its graceful arches can be seen through the window

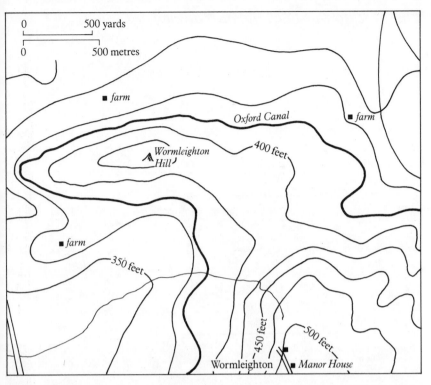

The map shows contour lines at 350 feet, 400 feet, 450 feet and 500 feet, with the Oxford Canal following the contours. Features marked include three *farm* symbols, *Wormleighton Hill*, the village of *Wormleighton*, and *Manor House*.

A section of the Oxford Canal, as surveyed by Brindley. To reduce the number of locks his canals followed the contours. This is an extreme example. What are the disadvantages of this technique?

Adapted from A. Burton, *The Canal Builders*, p. 76 (2nd edition 1981)

The network had been constructed without any central planning or standardisation, canals being built to serve local needs. There were variations in depths and in lock sizes. Brindley's canals were narrow with locks which catered for the narrow boat. Elsewhere, for instance in Yorkshire where the canals linked closely with the navigable waterways, there were broad locks which accepted the wider river barges. Where narrow canals met broad canals cargo had to be transhipped. This added to the expense, the slowness and the opportunity for theft.

Movement was slow. Queues at locks and tunnels ensured this. Early tunnels did not have towpaths and the barges had to be 'legged' through by bargees or 'leggers' lying on their backs and propelling the barge with their feet against the tunnel sides.

Although Pickford's flyboats operated to timetables, most barges, travelling at 2–3 miles an hour, did not. Canal companies maintained the waterways and collected tolls but they did not own barges. Freight charges were never standardised, and a long journey meant the payment of separate tolls on each new stretch of water.

It is hardly surprising that most canal companies found it impossible to compete with the greater convenience of railways.

8 Railways: the communica- tions revolution

Wondering crowds watch the fist train on the Stockton–Darlington Railway

On 27 September 1825 crowds of people turned out to marvel at the first train on the new railway.

. . . Throughout the whole distance the fields and lanes were covered with elegantly-dressed females, and all descriptions of spectators. The bridges under which the procession in some places darted with such astonishing rapidity, lined with spectators cheering and waving their hats, had a grand effect. At Darlington the whole inhabitants of the town were out to witness the procession.

. . . The procession was not joined by many horses and carriages until it approached within a few miles of Stockton; and here the situation of the Railway, which runs parallel and close to the turnpike road leading to Yarm and Stockton, gave them fine opportunity of viewing the procession. Numerous horses, carriages, gigs, carts, and other vehicles travelled along with the engine, and her immense train of carriages . . . and at one time the passengers by the engine had the pleasure of accompanying and cheering their brother passengers by the stagecoach, which passed alongside, and of observing the striking contrast exhibited by the power of the engine and of horses; the engine with her six hundred passengers and load, and the coach with four horses, and only sixteen passengers.

The first public railway to use steam locomotives, was built to carry coal from the South Durham collieries to the river port of Stockton. It passed through Darlington because the wealthy and influential Pease family, who owned woollen mills in the town, provided much of the finance. It was Edward Pease who engaged a colliery engineer from Killingworth, George Stephenson, to survey the route in 1821 and then to supervise its construction. In 1823 Stephenson persuaded Pease that steam locomotives were practical. The company had originally intended using horses and stationary steam engines along the track as motive power. Stationary steam engines would pull wagons attached to ropes up the gradients.

The railway locomotive and George Stephenson

Locomotives were still very new and untried in 1825. Richard Trevithick's invention of the high-pressure steam engine had made possible the use of steam-power in transport. In 1804 his first locomotive ran on an ironworks railway at Pen-y-darran in South Wales.

See Chapter 5 for the beginnings of railways on the coalfields

Eight years later, in 1812, John Blenkinsop's engine began work on the Middleton colliery lines near Leeds whilst in the North East William Hedley began building locomotives at Wylam colliery near Newcastle.

Colliery-owners quickly recognised the advantages of steam locomotives but there were many problems. The early engines consumed large amounts of coal, they were unreliable, breakdowns were frequent, and their weight too easily broke the brittle cast-iron rails.

George Stephenson was a self-educated man who had made himself into a respected and successful colliery engineer. Many north-east miners preferred his 'Geordie' safety lamp to the more famous Davy lamp. When his employers asked him to build a locomotive for the Killingworth colliery railway he eagerly turned his attention to solving the problems.

His first locomotive, *Blücher*, made its appearance in 1814. Others quickly followed. Stephenson did not invent the locomotive but he saw its possibilities as a means of transport. He made improvements to both it and the rails on which it ran. Between 1819 and 1822 he laid down the Hetton railway linking Hetton colliery with the River Wear at Sunderland. He claimed, in 1825, that he had built 55 engines of which 16 were locomotives. In that year he set up the firm of R. Stephenson and Co. as the first steam locomotive manufacturer. *Locomotion*, the engine that pulled the inaugural train on the Stockton to Darlington Railway, was the company's first locomotive.

Stephenson appreciated the extra strength of wrought-iron rails and recommended that these should be used on the SDR. The decision he took on the new line's gauge was to be particularly important. He chose 4 feet 8½ inches, probably because this was the standard axle width on colliery wagons in the North East. The same gauge was used on the Liverpool-to-Manchester Railway and then by the Stephensons and their pupils on the other lines they constructed.

Using the evidence: building the Liverpool-to-Manchester Railway

In 1824 George Stephenson was invited to become engineer for the proposed Liverpool and Manchester Railway.

The map shows that the transport links between these two cities before 1830 were inadequate to meet the needs of the rapidly growing cotton industry.

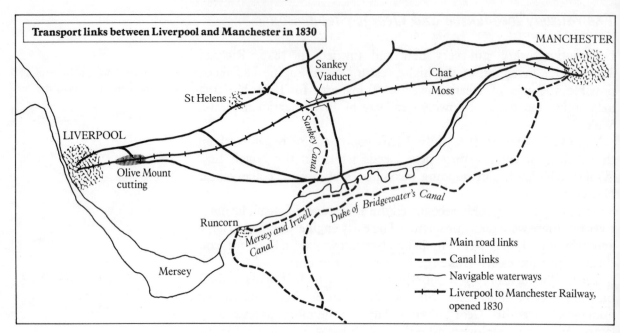

Transport links between Liverpool and Manchester in 1830

MANCHESTER

Sankey Viaduct

Chat Moss

St Helens

Sankey Canal

LIVERPOOL

Olive Mount cutting

Duke of Bridgewater's Canal

Runcorn

Mersey and Irwell Canal

Mersey

— Main road links
--- Canal links
— Navigable waterways
+++ Liverpool to Manchester Railway, opened 1830

A *The case for a railway*

The total quantity of merchandise passing between Liverpool and Manchester is estimated . . . at 1,000 tons per day. The bulk of this . . . is transported either by the Duke of Bridgewater's Canal, or the 'Mersey and Irwell Navigation'. By both of these conveyances goods must pass up the river Mersey, a distance of 16 or 18 miles, subject to serious delays from contrary winds, and not infrequently, to actual loss or damage from tempestuous weather. The average length of passage, by these conveyances . . . may be taken at 36 hours. . . . The average charge upon merchandise for the last 14 years has been about 15s per ton.

But it is not altogether on account of the exorbitant charges of the water-carriers that a railroad is desirable. The present canal establishments are inadequate to . . . the regular and punctual conveyance of goods at all periods and seasons. In summer time there is frequently a deficiency of water, obliging boats to go only half-loaded . . . while, in winter, they are sometimes locked up with frosts, for weeks together . . . There is still another ground for objection to the present system of carriage by canals, namely, the pilferage . . . whereas, a conveyance by railway, effected in a few hours . . . may be expected to possess much of the publicity and consequent safety of the King's highways.

Prospectus of the Liverpool and Manchester Railway Company, 1824

tempestuous: stormy

exorbitant: excessively high

B *The opposition*

There was plenty of opposition to the scheme. The Mersey and Irwell Navigation Company petitioned against the Liverpool-to-Manchester Railway Bill in 1824.

The vessels at present employed upon several canals between Manchester and Liverpool are capable of carrying, with ease and dispatch, a much larger quantity of goods every week than has ever been stated by the . . . promoters of the Bill, as the quantity passing in that period between Liverpool and Manchester; and it is submitted, that vessels can be loaded and discharged with much greater ease and expedition at the wharves of the carriers, than can possibly be the case from the Railway.

expedition: speed

. . . the rates charged by the carriers are as much overstated by the promoters of the Bill, as their means of accommodation are undervalued and misrepresented, both as to extent and dispatch. The distance upon the Petitioners' navigation . . . and also the periods of voyages, are in like manner greatly exaggerated.

C George Stephenson wrote to Joseph Pease in October 1824.

We have sad work with Lord Derby, Lord Sefton and Bradshaw, the great Canal Proprietors whose grounds we go through with the projected railway. Their ground is blockaded on every side to prevent us getting on with the survey. Bradshaw fires guns through his ground in the course of the night to prevent the surveyors coming in the dark.

The Railway Company's first Bill was defeated in the House of Commons, partly because of Stephenson's failure to master the details of the survey. He was humiliated in his cross-examination by the Bill's opponents.

George Stephenson's Sankey Brook Viaduct on the Liverpool-to-Manchester Railway

Making the Olive Mount cutting

D A year later, the opposition showed a different face as shown in this letter written by R.H. Bradshaw, the manager of the Bridgewater Canal, to J. Loch, the chief estate manager for the Earl of Sutherland.

The Manchester and Liverpool railroads are certainly going to Parliament again next session. The existing surveyor has just been here to show me their new plans, etc. and ask permission to go over our lands; to which (you will scarcely believe it) I have consented; but the man behaved so fairly and openly that I really could not refuse . . . .

Their new line is certainly a better one and much less objectionable than the former. They avoid Lord Sefton's land entirely and Lord Derby's land as much as possible. They do not cross the river Irwell at all . . . and they profess their great object to be getting over our canal (which they must cross) with the least possible injury or inconvenience to us. (27th September 1825)

The Act was passed in 1826 but the construction problems Stephenson faced were immense. There was to be a tunnel into Liverpool, a great cutting at Olive Mount on the approach to Liverpool, and the route across Chat Moss was ridiculed.

E Evidence of Francis Giles to the Parliamentary Committee on the Liverpool and Manchester Railway Bill, 1824:

No engineer in his senses would go through Chat Moss if he wanted to make a railroad from Liverpool to Manchester. . . . The surface of the Moss is a sort of long, coarse sedgy grass, tough enough to enable you to walk upon it, about half-leg deep. In the centre, where the railroad is to cross, it is all pulp from the top to the depth of 34 feet (10 metres); at 34 feet there is a vein of 4 or 6 inches (10-15 cm) of clay; below that there are 2 or 3 feet (60-90 cm) of quicksand; and the bottom of that is hard clay, which keeps all the water in.

1 Consult sources A and B.
   (a) Give four reasons why the Company thought the railway was needed.
   (b) How did the Navigation Company reply to the criticisms in the prospectus?
   (c) Both sources contain fact and opinion. Give examples of opinions. Give reasons for your choice.
2 Consult sources C and D.
   (a) What has the Railway Company done to try to reduce the opposition?
   (b) In what way had Bradshaw's attitude to the railway proposal changed? How do you explain his change of mind?
3 Consult source E and look at the illustrations. Briefly describe the construction problems and difficulties George Stephenson faced. How were they overcome?

The Rainhill Trials, October 1829

From the beginning it had been intended to use steam-power, in some form, on the line. By 1829 a decision had to be made but the directors

The Liverpool-to-Manchester Railway crosses Chat Moss. During construction the black spongy bog swallowed up men and animals. Drainage ditches filled with water and collapsed. The track was eventually floated on a raft of timber hurdles, brushwood and heather

were divided on whether to use stationary steam engines beside the track or locomotives.

The locomotive party had the support of Stephenson and his son Robert. Their opponents could point to the unreliability and wastefulness of existing locomotives. To settle the controversy the directors decided to hold a competition. Any engineer could enter a locomotive but the Company was interested in three things, speed, mechanical reliability and fuel economy.

Robert Stephenson's *Rocket* was the only locomotive to satisfy these three points. Its maximum speed was 29 m.p.h. and the average speed 16 m.p.h. The *Rocket* had a multi-tubular boiler which meant more steam could be produced and more power. Many other design features foreshadowed the shape of steam locomotives for the next hundred years. The *Rocket* demonstrated the potential of the steam locomotive. The Liverpool and Manchester Company gave the £500 prize to the Stephensons, purchased the engine and ordered two more. Plans to use stationary steam engines were abandoned.

The success of the Liverpool–Manchester Railway

The railway was officially opened on 15 September 1830. It was an instant success. Goods traffic soon reached the expected levels and the canal company had to reduce its charges. Passenger traffic exceeded all expectations. Within days of the opening most of the stagecoaches that ran between the two cities had been withdrawn and the railway was carrying an average of 1200 passengers a day. By 1833 this had tripled. Shareholders were paid good dividends as profits rose.

A developing railway network

There was no national plan for railway construction. The British railway network grew in a haphazard way, mainly to serve local needs.

The success of the Liverpool-to-Manchester Railway made George Stephenson's reputation. In the 1830s, he was much in demand surveying routes in the North and the Midlands. Amongst the first lines approved by Parliament in the 1830s, were the Liverpool to Birmingham Railway engineered by George Stephenson and his pupil, Joseph Locke; and the London to Birmingham Railway engineered by Robert Stephenson.

Once opened in 1838 this gave a direct rail link between London and the North West. Connecting lines at Rugby gave access to the North Midlands and the North East.

In the South the London and Southampton got its Act of Parliament in 1834. Joseph Locke was its chief engineer.

Brunel and the London-to-Bristol Railway (the Great Western Railway)

The London-to-Bristol Railway was completed in 1841. Its chief engineer was Isambard Kingdom Brunel. Brunel had designed a bridge to cross the River Avon as it passed through the Clifton Gorge. This had brought him to the attention of the Bristol businessmen who wanted the railway. He had considerable engineering experience having assisted his father's construction of the Thames Tunnel, but he had not worked on a railway.

Brunel planned a magnificent railway. His employers were in direct competition with Liverpool for the transatlantic passenger traffic and he set out to build the first stage of a route from London to New York which would be continued by steamship from Bristol.

Coming fresh to railway construction Brunel brought new ideas. The most controversal of these was his 7 feet gauge. He argued that the 'coal-waggon gauge' of the Stephensons was too narrow for fast, safe and stable travel. Brunel wanted to build bigger locomotives to get more speed on the straight level line he had surveyed. A broader gauge was essential.

By 1845 it was clear that the government would have to decide on a standard gauge for British railways. Difficulties had arisen at Gloucester, the first junction of broad and narrow gauge lines. All goods and all passengers had to be transferred. Passengers grumbled. Merchants claimed that goods were damaged. As the Great Western Railway extended its network it was clear that there would be several interchange points like Gloucester.

A Royal Commission was set up. Its members visited Gloucester, where, it was alleged, the narrow-gauge goods manager deliberately

created extra chaos by unnecessarily loading and unloading trains. A series of trials proved Brunel's points about speed and safety.

Additionally the Great Western began running expresses from London to Exeter in five hours, and then in four and a half hours. To do this, speeds of over 50 m.p.h. had to be reached and maintained – something that the narrow gauge locomotives of the time could not attain.

However, the Commissioners were more impressed by the chaos at Gloucester and the cost of converting over 1900 miles of narrow gauge to the broader gauge. Parliament passed the Gauge Act in 1846 making Stephenson's 4 feet 8½ inches the standard gauge for future railways. Only the Great Western, with about 270 miles, could continue with the broad gauge. Increasingly narrow gauge lines had to be laid on the Great Western's routes until finally, on one Sunday in 1892, the complete system was converted to narrow gauge.

Brunel's magnificent railway had impressive buildings. This is the station he designed at Bristol. A massive broad-gauge locomotive stands at the platform. Note the gentleman's carriage at the end of the train

Railway mania

Year	Mileage	Year	Mileage
1832	39	1841	14
1833	218	1842	55
1834	131	1843	90
1835	201	1844	810
1836	955	1845	2816
1837	544	1846	4540
1838	49	1847	1295
1839	54	1848	373
1840	—	1849	16
		1850	7

The table shows the total mileage of railway construction sanctioned by Act of Parliament in the 1830s and 1840s

Questions

There were two periods of railway mania (speculation in railway construction).
1 When were they?
2 Which was the greater of the two?
3 How do you explain the lack of interest in the intervening years?

A contemporary account gives us the atmosphere of these years.

avarice: greed

The most cautious were deceived . . . and men estimed good citizens . . . were drawn into acts which avarice urged but conscience condemned. They . . . heard the cry of railways at every turn; they listened to speeches at dinners, uttered by solemn, solid men, upon the glories of the rail; they read of princes mounting tenders, of peers as provisional committee men, of marquises trundling wheelbarrows, and of privy councillors cutting turf. . . . Their clerks left them to become railway jobbers. Their domestic servants studied railway journals. Men were pointed out in the streets who had made their tens of thousands. They saw the whole world railway mad. The iron road was extolled at public meetings; it was the object of public worship. . . . It penetrated every class; it permeated every household; and all yielded to the temptation. . . .

jobbers: dealers in railway shares

extolled: praised

The last day for the submission of plans to the Board of Trade in 1845 was 30 November, a Sunday. The Great Western ran ten special expresses to get railway promoters to London by the noon deadline.

The Eastern Counties ran eighteen or twenty special trains for the various projected lines. Engines with the steam up, and ready at a minute's warning, were kept for the expected wants of the projectors. Horses were scarce at the post towns, and two guineas a mile were paid for posting. . . .

Rival companies had to outwit each other.

. . . When an established company, with express trains at their command, refused one to the promoters of a competing line, the latter procured a hearse with all the paraphernalia of mourning, placed plans, sections and clerk inside, and dispatched it by special train to town.

J.A. Francis, *A History of the English Railway*, 1851

Many impossible schemes were proposed. Many schemes were never implemented. Some speculated in railway shares and made large profits, but many lost all they had. Nevertheless, by the early 1850s the main railway network had been established. Only central Wales and the north of Scotland were totally without railway lines.

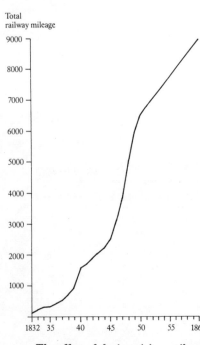

Total railway mileage

The effect of the 'mania' on railway construction

George Hudson, 'The Railway King'

At the centre of much of the speculation and investment during 'railway mania' was the substantial figure of George Hudson.

Hudson was a linen draper in York. In 1827 he inherited £30 000 and

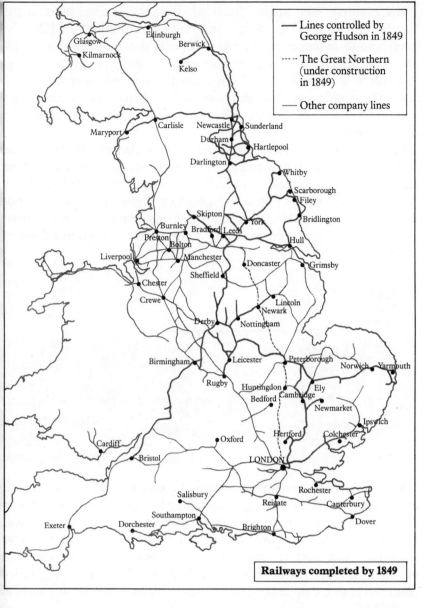

Railways completed by 1849

Legend:
— Lines controlled by George Hudson in 1849
---- The Great Northern (under construction in 1849)
— Other company lines

he used it to make himself a fortune by becoming involved in railway schemes. He helped get the railway to York in 1834 and was a leading promoter of the York and North Midland Railway which, through Derby and Rugby, gave a direct route to London.

Wherever he became involved in the affairs of a railway company it seemed to prosper. In 1844 he was at the centre of the first important amalgamation of railway companies to form a larger, more effective unit. Both the Midland Counties Railway and the Birmingham and Derby Junction Railway were competing for the traffic from the North Midland Railway to London. Fierce competition resulted in ruinous fare cuts. Hudson's solution was to form one company from the three – the Midland Railway.

Hudson tried to prevent the building of the Great Northern but failed. How did it threaten his railway empire?

His example was quickly followed. Competing companies in the North formed the Lancashire and Yorkshire Railway, whilst the Liverpool-to-Manchester Railway Company, the Grand Junction Railway and the London-to-Birmingham amalgamated to form the London and North Western Railway. Amalgamations ended competition and made the running of through trains easier. Many smaller companies found that they could not share in profits unless they became part of a larger company.

By 1849 Hudson controlled over 1000 miles of railway in the Midlands, the North East and in the Eastern Counties. He was MP for Sunderland. The greatest in the land sought the advice of 'The Railway King'. He was a man of power and influence. Nevertheless he could not stop the Great Northern Railway Company planning a route from London to the North that was thirty miles shorter than his line through Derby.

How Punch *saw Hudson at the height of his influence*

KING HUDSON'S LEVEE.

Shareholders welcomed his control of companies because dividends increased. Not all his dealings were totally honest. When profits fell in 1847 and 1848 he kept up dividends by making payments out of capital. In 1849 his affairs were investigated. The accounts were chaotic. Large sums had gone missing. Figures had been made up. Large expenses payments had been made. His fall was swift and Hudson was only saved from arrest as a debtor because he was re-elected MP for Sunderland until 1859.

The opposition to railways

Opposition to railways was vigorous. When the London to Birmingham line was being surveyed there was an outcry against it:

Hundreds of innkeepers, and thousands of horses . . . would be thrown out of employment; while hundreds of thousands would be ruined for the benefit of the few. Labour for the poor would be lessened, the rates for the poor increased. Canals would be destroyed; those who lived on them would be beggars; houses would be crushed by embankments, corn thrown out of cultivation, land made barren, landlords beggared. . . .

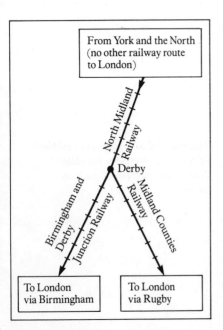

Railway competition at Derby

The London-to-Bristol Railway faced similar problems.

The people would be smothered in tunnels, and those that escaped suffocation would be burned in the carriages. Slopes were magnified into precipices, engines were to be upset, necks were to be broken. Eton College opposed it because it would be injurious to the discipline of the school, and dangerous to the morals of the pupils. . . . A farmer objected because his cows might be killed. . . . A gentleman objected because no public benefit would compensate for destroying the beauties of his estate. The water in the Thames . . . would be decreased, and the supply for Windsor Castle be destroyed. . . .

J.A. Francis, *A History of the English Railway*, 1851

Questions

1 Some of the opposition can be easily explained, Why would road and canal interests be against railway proposals?
2 Some of the reasons people were against railways seem ridiculous to us.
   (a) Pick out three examples of 'ridiculous' assertions against railways.
   (b) How do you explain this kind of opposition? Do you think people really had these fears? Explain your answer.
3 What is Francis's attitude towards these opponents of railways? Explain your answer.

Landowners who believed that the amenities of their estates would be destroyed by a railway were difficult to deal with. The London-to-Birmingham Railway had to by-pass Northampton because of this kind of opposition; Lord Exeter protected Burghley House but forced the Great Northern to take its main line through Peterborough rather than Stamford. Some made companies pay exorbitant prices for the land they needed and others, like Robert Gordon of Kemble House, made special terms. The Cheltenham and Great Western Union agreed to pay him £7500 compensation and to hide the line in an unnecessary tunnel.

By the 1840s, however, most landowners were recognising the advantages railways could bring to their estates and were actively encouraging them.

Building the line

There were three stages:
   1 Surveying the route.
   2 Getting the Act of Parliament.
   3 Constructing the line.
The chief engineer supervised both the survey and the construction. Robert Stephenson walked the route between London and Birmingham nearly twenty times during his survey. Brunel had a carriage made

to his specification as a kind of mobile office. This entry in his diary gives some indication of the many tasks he had to perform.

September 14 1833:
Up at 5 a.m. Joined Place and Williams ranged on to the Island east of Caversham. Breakfasted and mounted. Called on Mr Hawks, Surveyor. . . . Rode to meet Hughes; found him in barley stubble west of cottage. Directed him how to proceed and to meet me this evening at the Bear. Rode then to Purley Hall. Met Mr Wilder . . . spoke to him; found him very civil; gave him a prospectus. . . . Rode on to Streatley; tried in every way to find a line round instead of crossing the river at Goring; found it impossible. On looking at the country from the high hill south of Streatley . . . it was evident that much cutting might be saved by passing SW of Streatley Farm and winding a little more east of Halfpenny Lane.
   Returned to Reading . . . Hughes came at 7½. Agreed with him that he was to have £2.2 a day and pay his own expenses. . . . Pointed out to him the line he was to follow. Took him with me to Mr. Hawks to look at his large plan, Mr H—— to furnish him with a copy by tomorrow evening and is to make the survey of the line from Sonning to Streatley inclusive . . . Came to town by Mail.

Getting the necessary Act of Parliament could be a very expensive business.

. . . from returns which have been officially published it appears that, in the years 1845, 1846 and 1847, more than ten millions were expended in parliamentary contests.

Sir F.B. Head, *Stokers and Pokers*, 1849

After the Act was passed the contractor took over. Thomas Brassey and Samuel Morton Peto were the great railway contractors. Brassey alone was responsible for 1940 miles in the British Isles. Sections of the line were let out to sub-contractors who provided the labour. The navvies did the work.

. . . a full day's work consists of fourteen sets a day. A 'set' is a number of wagons – in fact, a train. There are two men to a wagon. If the wagon goes out fourteen times, each man has to fill seven wagons in the course of the day. Each wagon contains two and a quarter cubic yards. The result is, that each man has to lift nearly twenty tons weight of earth on a shovel over his head into a wagon. The height of the lifting is about six feet. This is taking it at fourteen sets a day; but the navvies sometimes contrive to get through sixteen sets, and there are some men who will accomplish that astonishing quantity of work by three or four o'clock in the afternoon. . . .

A. Helps, *Life and Labours of Mr Brassey*, 1872

The track had to be as level as possible. This meant filling valleys with long embankments, making cuttings and building tunnels. If the gradients were too steep or the curves too tight the early locomotives could not perform efficiently.

In determining whether the line should proceed by tunnelling or by cutting, the engineer's rule usually is to prefer the latter for any depth less than sixty

Hawks and Hughes were working for Brunel making the survey. Mr Wilder was a local landowner

feet; after which it is generally cheaper to tunnel. If, however, earth be wanted
for a neighbouring embankment, it becomes of course a matter of calculation
whether it may not be cheaper to make a cutting. . . .

> Sir F.B. Head, *Stokers and Pokers*, 1849

Earth from a cutting was taken in wagons to the embankment site.

There, the wagons were detached from each other. Afterwards they were
attached singly to the 'tip-horse', who would trot or gallop with them nearly to
the brink of the bank, where the horse being set free by a peculiar contrivance,
would step on one side, and the wagon, running on by its own impetus, and
coming against a sleeper placed at the end of the rails, shot out the earth into
the proper place. . . .

> A. Helps, *Life and Labours of Mr Brassey*, 1872

Tunnelling was slow and dangerous. A roof fall in the Watford
Tunnel during the construction of the London-to-Birmingham line
cost eleven lives. It took six years from 1839 to drive the Woodhead
Tunnel through the Pennines. Thirty-two men were killed and 140
seriously injured.

At last the proud directors could climb aboard the inaugural train.

31st May 1838. This being the day appointed for the opening of our railway,
the Directors and the company invited met at the depot before 11. A very
pretty sight it was. At 11.30 we entered the carriages of the first train, and
proceeding at a moderate pace reached Maidenhead Station in forty-nine
minutes, or at about 28 miles an hour. After visiting the works we returned to
Salt Hill, where a cold luncheon for about 300 was laid under a tent. After the
usual complement of toasts we returned to the line and reached Paddington (19
miles) in 34 minutes, or 33½ miles an hour. . . .

> J. Simmons, *The Birth of the Great Western Railway – Extracts from the Diary of
> George Henry Gibbs*, 1971 [Gibbs was a director]

Using the evidence: the Northbury line

The small manufacturing town of Northbury lies 20 miles from the nearest railway line. This line passes through Southchester. The two towns are linked by a canal and a turnpike but the manufacturers and leading citizens of Northbury want a railway. To the north of the turnpike there is a large undeveloped coalfield. To the south of the canal there is rich agricultural land and the main market town, Weston. Two routes have been surveyed. The advantages and disadvantages of each are shown on the map.

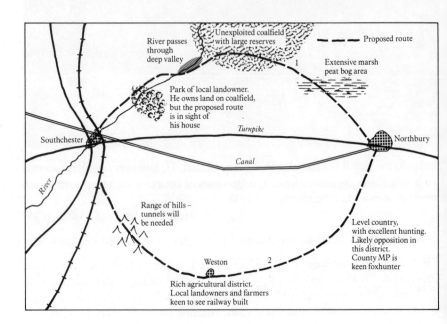

1 As a director of the new railway company decide which route you would recommend. Argue your case as fully as possible.
2 The canal company and the turnpike trust could petition Parliament against the railway company's bill. Write the statement they might make against the proposal.
3 As a landowner whose fox-hunting coverts would be crossed by route 2 write a letter to the local newspaper opposing the construction of the railway line.
4 As the company's engineer explain which line you would prefer to build. Describe the problems you expect and how you would have to overcome them.
5 Design a poster to encourage local people to invest in the railway company after you have decided which route to adopt.

Using the evidence: early railway travel

A A first journey was an adventure. In 1831 Colonel Phipps travelled from Liverpool to Manchester.

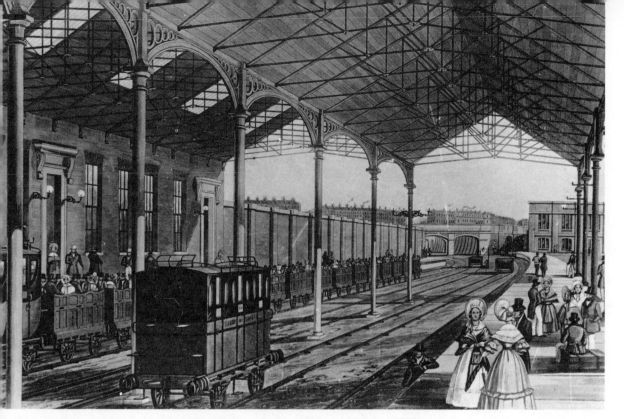

The ends of the carriages have strong leather mufflers to soften the force of the blow when they came in contact with each other, which frequently occurs when the engine stops. We stopped for water at a half-way house and once to regulate something out of order. The speed was by no means uniform, but varied considerably. At every mile a watchman is stationed to keep the way clear from stones. . . . We first passed on the road a string of carriages like our own, coming from Liverpool. The velocity with which both bodies are moving, separated only by a space of two or three feet, gave a terrific appearance to this occurence although, in reality there is no danger, when each person keeps his seat, and does not put the head out of the window . . . The last carriages we passed were platforms laden with merchandise and poultry. A gentleman's carriage was conveyed on one of these platforms.

Euston Station in 1837. How many third-class carriages are there? Why is their journey going to be unpleasant? The seat on the carriage roof is for the guard

velocity: speed

B Others were less impressed:

I cannot say that I liked it, the speed was too great to be pleasant, and makes you rather giddy, and certainly it is not smoother and easier than a good turnpike road. When the carriages stop or go on a very violent jolting takes place, from the ends of the carriages jostling together.

C Nevertheless rail travel quickly became popular.

Year	Millions of passengers carried
1838	5.4
1843	21.7
1848	54.4
1851	79.7

D First-class travellers were reasonably comfortable, and first-class carriages made up express trains. Second- and third-class passengers were less fortunate.

A passenger by the second-class carriages on the Manchester and Leeds complains that himself and a female relative have caught a severe cold from the holes in the floors of the carriages, which admit currents of air to the legs of the passengers; he asks if there is any use or object in these holes, except to drive passengers into the first-class carriages.

E Open third-class carriages were often attached to goods trains. On Christmas Eve 1841 a goods train with third-class carriages next to the engine crashed into a landslip in the Sonning Cutting on the Great Western Railway. Out of 38 passengers 8 were killed and 17 injured. The passenger carriages were crushed by the weight of the 17 goods wagons. The Board of Trade inspector's accident report described the carriages:

The third class carriages have seats 18 inches high, but the sides and ends are only two feet above the floor, so that a person standing up, either when the train is unexpectedly put in motion or stopped, is, if near the side or end, in great danger of being thrown out of the carriage, and those sitting near the sides are also in danger of falling; besides which, the exposure to the cutting winds of the winter must be very injurious to the traveller, who, if proceeding from London to Bristol, often remains exposed for ten or twelve hours, a great part of which is in the night time.

The GWR immediately boarded up the sides of its third-class carriages.

In 1844 the government gave some protection to third-class travellers. Since they were unprofitable the railway companies were reluctant to carry them.

In 1841, the fastest mail trains, carrying first-class passengers, took 4 hours 15 minutes for the journey from Paddington to Bristol. The day goods, with third-class passengers, left at 4.30 a.m. and arrived at 2.00 p.m.

The 1844 Railway Act

1 One train should run on every line, every day, in each direction, stopping at every station.
2 Its speed should be no less than 12 m.p.h.
3 The fare should be 1d a mile.
4 Third-class passengers should be protected from the weather and provided with seats.

F *Advice for travellers*
The following extracts are from *The Railway Traveller's Handy Book*, 1862.

1 Punctuality

. . . It should be . . . observed that the clocks at the various railway stations are universally set and regulated by 'London time'. . . . Most of our readers are aware that when it is twelve o'clock in the metropolis, it is either earlier or later than that hour elsewhere, according to the distance from London, and the

The comforts of first-class travel

direction of the compass. Thus the clock of a provincial town may point at five minutes to twelve, whereas it has already struck twelve in London, and the train appointed for departure at that hour has started when the unmindful traveller thinks that he has still a few minutes to spare. . . .

2 Comfort

. . . It would be as well for the traveller to provide himself with an over-coat, no matter what the season. . . . It is of the utmost importance to keep the feet warm; this may be accomplished by a pair of lambs'-wool socks and thick-soled boots, a pair of extra socks . . . or strips of flannel placed within the boots.

. . . A rug is certainly one of the greatest comforts of a railway traveller. . . . Not only does it keep the legs warm, but . . . it may be made to perform the part of a cloak, a counterpane, a cushion to sit upon. . . .

. . . A species of green or black spectacles, known as eye-preservers, are excellent things for a railway traveller . . . for if he be compelled to sit near the window, and opposite to the engine, he will find that by wearing these, the eyes will be preserved from the dust and ashes. . . .

3 Which class to travel?

The author recommended first-class. There would be plenty of room, greater comfort, and better companions. Third-class was cheapest, but the travellers

. . . may be destined to pass the next few hours . . . tightly compressed between two rough specimens of humanity. They may be doomed to semi-suffocation, to partial extinction of vision, and total deprivation of motive power by several large bundles, boxes, or baskets. . . . It may be that the shoulders, shins, toes, or other parts of the body, will from time to time be brought into contact with angularities or cubes. . . .

As for the 'parliamentary train':

. . . as this is the cheapest, so it is the slowest mode of railway conveyance. . . . The time of departure is usually early in the morning, so that a person having a distance of more than a hundred miles to go may calculate upon passing the best part of the day on the rail.

4 Safety

There were lamps in first-class carriages only. The great fear of the traveller was of attack in the darkness of a tunnel.

Male passengers have sometimes been assaulted and robbed, and females insulted. . . . And this has been most frequently the case when there have been only two occupants in the carriage. In going through a tunnel, therefore, it is as well to have the hands and arms ready disposed for defence, so that in the event of an attack, the assailant may be instantly beaten back or restrained.

The rush at the ten-minute restaurant stop. There were no toilets on the train

5 Refreshments

Refreshment stops had to be made on long journeys. On the London-to-Birmingham this was at Wolverton, on the London-to-Bristol at Swindon. In the ten minutes allowed, passengers had to struggle into the refreshment room, buy and consume their food and drink. *The Handy Book* recommended taking a packed lunch – it would be cheaper and of better quality.

Firth's painting shows a busy scene on the departure platform at Paddington in 1862

1 Consult sources A and B.
  (a) Find three pieces of information in Phipp's account which tell how the railway was operated.
  (b) Do you think he enjoyed his trip? Explain your answer.
  (c) What do both sources A and B agree on?
2 Study the illustrations and all the sources. Draw a chart to show the differences between the first-class, second-class and third-class travel.
3 Frith's painting shows Paddington Station in 1862. A cross-section of the travelling public are there – a working-class group in the background, a middle-class family piled high with luggage, boys returning to one of the new public schools, a soldier, a wedding party, a businessman. What else is happening in the picture?

  Using the sources write a letter from one of these travellers describing the journey to Bristol. Mention any anxieties the passenger may have had, the comfort or discomfort of the journey, the stop at Swindon. Base your letter on all the illustrations and sources.
4 Despite the fear of accidents, the discomforts and the unreliability of the early locomotives there was a dramatic increase in the number of passengers carried. How do you explain this?

The effects of railways

Questions

1 As you read this section design a chart to show 'The Effects of Railway Development'.
2 Here are some important railway facts:

1830	Liverpool-to-Manchester Railway opened
1836–7	The first railway mania
1841	London-to-Bristol Railway opened
1844–7	The second railway mania

By 1850, 6559 miles of railway were opened to traffic.
By 1870, 13562 miles of railway were opened to traffic.
Now look at these facts and figures about the coal and iron industries.

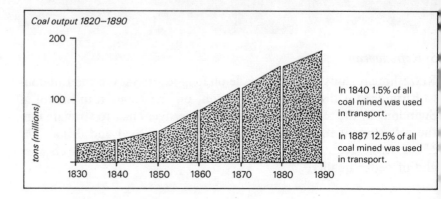

Coal output 1820–1890

In 1840 1.5% of all coal mined was used in transport.

In 1887 12.5% of all coal mined was used in transport.

Pig iron output 1820–60

1820	400 000 tons
1830	650 000 tons
1840	1 396 400 tons
1850	2 250 000 tons
1860	3 802 920 tons

(a) What happened to the output of coal and pig iron in the nineteenth century?
(b) Is there any connection between railway development and the growing demand for coal and iron? Explain your answer.

Road transport and related services declined steadily in the face of the new railways:

Only eleven mail coaches now leave London daily for the country. A few years since, before railways were formed. there were nearly eighty that used to leave the General Post Office. (1843)

EFFECTS OF THE RAIL ROAD ON THE BRUTE CREATION

Maidenhead is now in a miserable plight. The glories of 'The Bear', where a good twenty minutes were allowed to the traveller to stow away some three or four shillings worth of boiled fowls and ham to support his inward man during the night, are fast fading away forever. This celebrated hostelry is about to be permanently closed as a public inn. (1842)

Newspaper items quoted in W. M. Acworth, *The Railways of England*, 1899

There was a rail link between Hull and Manchester in 1840. Its effect on canal transport can be seen in the table below.

Canal charges per ton, Hull to Manchester		
	Before railways	*After 1840*
For corn, flour, etc.	£1 4s (120p)	13s (65p)
For cotton twist	£1 12s 6d (152½p)	£1 0s 0d
For manufactured goods	£2 5s 0d (225p)	£1 4s 0d (120p)

Business could only benefit from the new speed of travel.

A great part of the inland trade of the country is conducted by the agency of travellers; and here, what a revolution in the whole system and detail of business, when the ordinary rate of travelling shall be twenty miles instead of ten, per hour. The traveller will live double times: by accomplishing a prescribed distance in *five* hours, which used to require *ten*, he will have the other five at his disposal. The man of business in Manchester will breakfast at home – proceed to Liverpool by the Railway, transact his business, and return to Manchester before dinner.

H. Booth, *An Account of the Liverpool and Manchester Railway*, 1830

Packs of cotton, linen and woollen goods from Manchester are usually delivered in London almost with the regularity of letters. An immense quantity of fish from Billingsgate, and occasionally as much as 20 tons of fruit from Covent Garden market, are interjected into the country by the midday train. . . . Many tons of meat in hampers, and oftentimes a flock of a hundred dead sheep, wrapped up only in cloths, are also dispatched from the country to the London market.

Sir F. B. Head, Stokers and Pokers, 1849

Fishing ports like Grimsby, Lowestoft and Fleetwood were created by the railway. London's milk came on special trains from the West Country. Most farmers benefited although there were some exceptions:

The writer proceeded to say that the railway had greatly affected prices in the cattle-market at Southall, and had occasioned much discontent among the farmers, who complained that, in consequence of the facility that it afforded for the rapid transfer of stock from one county to another, they had been deprived of the advantages which they formerly possessed from their proximity to London. Five hundred head of sheep and 100 head of cattle had upon more than one occasion been suddenly introduced into the market from the West of England, and prices had been proportionately forced down.

Excursion trains began to run in 1840. An excursion from Leicester to Nottingham carried 2000 passengers in 65 carriages. Thomas Cook organised his first excursion from Leicester to Loughborough in 1841. Many thought that the cheap excursion was the greatest blessing of the railway age.

The most remarkable feature of this Whitsuntide was the larger numbers leaving Manchester rather than spending the holidays in the traditional way at Kersal Moor races.

Manchester Guardian, 1845

Seaside resorts benefited as the railway reached them.

The opening of the branch line from Blackpool to join the main railroad at Poulton, on the 29th of April, 1846, gave another marked impetus to the progress of the town; by its formation direct steam communication was completed with the populous centres of Lancashire and Yorkshire, and many, who had previously been deterred from visiting Blackpool by its comparative inaccesibility, now flocked down to its shores in great numbers.

J. Porter, History of the Flyde, 1876

Questions

How could these people be affected by the railways? Explain your answer as fully as you can.

1 The owner of a coaching business operating between London and Birmingham.
2 The owner of collieries in the East Midlands after the railway route to London was opened.
3 A dairy farmer close to a main line to London.

4 A shareholder in a canal which was facing competition from a railway.
5 A working man and his family in Manchester.
6 A middle-class family in London.
7 The editor of an important local newspaper like the *Leeds Mercury*.
8 A cotton manufacturer in Lancashire.
9 An unemployed man in the depression of the 1840s.
10 A landowner through whose estate a railway ran.

Towns and countryside were changed by the railway. The London and North Western Railway's viaduct crosses Stockport. Railways brought cheap and plentiful building materials

Railway towns grew up. Swindon was chosen for the Great Western Railway's locomotive works, Crewe developed from nothing because it became the site for the London and North Western Railway's workshops. Crewe was completely a company town.

There stands a plain neat building, erected by the Company, containing baths, hot, cold, and shower, for the workmen, as well as for their wives and daughters. . . . To a medical man the Company gives a house and surgery. . . . A clergyman, with an adequate salary from the Company, superintends three large day-schools for about three hundred boys, girls, and infants.

The town of Crewe contains 514 houses, one church, three schools, and one town-hall, all belonging to the Company.

Sir F. B. Head, *Stokers and Pokers*, 1849

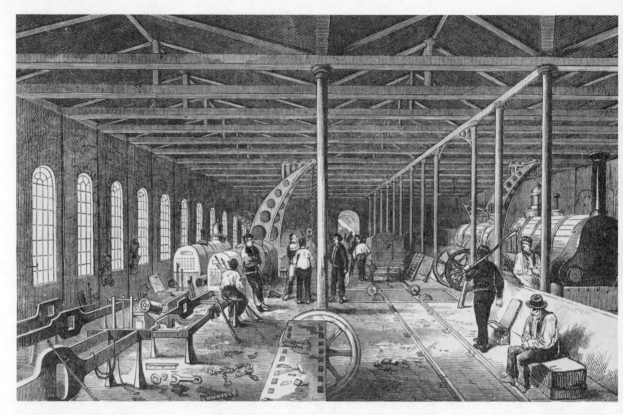

The engine building shop at Crewe – the railways created a new engineering industry

Britain made the world's first railways. Contractors like Thomas Brassey and Samuel Morton Peto took British navvies with them onto the continent or to Canada. They used British iron and materials, and so railway locomotives, wagons and equipment became important exports.

Perhaps the most important long-term consequences of railways was that they helped to break down differences within the British Isles. 'Railway time', or 'London time' became a standard national time, London newspapers had wider national circulations, the penny post allowed families to remain in contact with each other. The crowds who cheered and marvelled at Stockton and Darlington in 1825, and at Liverpool and Manchester in 1830 did not know what was beginning.

Working conditions

9 Pauper apprentices: a study of working conditions

Styal, Cheshire – a factory community

When Samuel Greg came to Styal he had to convert farm buildings to provide accommodation for his employees. What is the evidence that the cottages have been built into a barn?

By the 1820s the Gregs were building substantial cottages. Wages were lower than in the towns but so were rents, and living conditions were better. The school provided for employees' children can be seen. The grassed area in front of the cottages was divided up into allotments

The village shop supplied the workers with all their needs, from flour to bedsteads, from potatoes to silk handkerchiefs. Fresh produce came from the estate farm. Eventually the shop became a cooperative but those who got into debt had money stopped out of their wages. In 1838 Mary Howlett (was she John Howlett's wife?) owed £4. 1s (405p) and agreed that 2s. 6d (12½p) should be paid weekly.

A condition of employment was that all adult employees (excluding married women) were expected to join a sick club.

All this seems to have made a docile workforce. Between 1834 and 1846 there was only one stoppage because of industrial action when, on

20 August 1842, it was noted that the 'Mill stopped by rioters'. Four years later L. Bower reported to Robert Hyde Greg that he had been stopped and questioned about hours of work and conditions. Loyally he defended his employer:

. . . They said there was some bad reports about the Mill, that many left the place and would not stay. B. said few left and they were generally glad enough to come back again. . . . He had worked for 35 years under . . . Mr Greg and did not think there was any better master.

This is an example of the contract made between the Gregs and a family. In 1835 a number of families came to Styal from Buckingham under a scheme to move paupers from rural areas in the South to the North where jobs were available. What has been agreed? What do you know about John Howlett from this piece of evidence?

There were, however, many critics of places like Styal. What is Friedrich Engels suggesting here about employers like the Gregs?

. . . No doubt the mill-owner has provided a school and a church and a reading room. But he uses the school to inculcate strict obedience in the children's minds. He allows the reading room to stock only such books as support the middle-class point of view. The mill-owner dismisses workers who read Chartist and Socialist newspapers and books. . . .
F. Engels, *The Condition of the Working Class in England*, 1845

Chartists: see Chapter 12

Question

In view of Engels' comment, how do you explain L. Bower's attitude to his employer?

Using the evidence: pauper apprentices

In 1784 Samuel Greg began spinning cotton yarn in his new water-powered mill at Quarry Bank in the Cheshire village of Styal. He chose the site because the River Bollin was an ideal power source for the machines he planned to use.

Styal was a scattered farming community whose population could not provide Greg with the workforce he needed. As he prospered and the mill expanded so the labour shortages became more acute. Like other mill-owners Greg solved the problem in two ways. His agents toured nearby villages and towns attracting adult workers with their families promising regular wages and good accommodation.

Since both water frames and throstle frames could be supervised by children, Samuel Greg required large numbers of them. Hence he recruited children from parish authorities only too anxious to reduce the rates and to see the children in their care removed and placed in useful employment. These were the pauper apprentices.

A The Greg family appear to have taken their responsibilities seriously. In 1806 two apprentices, Joseph Fulton and Thomas Priestley, ran away and eventually reached London. Before returning them to Styal the Middlesex magistrates questioned the boys about their treatment. This is what Joseph Fulton, aged 17, told them.

My father . . . deserted me or went for a soldier when I was about 2 yrs old. . . . I had been in the workhouse of the parish of Hackney from an Infant About 3½ yrs since I consented . . . to be bound apprentice to Sam Greg. . . I was first employed to doff bobbins. . . . I used to oil the machinery every morning. . . . I did not spin. I liked my employment very well. I was obliged to make overtime every night. . . . I did not like this as I wanted to learn my books. . . . I wanted to go oftener to School. . . . This was the time that the straps and frames wanted mending. I have no reason to complain of my Master Mr Greg nor Richard Bamford who overlooks the work. There were 42 Boys &

Samuel Greg

throstle frames: a spinning machine developed from the water frame

doff: take off

more Girls apprenticed. We lodged in the Prentice House. . . . The Boys slept at one side of the house and the Girls on the other. . . . Our rooms were very clean, the floors frequently washed, the rooms aired every day, whitewashed once a year. Our beds were good. We slept two in a bed and had clean sheets once a month. We had clean shirts every Sunday we had new clothes for Sunday once in two years. We had working jackets new when these were worn out and when our working trousers were dirty we had them washed. . . .

On Sunday we went to church in the morning and to school in the afternoon after which we had time to play.

On Sunday we had for dinner boiled Pork and potatoes, we also had peas, turnips and cabbages in their season.

Monday we had for dinner milk & Bread and sometimes thick porridge, we had always as much as we could eat.

Tuesday we had milk and potatoes.

Wednesday sometimes Bacon and Potatoes sometimes milk and bread.

Thursday if we had Bacon on Wednesday we used to have milk and bread.

Friday we used to have lobs couse.   lobs couse: a stew

Saturday we used to dine on thick Porridge.

. . . . I had a shilling when we set out. . . . The shilling . . . arose from my overwork. I was paid 2d per week for which I worked nine hours. The money that the apprentices get . . . is set down in a book. They only have a little of it, the rest is saved until they come out of their term.

Thomas Priestley, age 13, added more details.

. . . I was set the same as the others to attend 2 machines Spinning Cotton, each of which spun about 50 Threads. My business was to supply these machines, to guide the threads occasionally and to twist them when they snapt. I soon became perfect in these operations. I also learned to take the machinery to pieces and apply the oil, a matter that required some care. . . . About 2 months before I left the place . . . one of the wheels caught my finger and tore it off. . . . I was attended by the surgeon of the factory Mr Holland. . . . I have no reason to complain of the usage. . . .

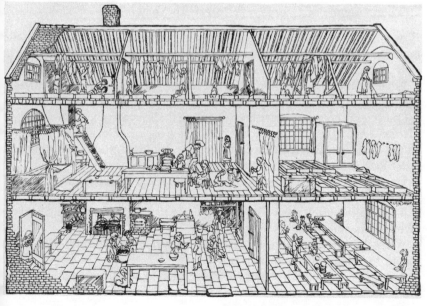

A reconstruction of the Styal Apprentice House in about 1830

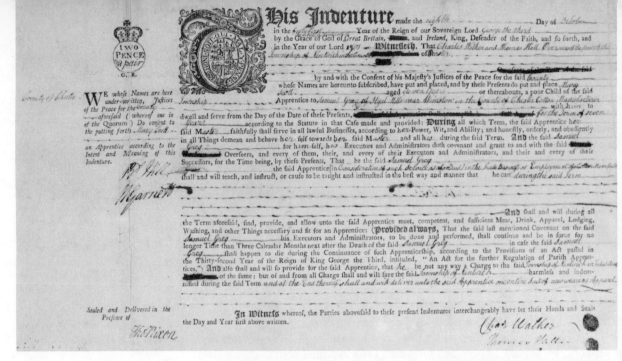

B *Samuel Greg agreed to provide 'Meat, Drink, Apparel, Lodging, Washing and other Things necessary and fit for an Apprentice' as well as instruction 'in the Trade Business or Employment of a Cotton Manufacturer'*

Our working hours were from 6 o'clock morning summer and winter till 7 in the evening. There were no night workers. We had only 10 Minutes allowed us for our Breakfasts. . . . 2 days in the week we had one hour allowed for dinner, while the machines were oil'd, for doing this I was paid half a penny a time. On the other days we were allowed half an hour for dinner. . . .

I had no reason to be dissatisfied . . . but during my illness I thot of my mother, and wanted to see her. . . . I . . . am very willing to go back again.

The Gregs were among the last mill-owners in the country to employ pauper apprentices. There were still about 80 at Styal in 1833, when George and Elizabeth Shawcross, the apprentice master and matron, gave evidence to the Royal Commission on Factory Conditions.

C The evidence of George and Elizabeth Shawcross:

How long do the children work in the mills? – Twelve hours, from six in the morning to seven at night; and hour at noon for dinner, and half an hour at eight o'clock for breakfast; they always go out of the mill for their meals.

What are the terms on which they are taken? – From nine to eighteen years of age: they are bound according to their ages, generally nine years of age. . . .

Can you say how many have been ill during the last year, and for what length of time? – We have very little sickness. Mr Greg pays the Doctor 20l. a year for all the medicine and attendance they receive. Children when they come first don't look so hearty as when they have been here some time. . . .

Do you teach the children? – No, the ladies teach the girls, and the school master the boys, three nights a week. . . .

Then do you teach them nothing? – Sewing to the girls, who all make their own clothes and the shirts for the boys.

When they are past eighteen do they generally remain in the mill? – Yes; and go out to lodgings or their friends.

Are any of the children deformed? – No, I don't know that we have ever had one.

D When the vicar of Biddulph in Staffordshire wrote to Samuel Greg in 1817 offering young children from the parish, he was informed that '. . . we keep them one month upon trial before bound to ascertain their probable healthiness' and that

Two guineas each will be expected from the Parish and clothing sufficient to keep the Children clean
   Say 2 Shirts
          2 Pair Stockings
          2 Frocks or Bedgowns
          2 Brats or Aprons
and 2 guineas to provide them other necessaries.

brats: a type of pinafore or apron

E Robert Hyde Greg opposed the Ten Hours Movement and its supporters were amongst his keenest critics. An incident involving an apprentice, Esther Price, provided them with an opportunity to discredit him. An anonymous pamphlet, dedicated to the reformer and philanthropist MP Lord Ashley (7th Earl of Shaftesbury) in 1837, alleged that

Ten Hours Movement: campaign to reduce hours of work for children in mills to ten a day. Robert Hyde Greg managed the mill after Samuel Greg's death in 1834

. . . One mode of punishment is to cut off their hair close to the head, especially of those who seem most anxious to preserve it. Another is of a rather more objectional nature. It is not long since a girl named Esther Price, a Liverpool apprentice, was ordered to be confined for five days for the grievous offence of going to Liverpool to see her father, during a temporary stoppage of the works, after she had asked permission to go, and was refused. . . .

Greg was seriously concerned by these accusations. A long, written explanation of the reasons for Esther Price's punishment was prepared

1 Consult source A. What do the accounts of Sefton and Priestley tell you about
(a) working conditions at Styal;
(b) living conditions of the apprentices;
(c) the attitude of the boys to their work, to Samuel Greg and to the mill overseers?
2 (a) How far does source C agree with the statements of the two boys?
(b) There are some differences. What are they? How do you explain them?
3 Now consult source E.
(a) What does this source add to our knowledge of conditions at Styal?
(b) Why do you think that neither source A nor source C mentioned punishment or ill-treatment?
4 Whose account do you think gives the most accurate picture of conditions at Styal, the two boys, the Shawcrosses or the anonymous writer of source E? Explain your choice.
5 Referring to all these sources in your answer, describe the attitude of the Gregs towards their pauper apprentices. What motives do you think they had for treating them in this way?

Caring for the apprentices was an expensive business. Beef, milk and vegetables were purchased from the village shop whilst large stocks of linen and woollen cloth, calico and other fabrics, shoes and stockings were kept at the Apprentice House. Pigs were kept in the garden to provide a regular supply of bacon. In 1842 Robert Hyde Greg calculated that it cost 6s. 5¼d (32p) to keep an apprentice for one week. At this time there were 52 children in the House. In 1847 the last apprentices completed their indentures. It was cheaper to employ children who lived with their parents in the village the Gregs had built. The wages book informs us that in February 1840 John Venables, age 14, a mule hand, received 3s. 6d (17½p) for a week's work and William Venables, age 13, working in one of the weaving sheds, received 2s. (10p). The apprentice system had ceased to be economic.

Pauper apprentices at Litton Mill, Derbyshire

Robert Blincoe (about 1792–1860) became an apprentice in 1799. He left Litton Mill in 1813. He worked in the cotton industry for the rest of his life, becoming a small manufacturer

F In 1832 the biography of Robert Blincoe was published. It was designed to shock and it gave an appalling account of the mistreatment Blincoe had suffered, in particular at Litton Mill in Derbyshire.

. . . few apprentices had either knife, fork, or spoon . . . or hats, shoes, or stockings. . . . Little attention was given to personal cleanliness. . . . Their bodies were literally covered with weals and contusions. . . . No soap was allowed. . . . The apprentices had their breakfast generally of water-porridge . . . and oaten cake, which they took in the mill. The breakfast hour was eight o'clock; but the machinery did not stop. . . . Forty minutes was allowed for dinner; of which time full one half was absorbed in cleaning the frames. . . .

Sixteen-hour days were common and the overlookers would,

. . . when Blincoe could not, or did not keep pace with the machinery, . . . tie him up by the wrists to a crossbeam and keep him suspended over the machinery. . . . Lift the apprentices up by their ears, shake them violently, and dash them upon the floor. . . .

. . . He had often been compelled, on a cold winter's day, to work naked, except his trousers, and loaded with two half hundredweights slung behind him, hanging one at each shoulder. . . .

R. Brown, The Memoir of Robert Blincoe, 1832

G Blincoe seems to have left Litton in 1813. In 1811 the local magistrate, M. M. Middleton, inspected the mill.

I found the house in which the apprentices board and lodge very clean; but two of them having come to me with a complaint of being worked too hard, and of not having sufficient support, I thought it right to examine some of the apprentices upon oath as to the facts they complained of, and the substance of their deposition is as follows, viz., that they go into the mill about ten minutes before six o'clock in the morning, and stay there till from ten to fifteen minutes after nine in the evening, excepting the time allowed for dinner, which is from half to threequarters of an hour; that they have water porridge for breakfast and supper, and generally oatcakes and treacle, or oatcake and poor broth for dinner; that they are instructed in writing and reading on Sunday.

House of Lords Account of Cotton Mills, 1819

H *Pauper apprentices feeding at a pig trough. Robert Blincoe described an incident like this*

I *Factory workers*

1 (a) What do Blincoe and Middleton agree on about Litton Mill?

(b) They differ on some very important points. How do you explain the failure of Middleton to learn about the ill-treatment Blincoe describes?

(c) Why would a historian writing about the cotton mills have to treat these sources carefully?

2 Sources H and I are illustrations from a book published in 1840, *The Life and Adventures of Michael Armstrong the Factory Boy.*

(a) What impressions do these illustrations give of life in a textile mill? Are they supported by Blincoe or the Styal evidence? Explain your answer.

(b) Compare source I with source C on page 56 (spinning mules in a mill). What are the differences? Which, in your opinion, is the more accurate illustration? Give reasons for your answer.

(c) What do you think Frances Trollope's purpose was in writing her book and illustrating it in this way?

Children and work

There was nothing unusual about the employment of young children. Describing the domestic system in the woollen industry around Halifax at the beginning of the eighteenth century Daniel Defoe wrote approvingly,

Among the manufacturers houses are likewise scattered an infinite number of cottages or small dwellings, in which dwell the workmen . . . the women and children of whom, are always busy carding, spinning, etc, so that no hands being unemploy'd, all can gain their bread, even the youngest to the ancient; hardly anything above four years old, but its hands are sufficient to itself.

A Tour Through the Whole Island of Great Britain, 1726

George Crompton, the eldest son of the inventor Samuel Crompton, began helping his mother by treading raw cotton in a tub of soapy water 'soon after I was able to walk'. Wherever the domestic system operated, in whatever trade, children were a part of the family work unit. One observer remembered,

The creatures were set to work as soon as they could crawl and their parents were the hardest of task masters.

In agricultural districts children could earn pennies scaring birds off the crops and helping with light farm work as one country boy, born about 1820, recalled:

When I got older I went to tending sheep. I was seven years old then.

Charles Shaw was seven when he began as a 'mould-runner' in a pottery works in 1839. For one shilling a week he worked up to fourteen hours a day with a platemaker:

. . . wedging clay was . . . the work of the boy. . . . What is now done by hydraulic pressure was then done by the bone and muscle of, perhaps, a half-fed boy. He had to take a lump of raw clay upon a plaster block, cut it into two with a piece of wire, lift one half above his head, and then bring it down upon the lower half, to mix them, with whatever force he could command. This had to be repeated till the clay was brought to the consistency of . . . putty. Doing such work as this was 'rest' from the mould running. Imagine a mere boy, running in and out of this stove room, winter and summer, with its blazing iron stove, his speed determined by his master's speed at his work. Coarse oaths, and threats, and brutal blows in many cases followed any failure to be at the bench at the required moment. . .

The few laws which protected children were ineffective. A House of Commons committee enquiring into the employment of boys as chimney sweeps in 1817 discovered that an Act of Parliament of 1788 requiring apprentices to be at least eight was completely ignored by both parents and employers. Boys as young as four, five or six years old were being forced into the trade.

Child brickyard workers were also expected to carry heavy loads of clay and finished bricks

THE LONDON SWEEP

Children in factories – a matter for concern

Legislation protecting apprentices, passed in 1802, proved ineffective. Mill-owners evaded its provisions or were ignorant of it whilst the magistrates failed to enforce it. However, the cotton industry was changing. Freed from water-power by the steam engine, manufacturers built their factories in the Lancashire towns. Their workers lived in the streets surrounding the mills and the large numbers of children still employed were 'free' living at home and receiving wages.

The new factories attracted public attention. This meant that the exploitation of children could not be hidden or overlooked. As evidence emerged that children were being overworked and abused, public opinion focused on the problem. Sir Robert Peel's Committee heard a mass of conflicting evidence in 1816.

Sir Robert Peel had made his fortune as a cotton manufacturer at Bury in Lancashire

Using the evidence: the 1816 Report of the Select Committee on the Employment of Children

1 As you read through the sources, list all the unfavourable aspects of factory work for children.
2 Collecting evidence from these sources, write two letters to a newspaper, one from a reformer arguing that children need protection and shorter hours, the other a reply from a mill-owner.

A *The mill-owners*
(i) James Pattison, a silk manufacturer of Congleton, Cheshire employed 54 children under the age of 10 out of a total workforce of 320–330. They earned from 1s. 6d (7½p) to 4 shillings (20p) a week for 12½ hours a day. This included two hours for meal breaks.

Why do you take the children so young? – The motive . . . is partly to oblige their parents; in a great degree to relieve the township; and also, because at that early age their fingers are more supple, and they are more easily led into the habit of performing the duties of their situation. . . .

Factory children – the cause of all the concern

Have you ever observed any inconvenience to the health of those very young children from being employed so many hours? I can only state . . . that they enjoy very excellent health. . . .

Do you conceive that working in the factories is favourable to the morals of young people? – It keeps them out of mischief; and while they are industriously employed, they are less likely to contract evil habits than if they are idling their time away.

(ii) William Sidgewick, a cotton spinner of Skipton, explained that his workers were expected to stand throughout the working day.

How many hours are they on their feet? – I cannot answer that, because they may occasionally sit down. . . . When the overlooker is not there, they may sit down. . . . We have no seats made for their convenience to sit upon. . . .

If the threads were not breaking, and the work was going on properly, you would have no objection to their sitting down? – No, I should not occasionally; but it might become a habit.

If there was a restriction as to the working of children under ten years of age, would not it lead to no child of that age being employed in the works? – My answer would be that I think the parent would be injured thereby, because many children under ten years aid the sustaining of the family by their wages.

(iii) Robert Owen had taken over the New Lanark mills from his father-in-law, David Dale in 1800. He ended his employment of children under ten and reduced hours of work to 10¾ hours. His views were very different to those of his fellow mill-owners.

What . . . period would you recommend for . . . admission to full work? – 12 years. . . . For the 2 years preceding, to be partially instructed; to be instructed one half the day, and the other half to be initiated into the manufactories by parties employing two sets of children. . . .

What time would you recommend? – About 10 hours of actual employment . . .

Do you think, if such an arrangement were made . . . the manufacturers

The schoolroom at Robert Owen's New Lanark factory. It was frequently visited and was unusual in the subjects taught. Owen tried to attract the children to school by making the teaching amusing and interesting

would suffer in any consequence? – My conviction is, that no party would suffer in consequence of it. . . . I have found . . . that there has been a very sensible difference in the general health and spirit of the whole mass of the population so employed. . . .

What employment could be found for the children of the poor, in those situations, till 10 years of age? – It does not appear to me that it is necessary for children to be employed under 10 years of age, in any regular work.

If you do not employ them . . . what would you do with them? – Instruct them, and give them exercise.

Would there not be a danger of their acquiring, by that time, vicious habits,   vicious: evil
for want of regular occupation? – My own experience leads me to say that I have found quite the reverse, that their habits have been good in proportion to the extent of their instruction. . . .

B *The magistrate*

Theodore Price had visited and inspected a mill at Emscott near Warwick. He found the mill to be hot and stuffy with all the windows fastened. He was informed that the windows had to be shut to prevent the draught blowing the cotton dust about.

Was it very minute in its particles? – So minute I did not see it, except where it had gravitated in quantities about the greasy parts of the mill.

What was the general state and complexion of the children employed. . .? –   hectic: flushed
I thought the children short in stature and they had a hectic appearance, probably from constant work and the warmth of the room; they were going backwards and forwards twisting the threads when they broke, and they were obliged to move quickly across a large room; there was a moisture about their faces. . . .

C *The doctors*

i) George Leman Tuthill MD stated that mill conditions would damage the health of children.

Have you, at any period of your life, had an opportunity of practising in any manufacturing country? – I never practised in any manufacturing country.

Or been in the habit of attending any poor houses or manufactories in the Metropolis? – I have not; the greatest opportunity I have had of seeing children, has been in consequence of my being physician to the Westminster Hospital.

ii) Sir George Blane, MD:

Supposing that children are employed in close rooms, regularly day by day for thirteen hours and a half . . . is it your opinion that the children, so employed, at the early age of from six to twelve, would receive no injury to their health? –
. . . I have no experience as to manufactories. . . . From what I have observed in the course of my experience. . . . I certainly should say it was greatly too much for the health of children. . . .

iii) Kinder Wood, a surgeon from Oldham, had visited two factories, one of which belonged to his father-in-law. He was critical of the long hours worked and agreed that the high temperatures and lack of ventilation could harm the health of children.

What effect had this employment on the growth of children? – I believe my opinions differ from those of many other persons; I believe that their growth is not at all stunted by this employment. . . .

Can you inform the Committee what effect the employment of children in Cotton mills has upon their mental organs or capacities? – They are not deficient in capacity, but on the contrary are very sharp. . . .

1 Consult the evidence of the mill-owners in source A.
 (a) How do Pattison, Sidgewick and Owen differ in their attitudes and opinions on the employment of children?
 (b) Whose opinions would another mill-owner agree with?
 Remember to give reasons for your answer.
 (c) From the evidence you have seen elsewhere in this chapter, do you think that Owen's attitude to children was usual?
 Explain your answer making reference to those sources.
2 Consult sources B and C.
 (a) Three out of four of these witnesses are critical of the employment of children. What is the weakness of their evidence?
 (b) Kinder Wood did not totally condemn the employment of children. Why would a reformer regard his evidence as worthless?

The Ten Hours Movement

The 1819 Factory Act, one consequence of the concern created by the 1816 Report, attempted to regulate the hours of work of children in cotton mills. Unfortunately Owen's proposals for regular inspection were abandoned. The Act was to be enforced by magistrates who were often uninterested, overworked or friendly with the mill-owners.

Although there was some protection for children employed in the cotton industry, those working in other branches of textiles – woollens, linen or silk – had none. In 1830 Richard Oastler launched a harsh attack on the West Riding mill-owners through the correspondence column of the *Leeds Mercury*. Accusing them of hypocrisy, he contrasted their concern for the black slaves of the West Indies with their exploitation of white slaves in their woollen and flax mills. Oastler became the propagandist and leader of the movement to reduce the working hours of children in textile mills to ten a day.

Adult workers supported this campaign. They knew that a reduction in the working hours of children would give every worker a ten-hour day since the mills could not operate without them. Short-time committees were organised and the West Riding became a hotbed of agitation.

Matthew Sadler took up the cause in Parliament. He prepared a Ten Hours Bill and obtained a Parliamentary Committee of Inquiry in 1831 to examine the evidence. His opponents alleged that the witnesses were carefully selected and trained in their answers. Their criticism could not lessen the impact the committee's report had on public opinion.

Witness after witness told of excessive hours, of beatings to keep

Richard Oastler was a land agent who sympathised with working people against their employers. He led their opposition to the New Poor Law Act (1834) in West Yorkshire (Volume 8, Chapter 1)

A CODRINGTON LABOURER.   A MORETON SLAVE.

exhausted children awake, of sadistic overlookers and employers, of deformities and of appalling injuries caused by the unfenced machinery.

Sadler contested Leeds in the 1832 general election as the workers' candidate. The middle-class mill-owners and their supporters made sure he was defeated. A new parliamentary champion had to be found.

Lord Ashley had never visited the North, and had not considered the problem of child labour until he had read the Select Committee's report. It appalled him, and he readily agreed to the suggestion that he should reintroduce Sadler's Ten Hour Bill in the 1833 session.

The 1833 Factory Act

Pressed by the mill-owners among its supporters, the government acted to forestall Ashley. It claimed that more information was needed. A Royal Commission was quickly set up and sent to the North to collect additional evidence. Its task was hampered by the opposition of workers and the short-time committees organised demonstrations by factory children in many of the towns they visited.

Although the Report concluded that much of the original evidence was biased and exaggerated it did recommend protection for the youngest children and the appointment of government inspectors to enforce any legislation.

The mill-owners were often opponents of West Indian slavery. The factory reformers contrasted the way in which the mill-owners treated their workers with the conditions they claimed existed in the West Indies. Who, according to this cartoon, is worst off?

The Factory Act restricted the youngest children aged from 9 to 13 to an eight-hour day, or forty-eight hours a week. Young persons aged from 13 to 18 were limited to twelve hours. Factory-owners were to provide school facilities for the youngest children and inspectors were to supervise the operation of the Act. Cotton, woollen and flax mills were to be controlled.

Ashley unsuccessfully persisted with his Ten Hours Bill but he, Oastler and the other activists did not accept their defeat. The government's measure gave greater protection to the very young children than did the Ten Hours Bill but since employers could work the children in relays there was no reduction in the hours of adults. Agitation was to continue.

Using the evidence: The opposition to reduced hours

A The *Leeds Mercury* opposed Oastler and the Ten Hour campaign.

. . . . There are the strongest possible objections to any legislative interference between the master and the workman – to any law that would constrain the free course of industry, or pretend to adjust either wages or the time of labour. The true policy is to leave the workman to get as much as he can for his labour, and the master to purchase labour as cheaply as he can. But . . . children under fourteen . . . are not *free agents*, . . . and their tender age requires that they should be protected from a combination of parents and employers to extract from them an undue amount of labour.

16 October 1830

. . . extreme hardship would be inflicted upon thousands and tens of thousands of families in Lancashire and Yorkshire, by a law fixing the hours of labour at eight or even ten hours, and *absolutely forbidding* the employment of any one child, whatever may be the circumstances, for a minute longer.

3 December 1831

On Lord Althorp's Factory Bill which became the 1833 Act:

This measure seems to us to be dictated by the best intentions, but to be a crude piece of legislation, calculated greatly to harrass the manufacturers by the strict *surveillance* and minute interference which it establishes, whilst it secures for the children more leisure and less wages than their parents will approve. . . .

10 August 1833

B Robert Hyde Greg protested against further legislation in 1837.

It is proposed . . . by the 'Short Time Committee', and Lord Ashley . . . *to limit the productive energy of the . . . great staple manufacturers, including steam engines, machinery, and grown-up men,* TO NINE HOURS AND A HALF DAILY.

Our only advantages consist in cheap machinery and low rate of interest. By restricting our mills to 69 hours a week, we have given up these advantages; by restricting them to 58, we not only annihilate them, but *hand them over to the enemy.* . . . .

surveillance: inspection

staple: textile

. . . It is much to be regretted that the present Factory Law, and the regulations of the Inspectors, tend to destroy *all good feeling*, and *to aggravate misunderstandings where they exist*. The Inspector's regulations are founded upon the principle of the master being *a tyrant and a cheat*. . . .

> Robert Hyde Greg, *The Factory Questions, considered*. . . .

C A contemporary economist's argument:

. . . in a mill . . . the whole net profit is derived *from the last hour*. . . .If the hours of work were reduced by one hour per day . . . profit would be destroyed. . . .

The exceeding easiness of cotton factory labour renders long hours of work practicable. With the exception of the mule spinners . . . the work is merely that of watching the machinery and piecing the threads that break. . . . The work . . . is scarcely equal to that of a shopman behind a counter in a frequented shop – mere confinement, attention, and attendance.

Any plan, therefore, which should reduce the present comparatively short hours, must either destroy profits, or reduce wages . . . or raise the price. . . .

. . . . The increase of price would be such as to occasion, even in the home market, a great diminuation of consumption. . . . I believe it would, in a great measure, exclude us from the foreign market, which now takes three-fourths of our annual production.

> Nassau Senior, *Letters on the Factory Act*, 1837

D (i) Leonard Horner wrote to his daughter soon after his appointment as a factory inspector in 1833 that although the mill-owners

. . . naturally dislike the Act . . . nothing would be kinder than the way they have received me, and one of them, Mr Lepper, has placed his little carriage at my disposal, and I am to dine with him today.

The factory inspector checks ages. Is the employer looking worried? Does employment seem to have had any ill effects on the children?

(ii) The terms of the 1833 Act were to be implemented gradually. . . .
In their 1834 Report the inspectors wrote:

. . . it will be found extremely difficult . . . if not wholly impossible, to limit
the labour of children, who are 12 years of age to 48 hours in the week, without
serious injury to the masters and work-people; as in many situations it will not
be possible to find a sufficient supply of children to work by relays and . . .
adult labour must necessarily be interfered with.

E In his report of 18 January 1837 Horner listed the offences he had
prosecuted West Riding manufacturers for during the last six months of
1836.

Description of the offence	Informations	Convictions	Withdrawn	Dismissed
1 Employing children under nine years of age	8	6	–	2
2 Employing children under 13 years of age longer than 48 hours in the week	69	58	5	6
3 Employing children in silk-mills more than 10 hours in the day	14	13	1	–
4 Employing children in the night-time	5	4	1	–
5 Employing young persons more than 12 hours in the day	24	19	4	–
6 Employing children without certificates of age	24	18	3	3
7 Employing children without requiring them to attend school	68	55	7	6
8 Not giving the time for meals prescribed by the Act	9	8	–	1
9 Not keeping the register required to be kept, in order to show the workers in the factory who are subject to the Act	32	31	1	–
10 Not keeping the register of time required to be kept, in order to show the hours when the children and young persons are employed	65	51	10	5
11 Making false entries in these registers	7	6	–	1
12 Giving false certificates of school attendance	2	1	1	–
13 Not fixing up the Abstract of the Act and the Regulations of the Inspectors	10	6	4	–
14 Not whitewashing the interior of the factory for more than 12 months	5	5	–	–
15 Various minor offences	18	10	7	1
	360	291	44	25

In 1837 Horner was transferred to Lancashire. In four months he prosecuted mill-owners for 504 offences. He found children hidden in wool bags and in the 'necessaries' and many mills had early-warning systems. Do you think he discovered all the breaches of the law?

necessaries: toilets

1 Which source could be used to support each of these statements?
Opponents of the Ten Hour Movement:
(a) believed that the government should not interfere between an employer and his workpeople;
(b) claimed that shorter hours would mean lower wages;
(c) claimed that the textile industry would not be able to compete with its rivals overseas;
(d) alleged that the inspectors destroyed the relationship between master and worker;
(e) asserted that the mill-owner's profit was made in the last hour of the twelve-hour day.

2 *Laissez-faire* was the belief that government should not interfere in the lives of the people. It was not the business of government to provide education, to improve public health, or to pass laws to protect workers. A worker was a free agent who could negotiate wages and conditions with the employer and leave if these were unsatisfactory.
From this evidence what can you learn about the attitude of the *Leeds Mecury*, Greg and Senior to:
(a) the workers;
(b) the arguments of the reformers.

3 Greg wrote that the evidence given to Sadler's Committee 'is *radically defective*, for it contains the statement of *one side only*. . . .'
(a) Could this same charge be made against Greg, Senior and the *Leeds Mercury*? Explain your answer.
(b) What kind of people are Greg and Senior hoping to convince by their arguments? Do you think it is the workers? Give reasons for your answer.
(c) What effect does Greg have by using words like 'enemy', 'tyrant' and 'cheat', italics and capital letters in his text?

4 Consult sources D and E.
(a) Compare these with the comments about inspectors in sources A and B. Do they confirm the *Leeds Mercury*'s fears or the comments of Greg? Explain your answer.
(b) The 1833 Factory Act has been described as the first effective Factory Act because inspectors were appointed. At first there were only three for the whole country, and there was no register of births until 1837. What do these facts and the sources suggest to you about (i) the effectiveness and impartiality of the inspectors; (ii) the effectiveness of the 1833 Act?

'Ten Hours' achieved

Ashley maintained the pressure for a Ten Hours Bill in the House of Commons. The strength of the agitation in the industrial areas declined during the 'Hungry Forties', but in 1844 Sir James Graham, the Home Secretary, introduced a new Factory Bill. Ashley's ten-hour amendment was defeated by the government but the new Act gave protection to female workers by limiting their hours to twelve a day. For the first time adult male workers benefited because machinery now had to be fenced. The hours worked by the youngest children were further reduced to six-and-a-half to give them ample time for schooling.

Finally, in 1847, John Fielden a mill-owner from Todmorden, and a colleague of Oastler from 1830, got a Ten Hours Act for young persons and women through Parliament. Mill-owners, however, exploited loopholes in the law operating young people and women in relays so that adult male workers did not benefit from the shorter hours.

Three years later Ashley persuaded the mill-owners to accept a compromise measure. In return for a ten-and-a-half-hour working day for women and young persons the mill-owners agreed to clear restrictions on working hours, mills being opened from 6 a.m. to 6 p.m. with one-and-a-half hours for breaks. The half-day on Saturday became compulsory.

Ashley was accused of deserting the cause by his former allies but textile workers were amongst the best protected in the country. Over the next eighteen years the provisions of the factory acts were gradually extended to other industries.

Working conditions underground – the Report that shocked

In 1840 Ashley pressurised the government into appointing a Royal Commission of Inquiry into Children's Employment. Its first Report published in 1842 dealt with the conditions under which children worked in the mining industry. Illustrated with line drawings, it shocked even more than the earlier reports on factory conditions.

Betty Harris, aged 37, drawer: 'I have a belt round my waist, and a chain passing between my legs, and I go on my hands and feet. The road is very steep, and we have to hold by a rope. . . . The pit is very wet . . . my clothes are wet through almost all day long. . . . The belt and chain is worse when we are in the family way. . . .'

Girl miner

(Far left) This shocked people in 1842. Why?

(Left) A woman bearer in Scotland. Agnes Kerr, age 15, 'was nine years old when commenced carrying coal; carry father's coal; make 18 to 20 journeys a day; a journey to and fro is about 200 to 250 fathoms; have to ascend and descend many ladders; can carry 1½ cwt' (Fathom: 6 feet or nearly 2 metres)

(Below) What is the job of the boy on the right? Why might the boy pushing the truck find it easier than Betty Harris?

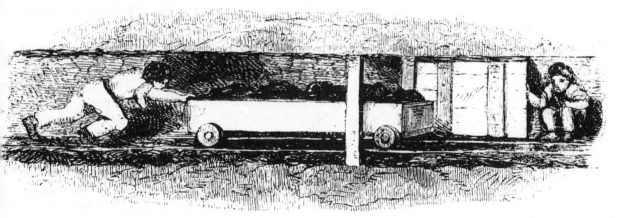

Children go to the iron and coal works at as early an age as six; at all ages from six to ten. (Shropshire)

Where they are much distressed, and there are large families, they will go as early as six or seven years old. (West Riding)

Some of six years old go down now. Lads six years old can keep doors well enough, and soon learn as well as old persons the ways of a pit. Parents could not keep their children if they were not allowed to go down. (A collier in the North East)

I started work when I was seven. I get very tired sitting in the dark by the door so I go to sleep. . . . Nearly a year ago there was an accident and most of us were burned. . . . All the skin was burnt off my face. . . . (Phillip Phillips, age 9, from Merthyr)

I don't know how old I am but I have been down here about three years. When I first came down I couldn't keep my eyes open but now I sit by the door and smoke my pipe. I smoke about 2oz a week and it costs about twopence. . . . (William Richards, from Monmouthshire)

Trappers, minding a ventilation door, had to remain down the pit until all work had finished for the day. This might seem light work but, as one assistant commissioner pointed out, sitting in the dark was a monotonous and lonely existence.

Most boys were employed as putters or hurriers moving coal in corves on sledges or wheeled wagons on rails from the coal-face. What appalled public opinion, however, was not the age, conditions and injuries these suffered but the employment of women and girls at the same task.

. . . One of the most disgusting sights I have ever seen was that of young females, dressed like boys in trousers, crawling on all fours, with belts round their waists and chains passing between their legs at clay pits at Hunshelf Bank, and in so many small pits near Holmfirth and New Mills. . . .

. . . On descending Messrs Hopwood's pit at Barnsley, I found assembled around the fire a group of men, boys and girls. . . . The girls as well as the boys stark naked down to the waist, their hair bound up with a tight cap, and trousers supported by their hips. . . . In the Flockton and Thornhill pits the system is even more indecent; for though the girls are clothed, at least three fourths of the men for whom they 'hurry' work *stark naked*, or with flannel waistcoats only. . . .

The report was very factual, but the evidence shocked middle-class readers. Despite this, Ashley was fiercely opposed by the mine-owners as his Mines Bill went through Parliament. The Act forbade the employment of women and girls underground, the employment of boys under the age of 10 and the operation of winding gear by boys under 15. An inspector was appointed to enforce this Act, but he was not a mining engineer and had no authority to establish safety standards.

Eight years later a properly qualified Mines Inspectorate was formed and in 1852 the inspectors were given power to close down collieries they considered unsafe or whose owners refused to implement their recommendations. The gradual widening of their powers contributed to the improving safety record in the country's mines.

Deaths in mining accidents
per million tons of coal mined

1851	19.35
1861	10.95
1871	9.15

By 1878 the protection given by government to young workers and women in the textile and mining industries had been extended to those working on the land, in metal works, in brickfields, in fact to most of those who worked in factories or large workshops. Domestic servants, people employed in small backstreet workshops and shop assistants were amongst those who still worked excessive hours and were not protected.

Using the evidence: the Felling colliery disaster

A List of the Persons killed by the Explosion.

Numbers on the Plan.	Name.	Day of Burial.	Years old.	Employment.	Numbers on the Plan.	Name.	Day of Burial.	Years old.	Employment.
1	John Knox	May 27		Trapper	m 47	John Wood	22	27	Hewer
2	Robert Harrison	27	14	Waggon Driver	m 48	Jeremiah Turnbull	22	43	Hewer
3	John Harrison	27	12	Waggon Driver	m 49	John Haswell	22	22	Hewer
4	George Ridley	27	11	Waggon Driver	50	John Burnitt	22	21	Hewer
5	Robert Hutchinson	27	11	Trapper	51	George Culley	22	14	Trapper
6	Thomas Robson	July 8	18	Putter	m 52	Joseph Wilson	23	25	Hewer
m* 7	John Pearson	8	58	Shifter	m 53	John Boutland	23	46	Hewer
8	Philip Allan	8	17	Putter	54	George Reay	24	9	Trapper
9	Geo. Bainbridge, unk.	8	10	Putter	55	William Gardiner	24	10	Trapper
10	Isaac Greener	9	24	Hewer	m 56	Thomas Craggs	24	36	Hewer
11	James Craigs	13	13	Waggon Driver	57	Thomas Craggs	24	9	Trapper
12	Edward Bell	15	12	Putter	58	John Greener	24	21	Hewer
m 13	Ralph Harrison	15	39	Horse-keeper	m 59	Edward Richardson	24	39	Hewer
m 14	Matthew Brown	16	28	Hewer	60	Robert Dobson	24	13	Trapper
15	James Kay	16	18	Putter	m 61	William Dixon	25	35	Hewer
16	George Bell	16	14	Putter	62	George Robson	25	15	Putter
17	Thomas Richardson	16	17	Putter	63	Andrew Allan	25	11	Trapper
18	Henry Haswell	16	18	Putter	m 64	John Thompson	25	36	Hewer
19	Joseph Anderson	16	23	Putter	m 65	John Pearson	25	64	Hewer
20	Joseph Pringle	16	16	Putter	m 66	Thomas Bears	25	48	Hewer
21	—— Dobson, unknown	16	a boy	Trapper	67	Charles Wilson	25	20	Hewer
22	George Pearson	16	26	Hewer	m 68	Michael Gardiner	25	45	Hewer
23	Robert Hall	16	15	Putter	m 69	James Comby	25	28	Hewer
24	Gregory Galley	16	10	Trapper	70	Joseph Gordon	25	10	Trapper
25	Benjamin Thompson	17	17	Craneman	m 71	Robert Haswell	25	42	Hewer
26	George Mitcheson	17	18	Putter	m 72	Joseph Wood	27	39	Hewer
27	Matthew Pringle	17	18	Putter	m 73	John Wilkinson	27	35	Hewer
m 28	Nicholas Urwin	17	58	Braking inclined plane	m 74	John Turnbull	27	27	Hewer
m 29	John Wilson	17	32	Hewer	m 75	Matthew Sanderson	27	33	Hewer
m 30	Thomas Young	17		Putter	m 76	Robert Gordon	27	40	Hewer
31	John Jacques, unknown	17	14	Putter	77	Thomas Gordon	27	8	Trapper
32	Edward Pearson	17	14	Putter	m 78	Christopher Mason	27	34	Hewer
33	William Richardson	17	19	Putter	79	Robert Gray Leck	28	16	Putter
34	Christopher Culley	17	20	Putter	m 80	William Jacques	28	23	Putter
35	William Boutland	17	19	Crane On-setter	81	William Hunter	29	35	Deputy
36	Jacob Allan	17	14	Putter	82	Thomas Ridley	29	13	Putter
m 37	Isaac Greener	17	65	Hewer	m 83	William Sanderson	30	43	Hewer
38	Thos. Bainbridge, unk.	17	17	Putter	84	George Lawton	30	14	Lamp-keeper
m 39	John Wilson	18	30	Hewer	85	Michael Hunter	30	8	Trapper
40	Matthew Bainbridge	18	19	Putter	86	William Dixon	31	10	Waggon Driver
41	John Surtees	18	12	Trapper	87	Edward Haswell	Aug. 1	20	Hewer
42	Ralph Hall	18	18	Putter	88	Joseph Young	3	30	Trapper
43	Paul Fletcher	18	22	Hewer	89	George Kay	26	16	Putter
44	William Galley	18	22	Putter	90	Robert Pearson	Sept. 1	10	Trapper
45	John Hunter	18	21	Hewer	91	John Archibald Dobson	19	15	Trapper.
m 46	Thomas Bainbridge	22	53	Hewer	92	Not yet discovered.			

1 List all the occupations mentioned. Find out what these did: trapper, putter, hewer.

2 What were the commonest occupations of those under 20?

3 Count up the number of people in different age groups from 6–10 to 61–65. Draw a bar graph to show your findings.

4 Using the information on your graph describe the age of the workforce – is it young, middle-aged or elderly? Try to explain your answer.

5 Felling was a colliery in the North East. What does this evidence tell us about women and pit-work in that coalfield?

This list of people working underground at Felling colliery was drawn up after the explosion in 1812. Ninety-two men and boys were killed. The age and occupation of each worker is given

Parliament protects the workers

Year	Events	Legislation	Terms
1802		*Health and Morals of Apprentices Act* sponsored by Sir Robert Peel.	1 Apprentices to work no more than 12 hours a day including meal breaks. 2 No night work. 3 Attempted to lay down minimum standards of care, e.g. no more than two to a bed, girls and boys in separate dormitories, two suits of clothing a year to be provided. 4 Local JPs who were not mill-owners were to inspect mills. Difficult to assess its effectiveness. Inspection and control inadequate. Outdated as fewer and fewer paupers were apprenticed.
1806	Joseph Fulton and Thomas Priestley run away from Styal.		
1813	Robert Blincoe leaves Litton Mill		
1816	Parliamentary Committee of Inquiry into the Employment of Children		
1819		Peel's and Owen's *Factory Act*	Children aged 9–18 to work 12-hour day. Limited to cotton mills.
1825		Hobhouse's *Factory Act*	Introduced the half-day on Saturday (9 hours)
1830	Oastler's letters to the *Leeds Mercury*. Ten Hours Movement begins in West Riding.		

Year	Events	Legislation	Terms
1832	Sadler's Select Committee evidence totally condemns the system.		
1833	Ashley becomes Parliamentary spokesman of the agitation.		
	Royal Commission on Employment of Children in Factories.		
	Ashley's Ten Hour Bill defeated.	Althorp's *Factory Act*	1 Children 9–13 to work 8-hour day.
			2 Children 13–18 to work 12-hour day.
			3 Inspectors to be appointed.
			4 Factory owners to provide schooling for the youngest children.
1836	*Registration Act* – registers of births to be kept which would make enforcement easier.		
1840	Royal Commission on Children's Employment		
1842	Commission reports on the mining industry.	*Mines Act* (Ashley)	1 boys under 10, girls and women not to work underground.
			2 An inspector appointed.
1844		Graham's *Factory Act*	1 Children 9–13 to work 6½-hour day.
			2 Women and young persons, 13–18, to work 12-hour day (69-hour week).
			3 Machinery to be fenced.
1847		Fielden's *Ten Hour Act*	Ten-hour day for women and young persons.

Year	Events	Legislation	Terms
1850		The compromise *Factory Act*	1 Mills to be open 6 a.m. to 6 p.m. – 12 hours. 2 1½ hours for meal breaks. 3 10½-hour working day for young persons and women.
1853		*Coal Mines Inspection Act*	Regular safety inspections.
		Factory Act	Relay working by young children forbidden.
1860		*Coal Mines Regulation Act*	Boys under 12 not to be employed. Safety rules clarified.
1860s	Legislation extended to other aspects of textile industry, e.g. bleaching, calico printing, dyeing.		
1862	Royal Commission on Children's Employment		
1867		*Factory Extension Act Hours of Labour Regulation Act*	Extended the legislation of 1840s to other factories and workshops.
		Gangs Act	Gave protection to women and children working in agricultural labour gangs.
1873		*Agricultural Children's Act*	Children under 8 not to work on farms.
1874(1) 1878(2)		Disraeli's *Factory Acts*	1 Established the universal 10-hour day in factories and workshops. Nobody under 10 to work. Full-time work for over-14s only. 2 Consolidated and brought together in one code all the Acts of the previous thirty years.

Working-class reaction to change

THE FRIENDLY SOCIETY OF IRON FOUNDERS OF ENGLAND, IRELAND AND WALES,
ESTABLISHED FEBRUARY 6TH 1809, AT BOLTON LE MOORS, LANCASHIRE.

The changes of the Industrial Revolution put many pressures on the working-class people of England. They reacted in a variety of ways.

Some workers, who felt threatened by change, resorted to violence and machine breaking. Luddism, 1811–1812, and the Swing riots, 1830, are two examples of this. Such outbreaks often occurred during years of economic depression, high prices and hardship.

Others turned to politics for solutions to their problems. The difficult years after 1815 were a time of political unrest in the industrial districts, whilst the peaks of Chartist activity were in the depression years of 1838–9, 1842 and 1847–8.

However, when prosperity returned workers turned to trade union activity. Higher wages and better working conditions then became a priority and a possibility.

Annual average price of British wheat per quarter 1801/51. What is the link between high wheat prices and political agitation amongst working people? Why was the summer of the year after a bad harvest likely to be a dangerous time?

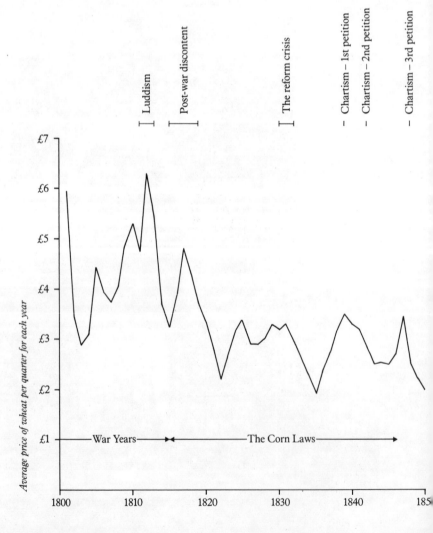

The attack on Rawfolds Mill

As you read the evidence list as many reasons as you can find why different groups of workers became Luddites.

William Cartwright of Rawfolds Mill was a hated man. He expected an attack on his mill and was prepared. He had four trusted workmen with him and five soldiers. They were well armed. The stairs to the upper floors were protected by rollers with large spikes. At the top there was a huge container of acid to be tipped on anyone attempting to ascend. The assault failed and the attackers withdrew leaving two of their number badly wounded in the millyard. Both died soon after without revealing the names of their fellows.

A reporter in the *Leeds Mercury* commented:

The assailants have much reason to rejoice that they did not succeed in entering the building, for we speak from our own observation when we say that had they effected an entrance the deaths of vast numbers of them, from a raking fire which they could neither have returned nor controlled, would have been inevitable.

RAWFOLDS MILL.

On the night of Saturday, 11 April 1812 this mill was attacked by about 150 men who wanted to destroy the machinery it contained

Rawfolds is in West Yorkshire, not far from Huddersfield. The attackers were croppers, highly-paid, skilled woollen-cloth finishers. Their livelihood was threatened by the gigmills and shearing frames Cartwright had installed.

Gigmills used rollers to raise the nap, and shearing frames were simple enough for children to operate. Gigmills had been attacked in the West Country in the 1790s, and in 1802 the Leeds croppers forced the masters to stop using the new machines in that town. Initially the West Riding croppers had looked to Parliament for help. In 1806,

John Wood's cropping shop, where
George Mellor the leader of the
attack worked. Most croppers
worked in small workshops like
this. Croppers used teazles to raise
the 'nap' on hairy, newly-woven
cloth. This was then shaved off
using shears that were four feet
long. It was a skilled craft, and a
full apprenticeship was required

however, MPs had shown little sympathy for the croppers' case and in
1809 all laws restricting the use of machinery in the woollen industry
were repealed. The croppers turned to other means of protecting
themselves.

The threat

This letter was received by a Huddersfield manufacturer.

Information has just been given in that you are a holder of those detestable
Shearing Frames, and I was desired by my Men to write to you and give you
fair Warning to pull them down. . . . You will take Notice that if they are not
taken down by the end of next week, I will detach one of my Lieutenants with
at least 300 Men to destroy them and furthermore take Notice that if you give
us the Trouble of coming so far we will increase your misfortune by burning
your Buildings down to Ashes and if you have Impudence to fire upon any of
my Men, they will have orders to murder you, and burn all your Housing, you
will have the Goodness to your Neighbours to inform them that the same fate
awaits them if their frames are not speedily taken down. . . .

Signed by the General of the Army of Redressers
NEDD LUDD

The 'organisation'

i) Verses from 'The Croppers Song':

And night by night when all is still,
And the moon is hid behind the hill,
We forward march to do our will
With hatchet, pike and gun!
Oh, the cropper lads for me,
The gallant lads for me,
Who with lusty stroke
The shear frames broke,
The cropper lads for me!

Great Enoch still shall lead the van
Stop him who dare! Stop him who can!
Press forward every gallant man
With hatchet, pike and gun!

Enoch: Nickname given to the sledge hammers used to smash machinery. Enoch Taylor was a partner in a firm that made shearing frames

The successful attack

By February 1812 there were nightly attacks in the Huddersfield area.

As soon as the work of destruction was completed, the Leader drew up his men, called over the roll, each man answering to a particular number instead of his name; they then fired off their pistols . . . gave a shout, and marched off in regular military order.

The assault on Rawfolds Mill

. . . witness was number 7, there was a man to put them in order. They were formed into companies; witness was in the pistol company. Mellor and Thorpe were the men who formed them into line; there were two companies of pistol-men; there were also a company of musket-men, which marched first, they were two deep and ten abreast . . . There were also hammers and mauls. When they got to Rawfolds they stopped and formed into lines thirteen abreast . . . and then advanced towards the mill. . . .

maul: heavy wooden hammer or mallet

> William Hall, giving evidence at the trial
> of eight men who took part in the attack

Benjamin Walker was another Luddite who turned informer. Here he describes the 'drilling' on the moors:

We were all marked with different sorts of marks . . . and we were all ordered . . to put pieces of white paper in our hats to see that no stranger or spy came among us . . . . When we had done we were all called over by numbers to know if all were come out but no man's name was mentioned.

The response of the authorities

Earl Fitzwilliam, the Lord Lieutenant of the West Riding, was inclined to dismiss many of the reports he received:

. . Having yesterday had occasion to converse with different persons I have the satisfaction of reporting that I am very confident the country is not in that

Clifton village had been raided and every gun taken

alarming state it has been supposed to be. That there is combinations for mischievous purposes, there can be no doubt: most recent events corroborate that belief – the sweeping off *every* gun at Clifton proves a system of enquiry and means of information: the manner in which the business was done, proves also a great degree of tactic in execution: but it goes no further than in the execution of robbery: it shows no symptom of preparation for resisting men in arms, military bodies. . . . Moreover, the reports of nocturnal training and drilling, when one comes to close quarters on the subject, and to enquire for evidence of fact, dwindles down to nothing; they are the offspring of fear, quite imaginary, and mere invention.

. . . . There is no evidence whatever, that any one person has yet established the fact of their having been assembled and drilling in a military way. . . .

(ii) The summing up of the judge at the trial of the Rawfolds Luddites January 1813:

a capital offence: punishable by death. statute: an Act of Parliament

. . . . He stated that his indictment was formed on a statute of George III. . . By this act it was made a capital offence to demolish any water, wind-mill, or mill of any other description . . . and it was also made a capital offence to begin to demolish any such mill. . . .

Seventeen men were executed at York after the trials. George Mellor and two others for the murder of William Horsfall a mill-owner who defied the Luddite threats, five for the attack on Rawfolds, and nine for seizing arms in raids on villages.

On 28 April 1812 William Horsfall, a mill-owner who ignored all the Luddite threats, was shot

Another reason for Luddism

A week after Horsfall's murder this appeared in the *Leeds Mercury*:

A . . . correspondent from Barnsley observes that, the army of General Ludd was the other day completely put to rout in the neighbourhood by the discharge of a substance called a *potatoe* into the stomachs of the refractory. A boat load of this kind of ammunition it seems arrived very opportunely, and being distributed to the labouring classes at 10d a peck, an instantaneous impression was produced, and the whole army dispersed. Our Correspondent recommends that funds should be formed in all the large Manufacturing towns to purchase ammunition of this kind, and that it should be distributed in a similar way.

refractory: troublesome people

peck: an old unit of weight

Luddism in the Midlands and Lancashire

Luddism had begun in Nottinghamshire in 1811, but not because the stocking-knitters were facing competition from new technology. At a time of rising food prices and trade depression, employers were cutting wages and increasing frame rents (the stockinger hired the stocking frame that stood in his cottage or in a small workshop). Stocking frames were broken in a very organised and disciplined manner.

They broke only the frames of such as have reduced the price of men's wages; those who have not lowered the price, have their frames untouched; in one house, last night, they broke four frames out of six; the other two which belonged to masters who had not lowered their wages, they did not meddle with.
                    Leeds Mercury, December 1811

In December the Luddites arrived at Ashover in Derbyshire.

. . . Two men came to this place . . . They went to every stockingers home and discharged them from working under such prices as they gave them a list of, and said they would come again in a few days, and in case any of them were found working without having a ticket from their master saying that he was willing to give the prices stated in their list, they should break their frames. They summoned all the stockingers . . . to a public house . . . for the purpose of collecting money from them for the support of those families who were deprived of getting their bread by having their frames broken. Where they found a frame worked by a person who had not served a regular apprentice-ship, or by a woman, they discharged them from working, and if they promised to do so, they stuck a paper upon the frame with these words written upon it – 'Let this frame stand, the colts removed' .. . .

colt: a worker who had not served an apprenticeship

Masters who produced 'cut-ups' – cheap stockings made of material woven on a wide loom rather than on the traditional stocking frame – were also attacked. Much less skill was needed to make them and skilled stockingers feared loss of employment. Employers who made truck payments, giving workers token or goods instead of money wages, had their frame broken.

In Lancashire Luddism appears to have been a movement of cotton

handloom weavers. There were attacks on power-loom weaving mills in Stockport, Middleton and Westhoughton in April 1812, although power looms did not present a serious threat to handloom weavers at this time. Food riots took place in many Lancashire towns in the spring of 1812 and there were many reports of men collecting arms and drilling on the moors. When news of the assassination of the Prime Minister, Spencer Perceval, reached Lancashire there was rejoicing in the mill-towns.

Alarmed, the authorities acted vigorously. Spies and informers hinted at links between Luddites in the three areas affected and letters like this only seemed to justify their fears.

To General Ludd Juner

Nottingham, 1812.

By Order of Genral Ludd . . .

I am requested to express the hye sence of honor entertained of the meretoreous movements you and your forses have so gallently mad in the neberood of Hudersfield to secure the rites of our pour starving fellow creturs

I am also desired to say that they lament with extrem regret the fate of the two *brave boys* who galantly spilt theire blod in a lodible cose at Rawfolds. . .

The Genral further auhtorises me to say that he trusts to the attachment of his subjects for the avenging of the death of the two brav youths who fell at the sege of Rawfolds. He also wishes me to state that though his troops heare are not at present making any osteniable movements that it is not for want of force . . . but that they are at present only devising the best means for a grand attack and that at present thay are dispatching a few indeviduals by pistol shot on or which fel last nite.

I am further ortherised to say that it is the opinion of our general and men that as long as that blackgard drunken . . . fellow, called Prince Regent and his servants have anything to do with government that nothing but distress wil befale us. . . .

The end of Luddism

Troops were moved into the troubled districts. An Act of Parliament made frame-breaking a capital offence. When Ludd briefly reappeared in the East Midlands in 1816 seven men were executed. In Lancashire and Yorkshire the courts acted harshly in 1812 and 1813.

Savage punishments help to explain the collapse of Luddism. More important was the end of the economic depression. Better harvests meant lower food prices and improving trade meant employment and higher wages. The stockingers, for a short time, got their way and the masters were intimidated into ending wage cuts, the employment of 'colts' and the manufacture of shoddy goods. Nevertheless, thirty years later the stockingers were amongst the lowest-paid of all handworkers and the croppers and handloom weavers could not stop the onward march of the machine.

In 1814, there were 1733 croppers in Leeds, all in full employment; and now, since the introduction of machinery, the whole of the cloth . . . is dressed by a comparatively small number, chiefly boys, at from 5s. [25p] to 8s. [40p] . . . and a few men at from 10s. [50p] to 14s. [70p] per week. The old croppers have turned themselves to anything they can get to do; some acting as bailiffs, water-carriers, scavengers, or selling oranges, cakes, tapes and laces, gingerbread, blacking, etc.

W. Dodd, *The Factory System*, 1841

Questions

1 It is the summer of 1812. As an official at the Home Office, write a report for the Home Secretary on the alarming news from the industrial districts. Explain what appears to be the cause of the trouble; why it is so threatening; and what recommendations you will make to end the disturbance.
2 Write a Luddite letter to an East Midland stocking-frame master warning him what will happen if he does not satisfy your grievances.

12

The working class and political change 1815–48

1 The post-war crisis, 1815–20

Napoleon was finally defeated at the battle of Waterloo in 1815. Immediately the war ended government contracts for war supplies were cancelled and depression hit the munitions, ironworking and ship-building industries. The rapid demobilisation of sailors and soldiers threw large numbers of men on to the labour market, particularly in London.

Other industries benefited from a short post-war boom as European markets were reopened, but this did not last. Wage cuts had to be accepted, and unemployment was widespread. The metalworking trades centred on Birmingham were badly hit and the cotton industry was seriously depressed by the fall in demand.

Things improved in 1818 but 1819 was one of the most disturbed years of the nineteenth century. Poor harvests in 1817 and 1818 aggravated the situation. After 1820 discontent lessened and disturbances ceased as prosperity returned.

THE YEARS OF CRISIS: 1815–20

Government measures	Events
1815 The Corn Law is passed by Parliament to protect agriculture from foreign competition.	Popular disturbances. The poor feared an increase in the price of food. Hampden clubs, to agitate for Parliamentary reform, were formed in many places.
1816 Abolition of the income tax introduced in 1797 during the war.	Excise duties and other indirect taxes on commodities purchased by the poor were increased. *December:* Spa Field meetings and riot in London.
1817 A Parliamentary Select Committee found evidence of a revolutionary plot. *Habeas Corpus* suspended (suspects could be held without charge) and the 'Gagging Acts' restricted public meetings.	*March:* the 'Blanketeers' set out from Manchester. They were unemployed weavers who intended marching to London to present a petition to the Prince Regent. They were soon dispersed. *June:* the 'Pentridge Rising' in Derbyshire. A government agent, Oliver, created the plot. Three were executed, fourteen transported and six imprisoned.
1818	A year of strikes as conditions improved. In Manchester the cotton spinners struck to get their wages restored to the 1816 level. There was a long weavers' strike.
1819 The Six Acts restricted public meetings, enabled magistrates to search for arms, forbade military-style drilling and restricted the freedom of the press.	*16 August:* the massacre of 'Peterloo'. Eleven were killed and over 400 wounded when troops dispersed a meeting of about 60 000 in Manchester.
1820	The Cato Street conspiracy – a plot to assassinate the Cabinet. Another government agent was involved.

A working-class reformer remembers

Samuel Bamford was a weaver from Middleton, near Manchester.

A series of disturbances commenced with the introduction of the Corn Bill in 1815, and continued with short intervals, until the close of the year 1816. In London and Westminster riots ensued, and were continued for several days, whilst the Bill was discussed; at Bridgeport there were riots on account of the high price of bread; at Bideford . . . to prevent the exportation of grain; at Bury . . . to destroy machinery; at Ely . . . at Newcastle-on-Tyne . . . at Glasgow . . . at Preston, by unemployed weavers; at Nottingham, by Luddites, who destroyed thirty frames; at Merthyr Tydfil on a reduction of wages. . . .

Corn Bill: the Corn Law being debated in the Commons

One view of England in 1815. The rich are prosperous and the poor will starve

One man, according to Bamford, became very influential.

. . . . At this time the writings of William Cobbett suddenly became of great authority; they were read on nearly every cottage hearth in the manufacturing districts of South Lancashire; in those of Leicester, Derby and Nottingham; also in many of the Scottish manufacturing towns . . . he directed his readers to the true cause of their sufferings – misgovernment; and to its proper corrective – parliamentary reform. Riots soon became scarce . . . Hampden clubs were now established.

Hampden clubs: clubs for reformers

One of these clubs was established in 1816, at the small town of Middleton. . . . The club prospered . . . we soon rented a chapel. . . .

On the first of January, 1817, a meeting of delegates . . . was held in our chapel, when resolutions were passed declaratory of the right of every male to vote, who paid taxes; that males of eighteen should be eligible to vote; that parliaments should be elected annually; that no placeman or pensioner should sit in parliament; that every twenty thousand inhabitants should send a member of the house of commons. . . .

S. Bamford, *Passages in the Life of a Radical*, 1841

placemen and pensioners: MPs who were given jobs or payments by the government so that they would support it

An election in the eighteenth century. There is no secret ballot

Intimidation at an election – why are the people being evicted from their homes?

WHO COULD VOTE IN ENGLAND IN 1815

The Constituencies	The Voters
Counties – each county returned two MPs	The owner of a 40-shilling freehold had the right to vote.
Boroughs – each borough returned two MPs	There was no standard qualification. 1 *Scot and Lot boroughs* – anyone who paid poor rates could vote. 2 *Potwalloper boroughs* anyone who 'had a family and boiled a pot there' could vote. 3 *Burgage boroughs* – the right to vote was attached to certain pieces of property. 4 *Corporation boroughs* – members of the town council voted. 5 *Freeman boroughs* – all freemen of the borough could vote.

Total number of MPs	
England	489
Wales	24
Scotland	45
Ireland	100
	658

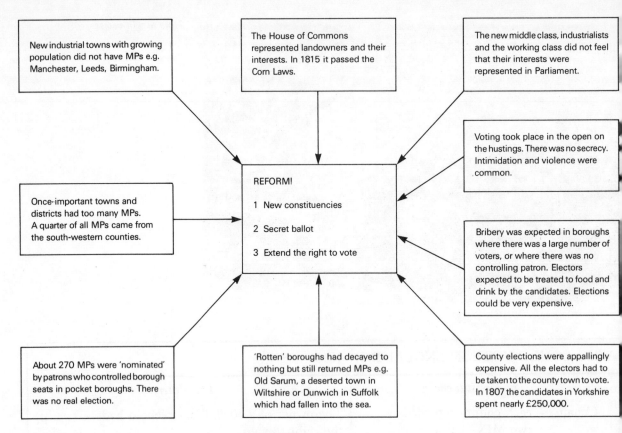

New industrial towns with growing population did not have MPs e.g. Manchester, Leeds, Birmingham.

The House of Commons represented landowners and their interests. In 1815 it passed the Corn Laws.

The new middle class, industrialists and the working class did not feel that their interests were represented in Parliament.

Once-important towns and districts had too many MPs. A quarter of all MPs came from the south-western counties.

REFORM!

1 New constituencies

2 Secret ballot

3 Extend the right to vote

Voting took place in the open on the hustings. There was no secrecy. Intimidation and violence were common.

Bribery was expected in boroughs where there was a large number of voters, or where there was no controlling patron. Electors expected to be treated to food and drink by the candidates. Elections could be very expensive.

About 270 MPs were 'nominated' by patrons who controlled borough seats in pocket boroughs. There was no real election.

'Rotten' boroughs had decayed to nothing but still returned MPs e.g. Old Sarum, a deserted town in Wiltshire or Dunwich in Suffolk which had fallen into the sea.

County elections were appallingly expensive. All the electors had to be taken to the county town to vote. In 1807 the candidates in Yorkshire spent nearly £250,000.

Pressure for electoral reform

The Political Register

William Cobbett's *Political Register* was priced at 1s. 0½d (5p) because of the high stamp duty on newspapers. Working people clubbed together to buy it. It was read aloud in public houses and clubrooms and then its contents would be discussed. In November 1816 Cobbett began publishing his leading article separately as a *Weekly Political Pamphlet*. This sold for 2d (under 1p) and he claimed a sale of 200 000 for the first one, an *Address to the Journeymen and Labourers*.

He told his readers that they were the creators of all national wealth and greatness, and,

. . . that the cause of our miseries is the *burden of taxes*. . . . The *remedy* . . consists wholly and solely of such a *reform* in the Commons or People's House of Parliament, as shall give to every payer of *direct taxes* a vote at elections and as shall cause the Members to be *elected annually*. . . .

The government's attitude

Magistrates saw conspiracy everywhere. After their investigation into the Spa Fields riot of December 1816 MPs concluded:

. . . It has been proved . . . that some members of these Societies . . conceived the project and endeavoured to prepare the means of raising an Insurrection, so formidable from numbers, as by dint of physical strength to overpower all resistance.

Concerned to maintain law and order the Tory government took firm measures to suppress any trouble. Possible local leaders, like Samuel Bamford, were arrested and Cobbett fled to America to escape a similar fate. The men from Pentridge were severely punished as a warning.

The use of spies

Evidence of any plot was scanty. Local magistrates relied on informers for information and the government had its own agents infiltrating the clubs in industrial areas. These men acted as *agents provocateurs*. In March 1817 Bamford was visited by 'a man dressed much like a dyer' who explained:

. . . that he was deputed, by some persons at Manchester to propose that, in consequence of the treatment which the blanketeers had received . . . 'a Moscow of Manchester' should take place that very night. . . . He said it would entirely depend on the co-operation or otherwise of the country people; that other messengers had been sent to every reform society within twenty miles of the town; that if the answers were favourable . . . the light of the conflagration was to be the signal for the country people to come in . . . the whole force was to be divided into parties, one of which was to engage the attention of the military . . . another was to take possession of the barracks and to secure the arms and magazine; another was to plunder and then set fire to the house of individuals . . . and a fourth was to storm the New Bailey and liberate the prisoners, particularly the blanketeers confined there. . . .

'a Moscow of Manchester': set Manchester on fire as the Russians had burnt Moscow in 1812 to force Napoleon to leave

conflagration: huge fire

magazine: ammunition store

New Bailey: the town prison. blanketeers: those who had set out to march to London with a petition for the Prince Regent

Bamford did not commit himself. Others did, in particular the stockingers and labourers around the Derbyshire village of Pentridge. They were persuaded by a man, who is only known as Oliver, that a national rising was to take place on the night of 8/9 June 1817.

. . . on the 1st or 2nd day of June, Oliver came to Nottingham. . . . He said, that all would be ready in London for the 9th of June . . . Oliver had a meeting with us . . . Brandreth . . . and many others were present. . . .
When Oliver had thus settled everything with us, he prepared to set off to organise things in Yorkshire, that all might be ready . . . in that County at the moment that the rising took place in London, where he told us there were Fifty Thousand Men with arms prepared, and that they would take the Tower. . . .

Jeremiah Brandreth: leader of Pentridge men

Oliver's journeyings were known to the authorities. The Derbyshire men's march on Nottingham was scattered by a troop of Hussars and the few hundred who rose in the Holmfirth area of Yorkshire suffered the same fate. On 14 June *The Leeds Mercury* reported

. . . the highly important fact . . . that the plot . . . has been got up under the instigation of an agent from London, and that the principal offender has been suffered to escape with impunity.

Public opinion was outraged at this revelation but that did not save the Pentridge men from execution or transportation.

The 'Peterloo Massacre' 16 August 1819

This was another disturbed year. The summer saw a series of reform meetings. These culminated in a great meeting planned for 16 August at St Peter's Fields in Manchester. Henry Hunt, a powerful and emotive speaker, was the main attraction. Throughout July and August the Manchester magistrates were alarmed at the reports they received of parties of men drilling on the moors. Bamford later explained:

. . . We had frequently been taunted by the press, with our ragged, dirty appearance . . . and the moblike crowds in which our numbers were mustered; and we determined . . . that we should disarm the bitterness of our political opponents by a display of cleanliness, sobriety, and decorum. . . .

Since large numbers were expected, there had to be organisation. Routes to be followed by columns from neighbouring towns were laid down. Banners were prepared. The people looked forward to a day out. Bamford's group from Middleton joined the Rochdale column:

. . . At our head were a hundred or two of women, mostly young wives. . . . A hundred or two of our handsomest girls, – sweethearts to the lads who were with us, – danced to the music, or sang snatches of popular songs: a score or two of children were sent back, though some went forward.

The sight of 60 000 people massed together caused the magistrates to panic and they decided to arrest Hunt. An eye-witness observed:

It seemed to be a gala day with the country people who were mostly dressed in their best and brought with them their wives, and I saw boys and girls taking their father's hand in the procession. . . . At length Hunt made his appearance . . . he was received with enthusiastic applause; the waving of hats and flags; the blowing of trumpets; and the playing of music. . . . I heard the sound of a horn, and immediately the Manchester Yeomanry appeared. . . .
. . . Their sabres glistened in the air, and on they went, direct for the hustings. . . . As the cavalry approached the dense mass of people, they used their utmost efforts to escape: but so closely were they pressed in opposite directions by the soldiers, the special constables, the position of the hustings, and their own immense numbers, that immediate escape was impossible . . .

Hunt was seized and taken away. Bamford described the scene:

In ten minutes . . . the field was an open and almost deserted space. . . . The hustings remained, with a few broken or hewed flag-staves erect, and a torn and gashed banner or two drooping; whilst over the whole field, were strewed caps, bonnets, hats, shawl, and shoes, and other parts of male and female dress: trampled, torn and bloody. The yeomanry had dismounted – some were easing their horses' girths, others adjusting their accoutrements; and some were wiping their sabres. Several mounds of human beings still remained where they had fallen, crushed down and smothered. Some of these were still groaning – others with staring eyes, were gasping for breath, and others would never breathe more. . . .

Eleven were killed and over 400 injured. The government congratulated the magistrates; the Home Secretary, Lord Sidmouth, took the

Manchester Yeomanry: part-time volunteer soldiers

hustings: speakers' platform

accoutrements: uniform and equipment

A *A detailed drawing of events at Peterloo*

opportunity to legislate against large organised public meetings.

Some alleged that the 'Peterloo Massacre' had been planned by the authorities:

... The Yeomanry Cavalry made their charge with a most infuriate frenzy; they cut down men, women, and children, indiscriminately, and appeared to have commenced a premeditated attack with the most insatiable thirst for blood and destruction. ... As a proof of premeditated murder on the part of the magistrates, every stone was gathered from the ground, on the Friday and Saturday previous to the meeting, by scavengers sent there by the express command of the magistrates, that the populace might be rendered more defenceless.

R. Carlile, *Sherwin's Weekly Political Register*

premeditated: planned in advance

B *Peterloo as the reformers saw it*

Questions

1 Samuel Bamford took part in the events he described. He wrote his memoirs in 1841. How good a source are they likely to be for the events of 1815–19? Explain your answer.

2 There are three different accounts of the events of Peterloo in this section and two cartoons.

(a) Which is most reliable as a factual account?

(b) Which is mainly opinion? Explain your answer.

(c) Study cartoon B very carefully. Explain as fully as you can what impression it gives of the event at St Peter's Field. What other evidence supports this interpretation?

(d) Are cartoon B and Carlile's comments convincing explanations of the massacre? Explain your answer very carefully.

2 The triumph of reform, 1832

The Tories, totally opposed to any reform of Parliament, had been governing the country since 1815. The other political group, the Whigs, whilst sympathetic to the demand for reform, were opposed to universal suffrage. They were, however, weak and divided, and seemed unlikely to defeat the Tories and form a government.

By 1829 the country was entering a new economic depression. A bad harvest forced up food prices. There was unemployment and discontent in the industrial districts. Lord Grey, leader of the Whigs, became alarmed. He feared that unless something was done to reform Parliament there would be a revolutionary outbreak.

His fears were increased by a movement that began in Birmingham in 1830. A Political Union was formed, uniting middle-class and working-class reformers. Soon monster meetings were being held in Birmingham and other towns and cities, demanding reform of Parliament.

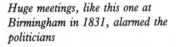

Huge meetings, like this one at Birmingham in 1831, alarmed the politicians

George IV, opposed to reform, died in 1830. He was succeeded by his brother, William IV, who was a supporter of moderate reform. The Tory government, however, maintained a firm resistance to all change. In November 1830 they were defeated in a House of Commons vote and resigned. Lord Grey formed a Whig government pledged to reform Parliament.

The Whig Reform Bill was presented to the House of Commons in March 1831. For over a year, until the Reform Act was passed in June 1832, the issue dominated public interest as the Tories in the House of Commons and the House of Lords tried to block reform.

A general election in 1831 proved that the public overwhelmingly supported the reform proposals. In October there were riots in Derby, Nottingham and Bristol in protest at the House of Lords' rejection of the Reform Bill. When in May 1832, the Tory Duke of Wellington tried to form an anti-reform government, popular opposition and talk of revolution forced him to stop. Lord Grey got his way, and the Act was passed.

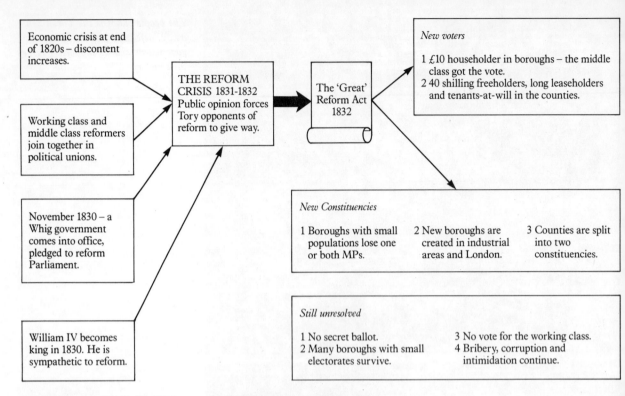

The following are the boxes in the flowchart diagram:

Economic crisis at end of 1820s – discontent increases.

Working class and middle class reformers join together in political unions.

November 1830 – a Whig government comes into office, pledged to reform Parliament.

William IV becomes king in 1830. He is sympathetic to reform.

THE REFORM CRISIS 1831-1832 Public opinion forces Tory opponents of reform to give way.

The 'Great' Reform Act 1832

New voters

1 £10 householder in boroughs – the middle class got the vote.
2 40 shilling freeholders, long leaseholders and tenants-at-will in the counties.

New Constituencies

1 Boroughs with small populations lose one or both MPs.

2 New boroughs are created in industrial areas and London.

3 Counties are split into two constituencies.

Still unresolved

1 No secret ballot.
2 Many boroughs with small electorates survive.

3 No vote for the working class.
4 Bribery, corruption and intimidation continue.

The 1832 Reform Act. Lord John Russell said that the Reform Act was a final measure. It did not satisfy everyone. The Chartists were demanding more by 1838

peck: unit of weight

gunpowder tea: a blend of tea

3 Chartism, 1838–48

What a row and a rumpus there is I declare,
Tens of thousands are flocking everywhere;
To petition the Parliament, onward they steer,
The Chartists are coming, oh dear, oh dear.
To demand equal justice, their freedom and rights,
Pump-handles and broomsticks, lawk, how they can fight;
The nation, they say, is o'erwhelmed with grief,
A peck loaf for two pence and four pounds of beef.

Such a number together was never yet seen,
Hurrah for the Charter and God save the Queen;
And when that the Charter old England has got,
We'll have stunning good beer at three halfpence a pot.
A loaf for a penny, a pig for a crown,
And gunpowder tea at five farthings a pound;
Instead of red herrings we'll live on fat geese,
And get lots of young women at two pence apiece.

Question

This ballad was probably on sale at the time of the great Chartist demonstration in London in 1848. What can we learn from it about
(a) the methods used by the Chartists,
(b) their aims and their motives?

Causes of Chartism

The 1832 Reform Act did not satisfy the working-class radicals. Working men whose support had helped to pressurise Parliament into passing the Act were ignored. They did not get the vote.

In 1836 the London Working Men's Association was formed. Two years later its secretary, William Lovett, was responsible for the production of the People's Charter. For ten years its Six Points were at the centre of an intermittent working-class campaign for reform of Parliament.

Disappointment with the 1833 Factory Act and anger in the North at the imposition of the workhouse system under the New Poor Law of 1834 contributed to the demand for the Charter. Working people, it was argued, could not expect justice until the House of Commons represented their interests.

A more important factor in explaining the popularity of Chartism was the extent of poverty and economic distress.

The Six Points of the Charter. Chartism failed – but how many of the Six Points are accepted today?

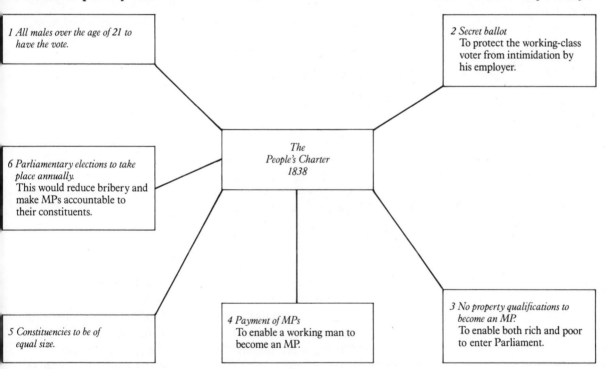

1 All males over the age of 21 to have the vote.

2 Secret ballot
To protect the working-class voter from intimidation by his employer.

The People's Charter 1838

6 Parliamentary elections to take place annually.
This would reduce bribery and make MPs accountable to their constituents.

3 No property qualifications to become an MP.
To enable both rich and poor to enter Parliament.

5 Constituencies to be of equal size.

4 Payment of MPs
To enable a working man to become an MP.

The Chartist James Rayner Stephens told a Manchester meeting in 1838 that

This question of Universal Suffrage was a knife and fork question . . . a bread and cheese question . . . and if any man ask him what he meant by Universal Suffrage, he would answer, that every working man in the land had a right to have a good coat to his back, a comfortable abode in which to shelter himself and his family, a good dinner upon his table, and no more work than was necessary for keeping him in health, and as much wages for that work as would keep him in plenty. . . .

CHARTISM – A TIMELINE

	Chartist developments	Economic conditions
1836	London Working Men's Association is formed.	A run of bad harvests begins in 1836.
1838	*May*: the People's Charter is published.	Textile industry at beginning of a severe recession.
	August: a huge public meeting in Birmingham is the first to adopt the Charter.	Profits in coal and iron industry begin to fall due to overproduction. Bad harvest. High bread prices.
	Autumn: delegates are elected to the Chartist Convention.	
1839	*February*: Chartist Convention meets in London.	Continuing depression. A second bad harvest.
	July: the House of Commons rejects the first Chartist petition.	
	August: the Chartist 'sacred month' or general strike has to be called off. There is no support.	
	November: The Chartist rising in Newport.	
1842	*May*: second Chartist petition with over 3 000 000 signatures is rejected by the Commons.	Economic crisis worsens. 1841 was another bad harvest. This is the beginning of the 'hungry forties'.
	August–September: strikes in the industrial areas. Chartists are blamed.	Trade begins to recover in the autumn. Conditions improve.
1847		Bad harvests in 1846 and 1847 meant high bread prices in 1848. A commercial crisis hits industry.
1848	*April*: great Chartist demonstration in London. Third petition presented to Parliament.	

General Sir Charles Napier was in command of the northern military district in 1839. He sympathised with the poor and with their demands, and wrote in his diary:

. . . The state of the unhappy hand-loom weavers is distressing in the greatest degree; an industrious man in full work and on the highest rate of wages starves: this is very dreadful and in such parts the Chartists are most numerous and most resolute. If this state of distress can be ameliorated one great source of Chartism will soon be tarried!

ameliorated: improved

At his trial in 1843 Richard Pilling told the jury that the great strikes of 1842 had been a protest at further wage cuts:

. . . I was twenty years among the handloom weavers, and ten years in a factory, and I unhesitatingly say . . . the longer and harder I have worked the poorer and poorer I have become every year. . . . Whatever it may have been with others it has been a wage question with me . . . Mr O'Connor has made it a chartist question. . . . But it was always a wage question and ten hours bill with me. . . .

Benjamin Wilson, of Halifax, remembered the revival of Chartism in 1848:

In this year flour was very dear . . . whilst trade was also very bad. This was the time to make politicians, as the easiest way to get into an Englishman's brains is through his stomach. It was said by its enemies that Chartism was dead and buried . . . they were doomed to disappointment. . . .

B. Wilson, *The Struggles of an Old Chartist*, 1887

The First Petition, 1839

The Chartist National Convention assembled in February 1839 to organise the presentation of the great petition. Delegates then debated what to do should the House of Commons reject it. There were wide differences of opinion and moderates left when physical force and violence were considered. It was finally agreed to hold a 'sacred month' or general strike to force the government to give way.

There were alarming reports from the industrial areas. From the North, General Napier wrote:

. . . we know that printed extracts from Maceroni's book on pike exercise are . . . in circulation; and we have information, though vague, that drilling without arms goes on nightly. We are also informed . . . that the purchase of firearms and the manufacture of pikes goes on. . . .

pike: a weapon like a spear

However, when the House of Commons received and rejected the petition on 12 July the Convention found it impossible to make the 'sacred month' effective. The plan was abandoned.

Feargus O'Connor

By now the Irishman Feargus O'Connor had emerged as the leader of the movement. He 'was a well-built strong powerful man, 6 feet in height, with large broad shoulders'. To this impressive appearance was added 'lungs of brass and a voice like a trumpet' which made him 'the most effective outdoor orator of his time, and the idol of the immense assemblages which were often brought together in those days.' His editorship of the Leeds-based *Northern Star* newspaper gave him a far wider influence.

Through the columns of the *Northern Star*, which reached a circulation of over 50 000 copies a week in 1839, and in his speeches O'Connor appeared to be the spokesman of the 'physical force' Chartists – those who were prepared to use violence to get the Charter.

William Lovett emerged as the leader of the 'moral force' chartists. Opposed to violence, they believed that working men should pressurise the government by proving their worthiness to have the vote. A programme of education was needed. O'Connor scornfully dismissed 'Church Chartism, Teetotal Chartism, Knowledge Chartism'.

bastille: the workhouse (the Bastille had been a Paris prison stormed at the beginning of the French Revolution in 1789)

. . . people who work sixteen hours a day from the age of nine to about thirty five, when they are thrown into a bastille as unfit for use, have very little relish for a protracted course of 'education' though it were certain in one hundred and twenty years to gain the Charter *for them*.

Northern Star, 24 April 1841

Using the evidence: was there a Chartist plot?

A The failure of the sacred month did not lessen the tension. One old Chartist remembered:

garret: attic

I was present in some part of nearly every Saturday at the pike market. . . The market was held in a long garret room. . . . In rows were benches or boards, supported on tressels, along which the Winlaton and Swalwell chain and nail makers brought in their . . . pikes, each a dozen or two, rolled up in the smith's apron. The price for a finished and polished article was two shillings and sixpence [12½p] . . . From that time (August to November 1839) . . . we counted sixty thousand shafted pikes.

Thomas Devyr, *The Old Book of the Nineteenth Century*, 1882

On 22 April 1839 Henry Vincent, a Chartist leader in South Wales, was arrested and imprisoned in Monmouth. John Frost, who had been mayor of Newport, was appalled at the ill-treatment Vincent received. At the Chartist Convention in London he discussed his fears with other delegates, that the South Wales miners, angered by Vincent's arrest, would attempt to release him. There must have been some violent talk because in September Peter Bussey, another Convention member, was travelling in the North saying that the Welsh intended to rise in support of the Charter.

B According to William Lovett, O'Connor was approached by some Yorkshire Chartists at the end of September.

Delegate: Mr O'Connor, we are going to have rising for the Charter in Yorkshire, and I am sent from —— to ask you if you will lead us on, as you have often said you would when we were prepared.

O'Connor: Well, when is the rising to take place?

Delegate: Why, we have resolved that it shall begin on Saturday next.

O'Connor: Are you well provided with arms then?

Delegate: Yes, all of us.

O'Connor: Well, that is all right, my man.

Delegate: Now, Mr O'Connor, shall I tell our lads that you will come and lead them on?

O'Connor (*Indignantly*): Why, man! When did you ever hear of me, or any of my family, ever deserting the cause of the people? Have they not always been found at their post in the hour of danger?

On 4 October O'Connor left for Ireland.

C The night of 3/4 November was very wet. A force of miners led by John Frost gathered in the hills above Newport and on the Monday morning, wet and cold, they entered the town.

(i) . . . . I saw Jenkin Morgan at Newport. . . . I . . . know him to be a Chartist. . . . On Sunday night, the 3rd of November . . . he came to my house and said he was a captain of men, and that I was appointed his man; he also said that Frost was on the hills, and was coming down with thousands of men to attack the soldiers. He said . . . that the Charter would be the law of the town of Newport on Monday night, and that it would be the law of the land before daylight. . . . He told me there was powder at Crossfield's warehouse, and I said it used to be kept at Pill, but we found no powder. He also told me that there was to be a rising through the whole kingdom on the same night, and the same hour. . . .

Report in the Charter, 17 November 1839

(ii) . . . At least eight thousand men, mostly miners . . . were engaged in the attack . . . many of them were armed. Their design seems to have been to wreak their vengeance upon the Newport magistrates, for the prosecution of Vincent . . . and . . . to advance to Monmouth, to liberate these prisoners. The ultimate design of the leaders . . . probably was to rear the standard of rebellion throughout Wales . . . until the people of England . . . should rise . . . for the same objects. . . . On entering Newport, the people marched straight to the Westgate Hotel, where the magistrates and about 40 soldiers were assembled. . . . The Riot Act was read, and the soldiers fired down, with ease and security, upon the people who had first broken and fired into the windows. The people . . . retired to the outside of the town . . . but ultimately returned home. About thirty of the people are known to have been killed, and several to have been wounded. . . .

Report in the Charter, 17 November 1839

(iii) The evidence of Edward Patton, a Newport carpenter, at Frost's trial.

The parcel of people I saw . . . were armed; they had guns, sticks, etc.; the sticks had iron points, I did not see many with guns. I saw of this body two hundred or three hundred. . . . I know the two bow-windows in front of the Westgate. I never saw anything done to the windows of the Westgate. I did not hear a crash of the windows. They were not very tumultuous. They drew up in front of the Westgate . . . and asked for the prisoners who were taken before

parcel: group

tumultuous: rowdy

daylight . . . then a rush was made. Then I heard firing, and took to my heels. I cannot say whether the mob had guns, pikes or clubs. I cannot tell whether they were armed for the biggest part . . . I could not say where the firing began. . . . Saw no smoke outside. It is likely enough the firing began from the Westgate inn. . . .

D *An artist's impression of events at Newport*

caltrops: cast-iron spikes to be thrown in front of horses to lame them

1 Compare the three extracts in C.
  (a) What are the differences between them? Compare them on numbers involved, the purpose of the Chartists, their arms and behaviour, how the shooting started.
  (b) Edward Patton was an eye-witness. What are the weaknesses of his evidence?
  (c) How does the illustration interpret what happened?
2 Here are five statements based on these sources. Do you agree with them? Explain your answer.
  (a) O'Connor supported a national rising.
  (b) The Newport men expected English Chartists to rise.
  (c) The Newport men only wanted to free the prisoners.
  (d) Most of the Chartists were armed.
  (e) The Chartists attacked first.
3 When Frost and his two lieutenants were convicted of treason the jury recommended mercy. On 9 January the Cabinet discussed this:

  . . . Lord Melbourne said he saw little in that recommendation; the jury were frightened, so was the judge. For his own part he felt certain that some decided measures were indispensable to prevent anarchy. He added that as for himself he was prepared for them. . . .

  Lord Melbourne was the Prime Minister. How would you describe his attitude towards the Chartists?
4 Does this evidence prove that Chartists were revolutionaries? Explain your answer.

After Newport, extremists continued to prepare for a rising. Napier had 'certain information that fireballs and caltrops are being prepared . . . for an outbreak' and that gunpowder sales were increasing. In Sheffield a bomb-making factory was discovered. Twelve hand grenades were found, 'the cases for which were stone bottles stuffed with blasting powder, pebbles and pitch.'

Hundreds, including O'Connor, were arrested. He was imprisoned for eighteen months. With all the important leaders locked up, and the three Newport men transported to Australia for life, Chartism seemed to die away.

Chartism after Newport

O'Connor's release from prison, and hard times, revived the movement. In May 1842 the second Chartist petition was presented and, once again, was overwhelmingly rejected by the House of Commons.

The summer of 1842 was the most violent of the nineteenth century. Discontent and bitterness mingled with resentment at the spurning of the petition. In August there were riots, strikes and marches in all the industrial areas. Factories and mines that continued to work were closed down by organised groups who pulled the plugs out of the steam-engine boilers.

Thomas Cooper, the leader of the Leicester Chartists, was in the Potteries when the trouble began. He hurriedly left for Manchester to attend a Chartist conference. As the train neared the city he and his travelling companions anxiously gazed out of the carriage window.

. . . So soon as the City of Long Chimneys came into sight, and every chimney was beheld smokeless, Campbell's face changed, and with an oath he said, 'Not a single mill at work! something must come out of this, and something serious too!'. . . . In the streets . . . were unmistakable signs of alarm on the part of the authorities. Troops of cavalry were going up and down . . . accompanied by pieces of artillery. . . . There were nearly sixty delegates present . . . it was evident they were, each and all, filled with the desire of keeping the people from returning to their labour. They believed the time had come for trying, successfully, to paralyse the Government. . . .

Thomas Cooper, *My Life*, 1872

Despite this optimism the strikes collapsed. The leaders were arrested and men drifted back to work. A good harvest and improving trade eased the situation.

The Chartists had failed again. O'Connor launched a scheme to settle Chartists on country smallholdings but the Charter was not forgotten.

. . . Amongst combers, handloom weavers, and other politics was the chief topic. *The Northern Star* was their principal paper, and it was a common practice . . . to meet at friends' houses to read the paper and talk over political matters. We met at a friend's at Skircoat Green . . . where there was sure to be a good many friends. We were only waiting for the time to come again . . .

B. Wilson, *The Struggles of an Old Chartist*, 1887

Taking the second Chartist petition to Parliament, 1842

O'Connerville seems a delightful place in this print, but most Chartists who moved into the countryside failed to make a living

That time came with bad harvest and depression; 1848 saw a third Chartist petition. A convention met in London. The authorities once again acted promptly. The Duke of Wellington took command of the capital's defence and large numbers of special constables were recruited. When the Chartists met at Kennington on 10 April, O'Connor accepted police advice and dispersed the demonstrators. This was the end of Chartism as a mass movement.

Questions

Here are three reasons why Chartism failed. Which do you think was the most important? Explain your answer.

1 Some old Chartists blamed O'Connor. He was too self-centred and conceited to allow any other leader to share his place.

2 The government acted promptly and sensibly at each crisis. In 1839 they were able to use the new London-to-Birmingham railway to transport Metropolitan Police to a troubled Birmingham. Men were imprisoned but there were no executions.

3 Support for the movement fluctuated with the price of bread and wage levels. As workers shared in the increasing prosperity of the 1850s, their interest in the Charter declined.

4 Extending the right to vote

After 1850 the popular demand for the reform of Parliament died. The country entered a period of prosperity and calm.

In 1866 there was a financial crisis, and important banks collapsed. The renewed economic crisis provided popular support for the Reform League. Agitation for reform culminated in serious disturbances in London in 1867 when Hyde Park was closed to prevent a reform meeting taking place there. The railings were uprooted as the demonstrators broke into the Park.

Meanwhile the politicians were determined to settle the question quickly. A Liberal Reform Bill had been defeated in 1866 but the new Conservative government led by Lord Derby and Benjamin Disraeli wanted to win popular support. They pushed a Reform Act through Parliament which gave the vote to the householders in the boroughs. Working men had the vote for the first time. Seats were redistributed to industrial districts and Birmingham, Manchester, Liverpool, and Leeds were given three Members of Parliament.

Voting was still public and open. Working-class electors needed the secret ballot to protect them from intimidation by employers. In 1872 the Secret Ballot Act was passed to safeguard the interests of voters.

The Second Reform Act (1867) had given the vote to working men in boroughs, but agricultural labourers still had no vote. The Third Reform Act, (1884) extended the right to vote to householders in rural areas. For the first time the country was divided up into equal-sized constituencies.

Nevertheless, the electorate was still small. Only men had the right to vote and they had to be householders. Universal male suffrage did not come until 1918 and the vote was not granted to all women over 21 until 1928.

The right to vote – a widening stream

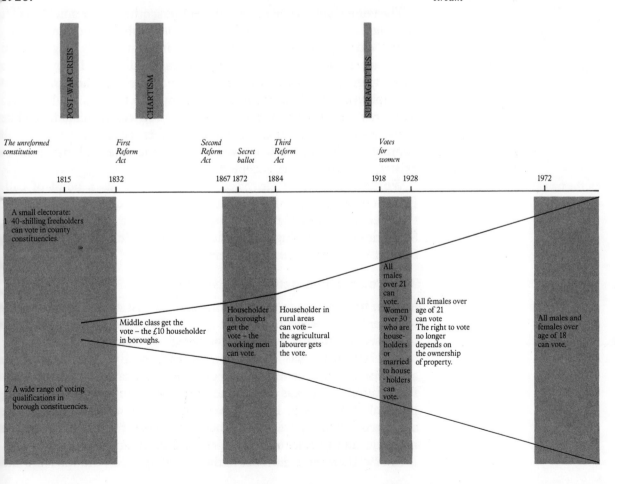

POST-WAR CRISIS

CHARTISM

SUFFRAGETTES

The unreformed constitution	First Reform Act	Second Reform Act	Secret ballot	Third Reform Act	Votes for women		1972
1815	1832	1867	1872	1884	1918	1928	1972

A small electorate:
1 40-shilling freeholders can vote in county constituencies.

2 A wide range of voting qualifications in borough constituencies.

Middle class get the vote – the £10 householder in boroughs.

Householder in boroughs get the vote – the working men can vote.

Householder in rural areas can vote – the agricultural labourer gets the vote.

All males over 21 can vote. Women over 30 who are house-holders or married to house -holders can vote.

All females over age of 21 can vote The right to vote no longer depends on the ownership of property.

All males and females over age of 18 can vote.

13

Trade unions 1750–1914

1 The beginnings to 1850

The eighteenth-century background

In the eighteenth century, workmen frequently united together to protect their interests against the employers. Usually this step was taken to deal with a particular crisis. For instance, on 25 August 1765, miners in the North East went on strike in a dispute with the employers over the renewal of the annual working contracts they had to sign. As soon as the problem was solved the 'trade union' collapsed.

Trade clubs, restricted to well-paid skilled workers in the handicraft industries, were more like modern trade unions. When a deputation from the Nottingham framework knitters was in London in 1812 they made contact with the London trade clubs. The carpenters, they were informed, had a fund of £20 000.

.... Look at other Trades! they all Combine ... See the Tailors, Shoemakers, Bookbinders, Gold beaters, Printers, Bricklayers, Coatmakers, Hatters, Curriers, Masons, Whitesmiths, none of these trades Receive Less that 30/- [£1.50] a week, and from that to five guineas [£5.25] this is all done by Combination, without it their Trades would be as bad as yours ...

The tailors had several thousand members; others were much smaller although they maintained links with other clubs in the same trade. Trade clubs protected their members' interests. This might mean taking an employer to court, as the shoemakers did in 1813, or calling a strike to get an increase in pay rates. The tailors kept their own list of unemployed men. The masters had to apply to the union when extra workers were required. Working hours were strictly regulated, and like other trades, tailors tried to restrict the entry of new men. Full apprenticeships had to be served and in some cases only the sons of existing workmen were accepted.

on the tramp: looking for work

Workers 'on the tramp' used the trade clubs as a point of call. Presentation of a membership ticket from his local club entitled the traveller to a few days' hospitality whilst he looked for work. Subscriptions were high and clubs provided sickness, old age and funeral benefits for their members.

The Combination Acts, 1799 and 1800

Most of these activities were illegal. Laws against workmen combining together to raise wages dated back to 1548. Employers were encouraged to prosecute striking workmen for breach of contract.

In 1789 there was Revolution in France. By 1792 the British authorities were becoming alarmed at the spread of revolutionary ideas from Europe. War was declared in 1793 and the following year leading political reformers in London were on trial for treason. They were acquitted but the government then took measures to restrict public meetings and to control newspapers and printing presses.

In 1797 there were mutinies in the fleet at Spithead and the Nore and

in 1798 rebellion in Ireland. In these circumstances associations of working men seemed very threatening. Rising bread prices and wartime inflation added to the discontent causing disturbances which worried magistrates and employers.

When the master millwrights of London petitioned Parliament in 1799 for legislation against a combination amongst their workers, MPs were ready to support them. A proposal that this should be extended to cover all trade union activity was taken up by the government and the Combination Act was quickly passed. In 1800 it was amended.

The Combination Acts clearly stated that any form of united action by workmen to raise wages or to alter working conditions was a criminal act. Picketing and intimidation to enforce a strike was illegal. The penalty for these offences was to be three months' imprisonment. Associations of employers were also forbidden. The Act of 1800 included an arbitration scheme which was never implemented.

Using the evidence: the cotton spinners' strike, 1818

The Combination Laws did not stop union activity. The London trade clubs survived and there were outbursts in the industrial areas. In July 1818 the Manchester cotton spinners went on strike demanding an increase in wages. The dispute spread to all the neighbouring towns.

A The spinners' case

It is asserted that our average wages amount to 30s or 40s per week – it is evident that this statement was made by some individual either ignorant or interested. In 1816, the average clear wages of the spinners in Manchester was about 24s, they were then reduced from 20 to 25 per cent, and have ever since laboured under that reduction.

What happened to the spinners' wages in 1816?

B *Their organisation*

The whole of the Spinners is out, Except about 500 . . . they marched By
piccadilly on Tuesday and was 23½ minets in going Bye . . . one man from
Eich shop is chose by the People and he commands them he forms them in
Ranks and atends them on the march and as the soal Command and they obey
him as Stickley as the armey do their Colonel . . .

Evidence of 'B', a government spy

. . . Four of five hundred or perhaps one or two thousand assembling from
different factories and at the hour of work, viz 4 or 5 o'clock in the morning, go
to a factory at the other end of town where they are not known, and so carry off
by force or intimidation, though without any violent breach of the peace, the
hands who might be disposed to go to work – and the parties assembled being
strangers, the masters have in no one instance . . . been able to identify
persons, so that no case can be made out under the Combination Act. . . .

James Norris, a Manchester magistrate, to Viscount Sidmouth,
the Home Secretary, 29 July 1818

C *The attitudes of the employers and of the authorities*
(i) Henry Hobhouse (Under-Secretary of State at the Home Office) to
Rev. W.R. Hay, a Manchester magistrate, 28 July 1818:

. . . I am not aware of any reason to doubt that the present discontent arose
exclusively from commercial causes, but there is strong ground to believe that
the political malcontents have been endeavouring to convert them to their own
wicked purposes, and it is of great importance to ascertain to what extent they
have succeeded, and by what means so large a body of mechanics has been
subsisted without any visible means of livelihood for so long a period. . . .

(ii) Henry Hobhouse to Major General Sir John Byng, 14 August 1818:

. . . Matters have certainly been better managed at Stockport than at
Manchester. The Masters have been more firm, and the convictions under the
Combination Act have done great service . . . the first object is to show to the
workmen that the law is strong enough, if it be put properly enforced, but this
principle has not been acted upon in Manchester, where the manufacturer
seems to rely more on your sword than on any other weapon. . . .

(iii) Henry Hobhouse to William Marriott, 19 August 1818:

. . . On the present occasion the master spinners appear to have acted with
very little discretion towards their men. . . . Government and the magistracy
must ever discountenance combination, but they have much to complain of
those who give rise to combination by relying on the support of the law instead
of considering the justice of the demands made on them.

D *Getting support*
A letter from the Staleybridge spinners to the local colliers, 7 August
1818:

Sir,
  The spinners of Manchester have authorized me to solicit you to join in their
union of trade, as all trades in England are uniting in one body for Trade and
Reform, and you are desired to send a delegate to all Meetings to consult
matters over and to inform you that you will be supported in your Trade in

malcontents: troublemakers

Byng was the military
commander in Manchester

turn; A letter was recieved from London this day from the Silk Weavers wishing to join them and offering their support. . . .

James Norris to Viscount Sidmouth, 11 October 1818:

. . . I am . . . now able to inform you that from all the information I can acquire, the General Union . . . is broken up. Delegates from Nottingham, Birmingham and Liverpool were here about a month ago, but they came after the spinners had gone in, and found the latter, I believe, so happy in being again employed, that . . . they left here in disgust. . . .

1 After reading source A what appears to you to be the main grievance of the cotton spinners?
2 (a) Outline the evidence in source B that shows the strikers were well organised.
(b) Why do you think it was necessary for the strikers to have this organisation and to parade in this way? What effect would it have?
3 Now read the extracts in source C.
(a) Hobhouse is very critical of the employers – why?
(b) How far does source B help to explain the failure of the employers to prosecute the strikers? Would Hobhouse accept this excuse?
(c) Hobhouse seems to blame the employers for what had happened. From the evidence you have seen, do you agree with him?
(d) From this evidence what aspect of the strike most worried the government?
4 (a) Why do you think the spinners wanted to form a general union of trades?
(b) How far do these sources show the difficulties trade unionists faced when they tried to link up outside their local areas?
5 What does this evidence tell you about the effectiveness of the Combination Laws? Explain your answer.

The repeal of the Combination Laws, 1824

The Combination Laws were unsatisfactory. Workmen who combined were prosecuted but employers who banded together to set wage rates escaped.

Francis Place, a London tailor, was determined to get the laws repealed. He began his campaign in 1814 but made little progress until he got the support of an MP, Joseph Hume. A Parliamentary Select Committee was obtained in 1824. Together they prepared the evidence, Place taking the leading role.

. . . Meetings were held in many places; and both masters and men sent up deputations to give evidence. The delegates from the working people had reference to me, and I opened my house to them. . . . I heard the story which everyone of these men had to tell. I examined and cross-examined them; took down the leading particulars of each case, and then arranged the matter . . . for Mr Hume; and . . . for the guidance of the witnesses, a copy was given to each. . . .

What does Place's account tell us about

1 the evidence presented to the committee?
2 Place's own opinions on trade unions?

The workmen were not easily managed. It required great pains and patience not to shock their prejudices. . . . They were filled with false notions . . . which I . . . dared not attempt to remove. . . . All expected a great and sudden rise of wages, when the Combination Laws should be repealed. . . . I had to discuss with them most carefully, to arrange and prepare everything. . . .

The committee recommended repeal and the legislation went through Parliament with scarcely any discussion.

Place expected workmen to abandon trade unions when they realised that wages were set by the law of supply and demand. Repeal, however, coincided with a period of prosperity and there was an outburst of union activity. Higher wages, better working conditions, and in some cases the dismissal of non-union labour were demanded. Strikes resulted.

Alarmed, the government appointed a new committee in 1825. It heard very different evidence. A new Trade Union Act was passed. Unions were allowed to exist but there were severe penalties to prevent intimidation and violence. 'Molesting' and 'obstructing' persons at work were forbidden, thus preventing any form of picketing.

Nevertheless unions were now legal associations. As Robert Peel, the Home Secretary, explained:

Men who . . . have no property except their manual skill and strength, ought to be allowed to confer together, if they think fit, for the purpose of determining at what rate they will sell their property.

The failure of national unions

After 1825 attempts to organise national unions either within a trade or of all trades were renewed. John Doherty, the leader of the Lancashire spinners, brought all the cotton spinners into one national union in 1829. The following year he formed the National Association for the Protection of Labour, a union open to all occupations. It was not a success. Its collapse was hastened when the secretary absconded with the funds.

The Builders' Union formed in 1831 had more initial success. At one time the union had 60 000 members and in 1833 a Builders' Parliament met in Birmingham. The union faced counter-attacks from the masters. In December 1833 the Derby employers agreed:

That each of them will immediately cease to employ every man who is a member of the Trades' Union, and will not receive or take back into his service any man who continues to be a member of that, or of any other Union. . . .

lockout: employers stop work and dismiss workers

The men were locked out and only allowed back when they agreed to sign the 'Document'. These tactics were repeated elsewhere and the union collapsed during 1834.

Robert Owen was a good employer. Refer back to Chapter 10

The ideas of Robert Owen influenced trade unions at this time. Owen believed that character was formed by the environment in which people lived. At his New Lanark mills he had tried to create a model community. He claimed that labour was the source of all wealth, but

A hostile view of trade union organisers from 1830. What is the cartoonist suggesting?

hat the wages paid by employers undervalued labour. He proposed hat large self-sufficient cooperative communities should be established, and in 1825 he went to America to try out his settlement at New Harmony.

When a disillusioned Owen returned to England in 1829 after the failure of his American schemes he discovered a growing interest in his cooperative ideas. There were some experiments with cooperative shops and in 1832 an Equitable Labour Exchange was set up in London. Workmen could bring articles they had produced, priced according to the hours of work involved, and exchange them for other goods. Labour notes were issued which some shopkeepers were prepared to accept.

In 1834 Owen was involved in an ambitious scheme to unite all workers in support of the Builders' Union. The Grand National Consolidated Trades Union (GNCTU) included cooperative proposals amongst its aims. A large membership was claimed but few subscriptions were paid and Owen quickly quarrelled with the union leaders. They distrusted his ideas and his moderation over wages and other issues.

The Tolpuddle Martyrs

Initiation ceremonies were a feature of early trade unions. They were to remind the new member of the need for secrecy. An informer joined the Yorkshire Trades Union:

. . . The first operation was to blindfold him . . . he was then required to give the password . . . he was then walked round the room, during which time a great rumbling noise was made by a sheet of iron – a hymn then sung – and he continued to walk . . . and was asked if his motive was pure – they then took the bandage from his eyes, and the first thing he saw was a picture of death as large as a man, over which was the inscription 'Remember Thy End'. Over this picture there was a drawn sword – his eyes were then bandaged again, and he was walked about the room, when, upon a signal being given, all the members made a great stamping noise with their feet – he was then ordered to kneel down beside a table, and the bandage was again taken from his eyes, when he saw a large bible before him, his hand having been placed upon it. . . . The 94th Psalm was then read, when the oath was administered . . . that he was to obey all the commands of the Union Committee, and to keep all secrets in every particular – the conclusion of the oath contained an imprecation, on which 'each person sworn is made to wish that if he violates the oath that his soul may be burnt in the lowest pit of hell to all eternity'. . . .

This branch met in the upper room of a public house. The ceiling of the room below was planked with thick boards and the joins were filled with wood shavings to prevent any sound filtering out.

imprecation: curse

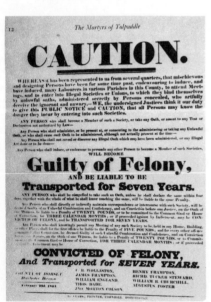

The Martyrs of Tolpuddle

This warning was issued by the
Dorset magistrates immediately
before the arrest of George Loveless
and the other Tolpuddle men

Questions

1 Look up Psalm 94. Why was this read?
2 This was in 1832 but these oaths had always been a normal part of trade-union life. Why do you think this was so?
3 Try to imagine the effect of this ceremony on the new member. What was it designed to do?

It is hardly surprising that when George Loveless organised the Friendly Society of Agricultural Labourers in Tolpuddle in 1833 new members had to take a solemn oath of secrecy. Trade-union activity in rural Dorset alarmed the landowners and magistrates.

They were determined to crush the society. Loveless and five others were arrested on 24th February 1834 charged with administering illegal oaths.

Lord Melbourne, the Home Secretary, was not sympathetic to trade unionism. In 1832, at the height of a miners' strike in the North East he had told the local magistrates to

. . exert themselves for the prevention and suppression of all meetings which shall be called together for an illegal purpose or which shall in the course of these proceedings become illegal; for the detection and punishment of all unlawful combination and conspiracy, as well as of all outrage and violence. . . .

Lord Melbourne was disturbed at the rise of the GNCTU, and the arrest of the Tolpuddle labourers seemed an opportunity to strike a blow against the spread of unionism. The magistrates were advised to proceed against the men under an Act passed in 1797 after the naval mutinies of that year. It made the administration of secret oaths punishable by seven years' transportation.

Despite the flimsy evidence against the men, the result was a foregone conclusion.

On the 15th March, we were taken to the County-hall to await our trial . . . the whole proceedings were characterized by a shameful disregard of justice and decency; the most unfair means were resorted to in order to frame an indictment against us. . . . The greater part of the evidence against us, on our trial, was put into the mouths of the witnesses by the judge. . . . I shall not soon forget his address to the jury in summing up the evidence: amongst other things, he told them, that if such Societies were allowed to exist, it would ruin masters, cause a stagnation in trade, destroy property . . . I thought to myself, there is no danger but we shall be found guilty, as we have a special jury . . . selected from among those who are most unfriendly towards us. . . . Under such a charge, from such a quarter, self-interest alone would induce them to say, 'Guilty'. . . .

indictment: charge

charge: instruction or advice

George Loveless, *The Victims of Whiggery*, 1838

Trade unionists protest at the harsh punishment imposed on the men from Tolpuddle, 1834

The conviction of the six Tolpuddle labourers and the determined opposition of the employers contributed to the short life of the GNCTU. In any case, poor and expensive communications made the organisation of national unions almost impossible at this time.

Unions in the shadows: the 1840s

During the latter 1830s and the 'Hungry Forties' agitation centred on political reform. Chartism absorbed all attention. Trade unions however, survived but tended to be local in their activities.

An exception to this was the Miners' Association of Great Britain. Founded in Wakefield in 1842 it soon claimed 70 000 members. I lasted until 1848 and employed a solicitor, W. P. Roberts, to fight cases against the employers through the courts.

Faced by the united oppositon of the mine-owners, the Association's achievements were limited. The Northumberland and Durham men went on strike in April 1844. They were forced back to work as winter approached. Their families had been evicted, blackleg labour was brought in by the employers, the Poor Law authorities were instructed not to assist the families of strikers and in his company town of Seaham Lord Londonderry ordered local tradesmen to refuse credit to miners. All the difficulties unionists had faced still existed. Combination was still unacceptable.

2 The struggle for acceptance

The New Model Unions

The Amalgamated Society of Engineers was formed in 1851. It survived a fierce onslaught from the London and Lancashire employers in 1852 to become the first of the New Model Unions. Its secretary, William Allen, and the secretary of the Amalgamated Society of Carpenters and Joiners, Robert Applegarth, were determined to win a respected place for trade unions in Victorian society.

The New Model Unions were unions for skilled men. They sought to retain apprenticeship, and opposed piece-rate payments and new working practices which reduced the status of the craftsman. These unions were centralised with headquarters in London. The railway network and the cheap postage service made this possible. Paid, full-time secretaries like Allen and Applegarth managed the unions' affairs. Local branches had some independence but all important decisions had to have the approval of the executive council in London. This was especially true of strikes.

The executive council does all it possibly can to prevent any strike, and where they have time and opportunity, generally . . . they cause a deputation of the workmen to wait on their employers to represent their grievances, and then the council gives advice afterwards. We endeavour at all times to prevent strikes. . . .

Membership card of the Amalgamated Society of Engineers

. . . we believe that all strikes are a complete waste of money, not only in relation to the workmen, but also to the employers.

Evidence of William Allen to the Royal Commission on Trade Unions

Applegarth and Allen knew that strikes turned public opinion against trade unions. But if the leaders of the new model unions were cautious in their use of the strike weapon, other unionists used it and more violent methods very freely.

Who would join a New Model Union?

The conditions of membership
The applicant:

● had to be a properly qualified craftsman.

● had to be known and proposed by another member.

● had to pay an entry fee and a weekly subscription of 1 shilling (5p).

● had to obey the rules and the authority of the Central Executive Council.

Strike rules

Strike action had to be approved by the Executive Council.

… under no circumstances will any branch be allowed to strike without first obtaining the sanction of the council, whether it be for a new privilege or against an encroachment of existing ones …"

(Robert Applegarth, secretary of the Carpenters and Joiners.)

In 1868 the Amalgamated Society of Carpenters and Joiners had 8,261 members.

The Amalgamated Society of Engineers had 33,600 members.

The benefits of membership

Unemployment benefit for 24 weeks.
Strike pay of 15 shillings a week.
Insurance of tools against loss.
Sickness benefit.
Funeral benefit.
A weekly pension on retirement.
Emigration assistance.
Payment of fare to district where work is available.
The Union will help unemployed members find work.

The 'Sheffield Outrages'

The New Model Unions appeared moderate and responsible. In Sheffield the activities of the small local unions were very different.

Many different crafts were employed in the cutlery trade and each craft was organised into a separate union. Non-unionists and members who offended against union rules were intimidated. 'Rattening' was used against them. An offender's tools and materials were taken and hidden. Once he had agreed to accept the union's demands these were returned. If this proved unsuccessful then other steps were taken. Thomas Fearnehough, refused to join the Saw Grinder's Union.

... Henry Skidmore, secretary of the Saw Makers' Society, and Joseph Barker, secretary of the Saw Handle Maker's Society, called on Broadhead, and represented to him that Fearnehough was working ... and thereby injuring the trade, and asked him 'if something could not be done to stop him working'. . . . On the 8th October 1866 a can of gunpowder was exploded in the cellar under Fearnehough's house. . . . Samuel Crooks was hired by Broadhead to commit this outrage, and was assisted by Joseph Copley, a member of the Saw Grinders' Union. A day or two after this occurrence, Baker and Skidmore, with the knowledge of Thomas Smith, Secretary of the Saw Markers' Union, paid Broadhead £7.10s. [£7.50], the share of each union for the expense of committing the outrage. . . .

Trades Union Commission: Sheffield Outrages Inquiry

Events in Sheffield undermined the work of Allen and Applegarth. Public opinion assumed that all unions used these tactics.

Legal difficulties – the case of Hornby *v* Close, 1867

Since the unions provided friendly-society benefits for their members, the union leaders believed that their funds were protected under the Friendly Societies Act of 1855. In 1867 the Boilermakers' Society sued the treasurer of its Bradford branch to get the return of money he owed. The magistrates, and then the appeal court, decided against the union.

The judges agreed that unions had the functions of friendly societies but since their main purpose was to act 'in restraint of trade', they were illegal associations. Their funds were not protected.

The Royal Commission on Trade Unions, 1867

In 1867 the Government set up a Royal Commission to examine trade unions and their activities.

Trade union leaders were anxious that the Commission's final report should be favourable. The secretaries of the London-based societies had been working together since the early 1860s and had formed an unofficial committee, the Junta. Allen and Applegarth were leading members. It had already campaigned for a change in the Master and Servant Laws because they made it impossible for a workman to strike without risking imprisonment for breach of contract. The Junta had played a leading part in the agitation which preceded the Second Reform Act in 1867. This gave the working man in boroughs the vote.

THE STRIKE.—HITTING HIM HARD.

Punch's *comment on trade unions, 1861*

The Junta persuaded the government to allow them to nominate one member of the Commission. In addition Applegarth was to attend the examinations of trade union witnesses as the Commission's expert. As two of the principal witnesses, Applegarth and Allen emphasised the beneficial aspects of trade unionism. Others witnesses made more damaging statements, but the Commissioners concluded that the violence of the Sheffield unions was exceptional and in decline.

The Report recommended that trade unions should be given full legal protection.

The Trade Union Congress is formed

Outside London many union leaders distrusted the moderate Junta members. Concerned at the proceedings of the Royal Commission the Manchester and Salford Trades Council proposed that unions should send delegates to a meeting in Manchester.

The first Trades Union Congress met on the 2 June 1868. Thirty-four delegates represented 118 000 members. Only two London trade unionists attended. The Junta feared a new rival to their authority. In 1869 Congress met in Birmingham.

The 1871 meeting was held in London and coincided with the parliamentary sitting. Delegates lobbied MPs on the trade-union legislation the government was expected to introduce.

REFORM OF LAWS ON TRADE UNIONS

Date	Government	Event	Unionist attitudes
1871	William Gladstone's Liberal Government	1 *The Trade Union Act* gave legal recognition to trade unions and protection to their funds as friendly societies.	
		2 *The Criminal Law Amendment Act* repealed the restrictions on picketing of the 1825 Act.	The TUC worked to get the repeal of this Act and some change in the Master and Servant Laws.
1872		Some London gas workers were sentenced to twelve months' hard labour for breaking their contract when they went out on strike.	
1874		The wives of twelve farm labourers were sentenced to hard labour for intimidating blacklegs during a strike.	At the general election of 1874 the TUC advised trade unionists to question candidates on their opinions. Since working men had the vote they could influence the result in some constituencies.
1875	Benjamin Disraeli's Conservative Government	1 *The Conspiracy and Protection of Property Act* legalised peaceful picketing and stated that in industrial disputes the law of conspiracy was not to apply unless criminal actions were involved. 2 *The Employers and Workmen Act* made breach of contract a civil, not a criminal offence.	The Conservative Government gave the trade unions the legal protections they needed.

Since the Criminal Law Amendment Act of 1871 was unsatisfactory, Congress appointed a Parliamentary Committee to continue the agitation for improvement in the law between its meetings. The Junta dissolved itself and the Trades Union Congress became the mouthpiece of trade unionism.

The Conservative legislative of 1875 gave unions a firm legal standing. The Junta had won the recognition of trade unions as respectable and responsible organisations, now the Parliamentary Committee of the TUC had secured legal recognition.

The growth of unionism in the 1870s

The craftsmen who joined the New Model Unions were only a small proportion of trade unionists. Unionism had always be strong in the cotton districts and the coalfields. In 1873 each of the two national miners' unions claimed 100 000 members but in the depression that began in the late 1870s both collapsed dramatically.

New groups of workers organised in the 1870s included railwaymen and agricultural labourers. The Amalgamated Society of Railway Servants got public sympathy because its main demand was a reduction in the hours railwaymen worked. There was evidence that long hours worked by drivers and signalmen contributed to accidents. Fiercely opposed by the railway companies, the union made little progress.

Joseph Arch founded the National Agricultural Labourers' Union in 1874. Farm-workers were difficult to organise. They worked in small scattered groups but their response in the South and East was enthusiastic. A series of strikes in 1874 forced wages up. Farmers responded with lockouts but the onset of the agricultural depression after 1877 fatally weakened the union.

Agricultural labourers who joined the union suffered severely in 1874. A family is evicted

3 Unions for unskilled workers

Will Thorne – unskilled labourer and union organiser

In the 1880s the vast majority of workers were not members of trade unions. Unskilled workers who frequently changed jobs and were easily replaced seemed impossible to organise.

Will Thorne, born in Birmingham in 1857, was typical in the range of jobs he had.

My first job came when I was only a little over six years of age; it was turning a wheel for a rope and twine spinner. . . . I received 2s 6d [12½p] per week and worked from six in the morning until six at night. . . .

At eight he was working in a brickyard. Periods with a plumber, a lath splitter, a cow- and pig-hair trader, in an ammunition works, in a wagon-works and navvying on the Burton to Derby railway followed. Eventually Will Thorne settled to brickfield work in the summer and labouring in Birmingham's Saltley gasworks in the winter where his first job was wheeling barrows of coke from the ovens.

The work was hot and very hard. As the coke was drawn from the retort on to the ground we threw pails of water on it, and the heat, both from the ovens and the clouds of steam that would rise from the drenched coke was terrific. Once cooled, the coke had to be wheeled away and pitched onto a big heap. For this we used a great six-pronged fork. It was gruelling work.

The men worked twelve-hour shifts, a fortnight of days followed by a fortnight of nights. Changeover Sunday meant a twenty-four hour shift.

Thorne persuaded his fellow-workers to ask Birmingham Corporation, which operated the gasworks, to end Sunday working. The

Mechanisation in the gas works persuaded unskilled labourers to join Will Thorne's union

Matchmakers were the first unskilled workers to fight a successful strike. Assisted by the socialists Annie and Eleanor Marx they won their demands from Bryant and May in 1888

Corporation agreed but his efforts to form a permanent union failed, even when mechanisation increased the stokers' work.

I was put to work on this machine. One machine was used on either side of the retorts. Four of the stokers worked with the machines, charging the retorts with coal and drawing off the coke, instead of using the old hand rakes and shovels.

The machines made the work heavier for the men. In fact, so hard and rapid was the work that we often had no time to eat our food between charges. The machine was constantly breaking down, and this would put us behind with the work, for breakdown or no, we had do our same number of charges. . . .

Moving to London, Thorne found the same long hours at the Beckton gasworks where he again encountered the 'iron man'. Its use so angered the men that in March 1889 they formed the National Union of Gas Workers and General Labourers. Will Thorne was elected General Secretary. His first demand was for an eight-hour day in the London gasworks. He had successfully negotiated this, without a strike by the summer.

Thorne had persuaded reluctant unskilled and semi-skilled workmen to join a union. Many were seasonal workers and all could easily be replaced but the companies gave way because the industry was expanding rapidly and the consequences of a long gas strike were unacceptable to the general public.

The dockers' strike, 1889

Dockers were a poverty-stricken group of London workers. Every day thousands of men gathered at the dock gates and fought for a day's work.

As a rule I have to struggle for employment. Yesterday I earned 2s. 3d. [11½p]; this is the first work I have done since last Friday . . . I have been down at the London Docks, No. 5 gate, every morning since last Friday, at the usual hour of calling on, that is, half-past eight, and I have been unsuccessful in obtaining employment until yesterday; yesterday I was there from half-past eight till half-past eleven. At half-past eleven I should say that there were something like 350 men waiting for employment. . . . A contractor came to the gate for, I think it was, 14 men . . . and of course there was a struggle . . . . they have a certain number of tickets to give out; and there was a struggle between us men at the gate who should be lucky enough . . . to gain one of these tickets.

> James Gray, dock labourer, giving evidence to a Parliamentary
> Select Committee in 1888

Ben Tillett's description was more dramatic.

At the 'cage' so termed because of the stout iron bars made to protect the 'caller on', men ravening for food fought like madmen for the ticket. . . . Coats, flesh, and even ears, were torn off, men were crushed to death in the struggle . . . The strong literally threw themselves over the heads of their fellows, and battled with kick and curse through the kicking, punching, cursing crowd to the rails of the cage, which held them like rats – mad, human rats, who saw food in the ticket. . . .

> B. Tillett, *A Brief History of the Dockers' Union,*
> *Commemorating the 1889 Dockers' Strike*

Questions

1 Using the descriptions explain how the dockers were employed.
2 How does Tillett's description differ from the docker's? Explain his use of words like 'madman', 'rats'.

In 1887 Tillett became secretary of the Tea Operatives and General Labourers' Association. Its membership was never large but Tillett became well-known in the docks. When the dockers' strike began on 14 August 1889 he became their leader.

The strike was a protest against conditions of employment but the strikers focused on a wage increase from 5d to 6d an hour – 'the dockers' tanner'. Other demands included an overtime rate of 8d an hour, a guaranteed minimum four hours work, and only two 'call ons' in a day.

Soon the London docks were at a standstill. All other dock and river workers came out in support of the dockers. The strikers tightly picketed the dock gates and prevented the use of blacklegs. Public

The dockers' demands   *The processions through the City of London were a feature of the dockers' strike*

sympathy was high and large sums of money were raised to feed the strikers' families. There were daily mass meetings and a daily procession through the City of London.

. . . . Our daily processions . . . were not only demonstrations and advertisements for our cause, but in the nature of relief expeditions. In our marches we collected contributions in pennies, sixpences and shillings from the clerks and City workers, who were touched perhaps to the point of sacrifice by the emblem of poverty and starvation carried in our procession – the 'dockers' dinner', a herring and dry bread. . . .

B. Tillet, Memories and Reflections, 1931

The dispute lasted five weeks before Cardinal Manning was able to negotiate a compromise acceptable to both dock employers and workers. The 'tanner' was won. Dockers had shown what could be done by unskilled workers if they were determined, well organised and had public support.

The 'New Unions'

In 1889 Tillett and Tom Mann organised a new Dockers' Union. Within a year they had 40 000 members. Thorne's Gas Workers and General Labourers' Union expanded rapidly. Other associations of unskilled workers or general unions catering for workers in a wide range of occupations soon emerged.

Setbacks followed the initial successes. Thorne's union lost £20 000 in an unsuccessful dispute with the South Metropolitan Gas Company in 1890 and the dockers suffered serious defeats in Hull and Bristol.

Members were unskilled and semi-skilled workers on low wages.

Low subscriptions – members of the Gasworkers Union paid 2d. a week.

"I do not believe in having sick pay, out of work pay, and a number of other pays, we desire to prevent as much sickness and men being out of work. The way to accomplish this, is firstly to organise, then reduce your hours of labour or work, that will prevent illness and members being out of employment."
(Will Thorne, 1889)

Aimed to improve working conditions. "New Unions" wanted the eight hour day. In 1890 it became T.U.C. policy.

"Physically the 'old' unionists were much bigger than the 'new' ... A great number of them looked like respectable city gentlemen; wore very good coats, large watch chains, and high hats ...
Amongst the 'new' delegates not a single one wore a tall hat. They looked workmen; they were workmen." (John Burns at the 1890 T.U.C.)

More militant than the craft unions. Thorne wanted closed shops to ensure that strikes would be successful.

"One Man, one Ticket and every man with a Ticket" (Will Thorne)

Leaders were socialists. The leaders of the craft unions were liberals.

The 'New Unionism'

Questions

1 Make a timeline of the important events in the development of trade unions from 1850 to 1890.
2 Draw a chart to compare the New Model Unions with the New Unions of 1889. Use these headings:
   Members; Subscriptions; Benefits; Aims; Leadership; Methods.
3 Between 1850 and 1890 the trade union movement had made great progress.
   (a) In what ways was trade unionism stronger in 1890 than in 1850?
   (b) Explain how these changes had been brought about.
4 Using the evidence in this section script a newspaper interview from 1889 with *either* a gasworker explaining why he has joined the Gas Workers Union *or* a docker in which he explains why he has come out on strike.

4 Trade unionism becomes political: the birth of the Labour Party

Working-class MPs

The first two working-class MPs entered the House of Commons in 1874. Alexander MacDonald and Thomas Burt were both miners. They supported the Liberals. They were soon joined by other miners and by Henry Broadhurst, a stonemason, the secretary of the Parliamentary Committee of the TUC. All were 'Lib-Labs'.

The early Socialists

Others did not believe that either the Liberals or the Conservatives understood the needs of working people. Influenced by the writings of Karl Marx, H. M. Hyndham founded the Social Democratic Federation in 1884. The SDF played a prominent part in the unemployment riots in London in 1886 and 1887 but it made little impact on the working class.

Its greatest influence was on men who became involved with the 'New Unionism'. Will Thorne was taught to read by Eleanor Marx, Ben Tillett had contacts with the SDF and John Burns was one of the SDF leaders charged after the 1886 riots. When these men attended the TUC they opposed the old reliance on the Liberals.

Eleanor was Karl Marx's daughter

Forming a working-class political party

In 1892 James Keir Hardie was elected MP for West Ham. He had attacked Broadhurst's liberalism and had campaigned for the TUC to support an independent working-class political party. He was ignored.

When he entered Parliament, Keir Hardie was determined to maintain his independence as a representative of the working classes.

Keir Hardie's election poster, 1895

VOTE FOR

Home Rule.

Democratic Government.

Justice to Labour

No Monopoly.

No Landlordism

Temperance Reform.

Healthy Homes.

Fair Rents.

Eight-Hour Day.

Work for the Unemployed.

KEIR HARDIE.

John Burns, also elected in 1892, soon joined the Liberals but Keir Hardie did not. His first arrival at Westminster dressed in a cloth cap and a tweed jacket caused a sensation.

Keir Hardie encouraged the founding of the Independent Labour Party at Bradford in 1893. The ILP was never a strong or a wealthy association and in the 1895 general election all its candidates, including Keir Hardie, were defeated.

Meanwhile socialist union leaders had been demanding TUC support for an independent political party. Eventually in 1899 Congress half-heartedly passed a resolution authorising the Parliamentary Committee

... to invite the co-operation on lines mutually agreed upon in convening a Special Congress of representatives from such ... organisations as may be willing to take part to devise ways and means for securing the return of an increased number of Labour members to the next Parliament.

On 27 February 1900 representatives from the socialist societies, the ILP and the trade unions met. They agreed to form a Labour Representation Committee (LRC) with the aim of establishing

... a distinct Labour group in Parliament who shall have their own whips, and agree upon their policy, which must embrace a readiness to co-operate with any party which for the time being may be engaged in promoting legislation in the direct interests of Labour, and be equally ready to associate themselves with any party in opposing measures having an opposite tendency. ...

Caught unprepared by the 1900 general election, only two of the LRC's fifteen candidates were elected. Success depended on trade unions. They had the money the Committee needed but their initial support was poor. Only 41 out of 1272 trade unions had joined the LRC after twelve months.

The unions turn to the LRC

The 1890s were difficult. Rising unemployment put unions at a disadvantage. Employers' associations successfully fought the unions. Blackleg labour was supplied to break strikes. After a long and bitter dispute in 1897, even the powerful Amalgamated Society of Engineers admitted defeat. Demands for a eight-hour day were dropped and increased mechanisation had to be accepted.

Legal decisions weakened the unions. Lloyds v Wilkins (1896) cast doubt on the legality of picketing. More seriously, in 1900 the Taff Vale Railway Company was awarded damages of £23 000 against the Amalgamated Society of Railway Servants. The Union appealed, but in 1901 the House of Lords confirmed the original judgement. A union was liable to compensate an employer for losses if its picketing prevented the use of blacklegs.

Trade unions needed to change the law. That could only be done through Parliament. Suddenly more unions began to take an interest in the activities of the Labour Representation Committee.

The beginnings of the Labour Party

Increasing support meant the LRC had the funds to finance both candidates and working-class MPs.

In 1903 Ramsay MacDonald, secretary of the LRC, made an agreement with Herbert Gladstone, the Liberal chief whip. Liberal and LRC candidates would not oppose each other. As a result, 29 LRC sponsored candidates won seats at the 1906 General Election.

At Westminster these new MPs formed themselves into the Labour Party. In 1909 they were joined by the miners' MPs. There were then over fifty Labour MPs.

The Labour Party in Parliament

The Party's main achievement was in persuading the Liberal government to pass the Trade Disputes Act in 1906. This gave unions immunity from claims for damages. The dangerous consequences of the Taff Vale judgement were removed. However, Labour MPs made little impact in the House of Commons or on the policy of the government. In 1908, moreover, the future of the Party was threatened by the Osborne Judgement.

Osborne, a member of the Amalgamated Society of Railway Servants, was a Liberal. He objected to his union paying contributions out of its members' subscriptions to another political party. The courts supported him. With no certain source of money the existence of all working-class MPs was at stake.

The problem was solved in two ways. In 1911 Parliament agreed to the payment of a salary of £400 a year to all MPs. Two years later the Trade Union Act allowed unions to have a political fund, provided members had the opportunity to contract out.

Using the evidence: dealing with strikes

In the autumn of 1910 there was a miners' strike in the South Wales coalfield over a dispute about payments to be made to men working difficult seams.

A By November 30 000 men were locked out or on strike.

By Sunday, November 6th, the workmen discovered that it was the intention of the owners to import blackleg labour for the Glamorgan Colliery at Llwynpia. On the night of Monday, November 7th, a body of strikers surrounded the colliery, and had a sharp brush with a body of police ensconced in the colliery premises. Reinforcements of police were rapidly sent into the valley, where their arrival aroused treatment, especially in Tonypandy. . . . Between midnight and 1 a.m. on the morning of November 8th, disturbances broke out with a certain amount of smashing of windows. The police used their truncheons freely and dispersed the miners. . . .

ensconced: guarding

R. Page Arnot, *The Miners: Years of Struggle*, 1953

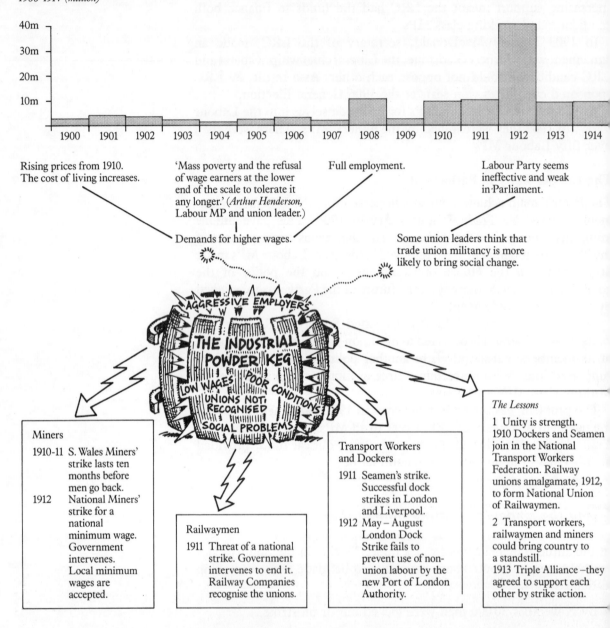

Total number of days lost by strikers
1900-1914 (million)

Rising prices from 1910.
The cost of living increases.

'Mass poverty and the refusal of wage earners at the lower end of the scale to tolerate it any longer.' (*Arthur Henderson,* Labour MP and union leader.)

Full employment.

Labour Party seems ineffective and weak in·Parliament.

Demands for higher wages.

Some union leaders think that trade union militancy is more likely to bring social change.

AGGRESSIVE EMPLOYERS

THE INDUSTRIAL POWDER KEG

LOW WAGES POOR CONDITIONS
UNIONS NOT RECOGNISED
SOCIAL PROBLEMS

Miners

1910-11 S. Wales Miners' strike lasts ten months before men go back.

1912 National Miners' strike for a national minimum wage. Government intervenes. Local minimum wages are accepted.

Railwaymen

1911 Threat of a national strike. Government intervenes to end it. Railway Companies recognise the unions.

Transport Workers and Dockers

1911 Seamen's strike. Successful dock strikes in London and Liverpool.

1912 May – August London Dock Strike fails to prevent use of non-union labour by the new Port of London Authority.

The Lessons

1 Unity is strength. 1910 Dockers and Seamen join in the National Transport Workers Federation. Railway unions amalgamate, 1912, to form National Union of Railwaymen.

2 Transport workers, railwaymen and miners could bring country to a standstill. 1913 Triple Alliance –they agreed to support each other by strike action.

1910–14: years of industrial strife

B The Chief Constable asked for troops to assist the police i▸ maintaining order. Winston Churchill, the Home Secretary, learnt o▸ this on Tuesday 8th November.

. . . . At 11 o'clock Mr Churchill . . . definitely decided to employ Polic◂ instead of Military to deal with disorder, and, while moving troops near to th▸ scene of disturbance, to keep them in the background . . . . 300 Metropolita▸ Police . . . were ordered to start for Pontypridd. . . . This force of picke◂ constables experienced in the handling of crowds, was for every purpose bette▸ suited to the needs of the situation than an equivalent body of military infantry soldiers can if attacked or stoned only reply by fire from long range rifles which often kills foolish sightseers . . . or innocent people. . . .

Letter from Winston Churchill to King George V

C Sir Nevil Macready was in command of the troops in the area.

During the rioting that occured on 21st November throughout the Tonypandy Valley the Metropolitan Police while driving the mob before them along the main road were heavily stoned from the side tracks, and suffered severe casualties. In order to counter these tactics on the part of the strikers on the next occasion when trouble was afoot, small bodies of infantry on the higher ground, keeping level with the police on the main road, moved slowly down the side tracks, and by a little gentle persuasion with the bayonet drove the stone-throwers into the arms of the police on the lower road. The effect was excellent; no casualties were reported, though it was rumoured that many young men of the valley found that sitting down was accompanied with a certain amount of discomfort for several days. As a general instruction the soldiers had been warned that if obliged to use their bayonets they should only be applied to that portion of the body traditionally held by trainers of youth to be reserved for punishment. . . .

Sir Nevil Macready, *Annals of an Active Life*, 1924

D In August 1911 there was a national railway strike.

. . . The Home Secretary, Mr Winston Churchill, kept the Government's promise to the companies by planting troops at the stations throughout the country. The dangerous method of attempting to overawe the men by a display of armed force was openly indulged in, and it was obvious to every observer that the most repressive measures would be adopted by the authorities if the slightest excuse was given. . . .

Rowland Kenney, *Man and Rails*, 1913

E Keir Hardie describes the events at Llanelli.

. . . A train was stopped by a crowd of strikers squatting down on the line in front of it. Some troops quartered at the station rushed up at the double, and lined up on both sides of the engine. Before they got there . . . a striker had boarded . . . the engine and drawn the fire, and so the engine was effectively disabled from proceeding. But for the presence of the soldiers nothing more

Troops escort vehicles through Liverpool during the railway strike in August 1911

Lloyd George was Chancellor of the Exchequer at this time

would have happened. Some boys and youths did pelt stones at the soldiers, and one of them was struck. Mr Lloyd George spoke of what happened as being undoubtedly a 'very great riot', and described the engine driver as lying bleeding and helpless from the violence of the mob. This, however, was all imagination. . . . The train was standing in a deep cutting, and the official story is that stones were coming in showers from both sides. Now, not one pane of glass in the carriage windows was broken, not one passenger was hurt or molested, in fact they were looking out of the windows, no civilian was struck, no property was damaged; there was no riot. But the officer in charge ordered the people to disperse; he gave them one minute in which to do so; at the end of the minute he ordered five rounds to be fired which killed two men outright and wounded four others. John Johns, one of the murdered men, was sitting on the garden wall of his own house in shirt and trousers, looking on; the other was also in his garden at the top of the railway embankment.

No one has ever alleged that either of them threw stones or took any part in what little stone throwing there was. Presumably, however, they made good targets, and so were picked off. For the troops are not to fire at random. They are not to use blank cartridges, even by way of warning, they are not to fire over the heads of the people, they are not to fire at the legs of the crowd; their instructions were to make every shot tell, they were to shoot to kill. . . .

J. Keir Hardie, *Killing No Murder*, 1911

1 Both these incidents involve the use of 'blacklegs'.
(a) What is a blackleg?
(b) Why were the strikers determined to intimidate them?
(c) Who was the 'blackleg' in source E?

2 Read sources A, B and C.
(a) The Chief Constable of Glamorgan wanted troops. Does source A suggest that they were really needed?
(b) Why did Churchill send more police rather than troops?
(c) To what extent does Macready's evidence (Source C) support Churchill's assessment of the situation?

3 Does source C tell us anything about Macready's attitude towards the strikers and towards the use of troops? Explain your answer.

4 Refer to sources B, D and E.
(a) After reading sources B how can you explain the Home Secretary's actions in source D?
(b) To what extent does source E justify the fears of Churchill expressed in his letter to the King?

5 After you have read source E use the clues it contains to reconstruct the incident from the viewpoint of an anti-trade union newspaper. Make up a suitable headline and write a newspaper report of the event.

6 Refer to sources C, D and E.
(a) How do the writers of sources D and E make their attitude to the strike and to the use of troops clear to the reader? Explain your answer and refer to the sources.
(b) These three sources present three very different impressions of the use of troops. Which account would a historian find the most useful? Which do you think is the most accurate?

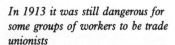

In 1913 it was still dangerous for some groups of workers to be trade unionists

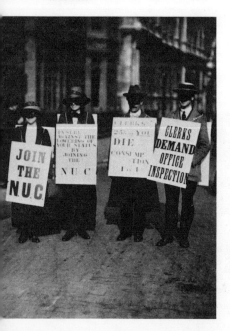

The 'Workshop of the World'

14 Industry and trade 1700–1870

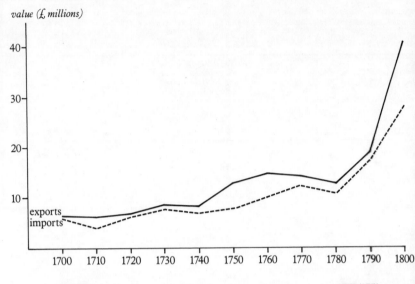

value (£ millions)

Table 1   English imports and exports, 1700–1800

Table 2   Trading customers
(a) Where exports went. Exports are articles manufactured in Britain and sold to customers abroad

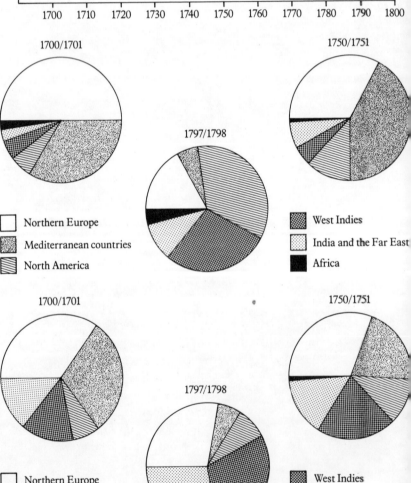

(b) Where the imports came from

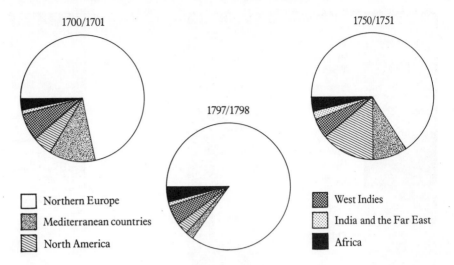

) What happened to re-exports. Re-exports were mainly tropical foodstuffs produced in the West Indies and the Far East, e.g. tea, sugar, coffee, tobacco. Under the Navigation Laws the goods grown in the colonies had to pass through Britain before they were sold to foreign customers

1700/1701

1750/1751

1797/1798

- ☐ Northern Europe
- ▦ Mediterranean countries
- ▨ North America
- ▦ West Indies
- ⬚ India and the Far East
- ■ Africa

The effect of the Navigation Laws. All trade from and to the colonies had to pass through British ports. The Navigation Acts of 1651, 1660 and 1662 gave protection and encouragement to British shipping. All European countries protected their empires and their trade in this way

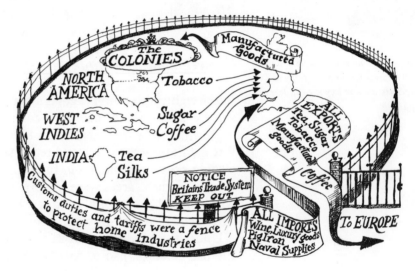

1 Study Table 1.

(a) What does it tell you about British trade between 1700 and 1800?

(b) What developments in the textile industry coincided with the steep rise in exports after 1780?

2 Study the pie graphs in Table 2.

(a) Which areas became less important as export markets during the eighteenth century?

(b) Which areas became more important as export markets?

(c) How do you explain the increasing importance of North America?

(d) What is the link between 2(b) and 2(c), between imports and re-exports?

(e) Historians write about a 'commercial revolution' in the eighteenth century. What do you think they mean?

3 Study Table 3 on the next page.

Describe the changes in exports and explain why these took place.

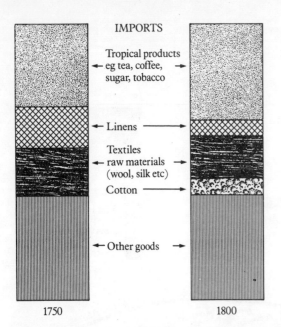

IMPORTS

Tropical products
← eg tea, coffee,
sugar, tobacco →

← Linens →

Textiles
← raw materials →
(wool, silk etc)

Cotton

← Other goods →

1750   1800

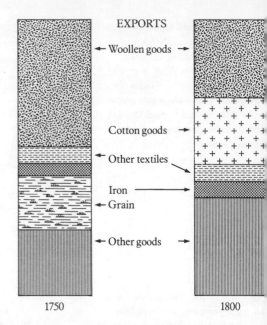

EXPORTS

← Woollen goods →

Cotton goods →

← Other textiles →

Iron
← Grain

← Other goods →

1750   1800

Table 3   The commodities imported and exported. Imported tropical products were re-exported in large quantities

Government and trade in the eighteenth century

In the eighteenth century, government encouraged trade by protection and by extending the country's colonial power.

During the Seven Years War (1756–63) the war policy of William Pitt the Elder was to destroy French sea-power and to capture French trading posts and colonies in India and the West Indies. Colonies and control in these areas were important because they supplied Europe with tropical agricultural products like tea, coffee, sugar and tobacco which could not be grown in cooler climates.

Under the Navigation Laws of 1651, 1660 and 1662 products from English colonies, had to be sent to England before they could be re-exported to Europe. This re-export of tropical products became an important element in British trade. Sugar refining and tobacco-curing became important industries in the importing ports of Glasgow, Liverpool, Bristol and London. The colonists were also forced to buy all the goods they needed from Britain. Since all goods travelling between the colonies and Britain had to be carried in British ships, as trade increased so did the merchant fleet. Shipbuilders prospered.

Government policies, however, could have adverse effects. The outbreak of the American War of Independence in 1774 caused a decline in trade which lasted into the 1780s. The American colonies had become important markets for British exports, and merchants feared that, once Americans were free to choose, British trade would suffer. When the war ended, however, Americans still bought British. Exports of woollens, cottons and other goods grew rapidly as the population of the United States expanded. By the end of the century the United States was the largest single export market for manufactured goods.

During the long French wars after 1793 Britain's export markets in

Europe were disrupted. After 1806 Napoleon's Continental System, which closed ports to British goods, was a serious threat. New markets were found in South America which compensated for the losses in Europe. The Royal Navy's control of the seas enabled merchants to prosper and to escape the worst effects of economic warfare.

Why overseas trade was important

Home demand provided a limited market for manufactured goods. Overseas trade increased that market. The rapid growth of a mass-production cotton industry at the end of the eighteenth century would not have been possible if extensive export markets had not existed. It was the 1820s before the British cotton industry faced realistic competition from European rivals, and they never threatened the vast market for British cottons in British India.

Trade also gave access to essential raw materials. The producers of these raw materials in the West Indies and in the southern United States (raw cotton) earned cash which they spent on British textiles and other manufactured goods.

Ports developed. London was always the most important but the three West Coast ports of Liverpool, Bristol and Glasgow benefited from the growth of the Atlantic trade.

	Population in 1700	*Population in 1801*
Bristol	20 000	64 000
Liverpool	6 000	88 358
Glasgow	12 600	83 769

Bristol docks in the early eighteenth century

In the 1720s when Daniel Defoe visited Liverpool he sensed that it was already mounting a successful challenge to Bristol.

The town now has an opulent, flourishing and increasing trade, not rivalling Bristol, in the trade to Virginia, and the English island colonies in America only, but it is in a fair way to exceed and eclipse it, by increasing in every way in wealth and shipping. They trade round the whole island, send ships to Norway, to Hamburgh, and to the Baltick, and also to Holland and Flanders; so that, in a word, they are almost become like the Londoners, universal merchants.

Glasgow, he learnt, sent

near fifty sail of ships every year to Virginia, New England, and other English colonies in America, and are every year increasing.

Trade also helped to finance industry. Banks and insurance companies set up originally to meet merchant needs were readily adapted to help industry. Profits made in trade were invested in the new industries. The Coalbrookdale ironworks was financed by the Bristol merchant families of Campion and Goldney. Richard Crawshay and Anthony Bacon, who invested in the Cyfarthfa Ironworks, were successful London merchants.

Using the evidence: the slave trade

The profits of the slave trade did not directly show up in the trade statistics, but it was an essential part of the colonial trade. Defoe summed it up:

No African trade, no negroes; no negroes, no sugars, gingers, indigoes etc.; no sugars etc. no islands; no islands no continent; no continent, no trade. . . .

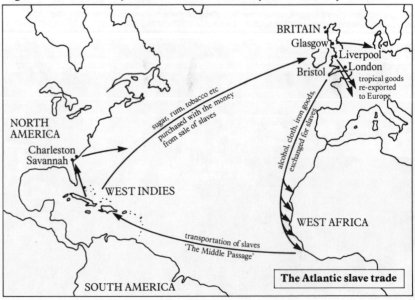

The Atlantic slave trade at the end of the eighteenth century. Defoe's comment, made at the beginning of the century, still seemed true. The rise of the cotton industry, however, made tropical products less important to the national economy. Even in Liverpool fewer ships were engaged in the slave trade

Merchants from Liverpool, Bristol and Glasgow were involved in the slave trade. In 1792 there were 133 Liverpool ships engaged in it. By this time, however, the trade was already being criticised by the Quakers, the Evangelicals and their supporters in Parliament.

William Wilberforce undertook the parliamentary leadership of the campaign to abolish the slave trade in 1787. The abolitionists had collected evidence of brutality and atrocities committed on the slaving ships. Abolition became a moral and religious campaign, but there was great opposition to it. The parliamentary struggle that began in 1788 did not end until 1807 when the slave trade was finally abolished.

Wilberforce was a leading member of the Evangelical group within the Church of England. He was a close friend of William Pitt, the Prime Minister who encouraged him in his anti-slave campaign

A *On the slave ships*

(i) The evidence of an African slave:

. . . . I was soon put down under the decks, and there I received such a salutation in my nostrils as I had never experienced in my life: so that with the loathsomeness of the stench and crying together, I became so sick and low that I was not able to eat, nor had I the least desire to taste anything. I now wished for the last friend, death, to relieve me; but soon, to my grief, two of the whitemen offered me eatables, and on my refusing to eat, one of them held me fast by the hands and laid me across . . . the windlass, and tied my feet while the other flogged me severely. I had never experienced anything of this kind before, and although, not being used to the water, I naturally feared that element . . . nevertheless could I have got over the nettings I would have jumped over the side, but I could not; and besides, the crew used to watch us very closely who were not chained down to the decks. . . .

windlass: a mechanism for hoisting or lowering the anchor

The closeness of the hold and the heat of the climate, added to the number in the ship, which was so crowded that each had scarcely room to turn himself, almost suffocated us. . . . The air soon became unfit for respiration from a variety of loathsome smells, and brought on a sickness among the slaves, of which many died. . . .

Olaudah Equiano, *Interesting Narrative of the Life of Olaudah Equiano, written by himself*, 1789

Wilberforce's model of a slave ship showing how the slaves were packed into the hold

rooms: spaces, holds

(ii) James Penny had made eleven slaving voyages. This was his evidence to Parliament in 1789.

. . . they are comfortably lodged in Rooms fitted up for them, which are washed and fumigated with Vinegar or Lime Juice every Day. . . . The Men Slaves are fettered when they first come on Board . . . but during the Passage, if they appear reconciled to their Condition, their Fetters are gradually taken off. The Women, Youths, and Children are always at Liberty, and are kept in separate Apartments. The Whole of the slaves are brought upon Deck every Day, when the weather permits, about Eight o'clock. If the weather is sultry, and there appears the least Perspiration upon their Skins, when they come upon Deck, there are Two Men attending with Cloths to rub them perfectly dry, and another to give them a little Cordial. The Surgeon, or his Mate, also generally attends to wash their Mouths with Vinegar or Lime Juice, in order to prevent Scurvey. (after being fed) They are then supplied with Pipes and Tobacco. . . . They are amused with Instruments of Music peculiar to their own Country, with which he provided them. . . . The Women are supplied with Beads . . . and the utmost attention is paid to keeping up their Spirits. . . . Particular Attention is paid to them, when sick, and the most airy Part of the Ship is appropriated for the Hospital. . . .

(iii) Another captain explained why the slaves were well treated.

If any of the slaves die, the surgeon loses his head money (usually one shilling for each slave sold) and the Captain his commission; if the slaves are bought in bad order to market they average low, and the officers' privilege slaves, which are generally paid them on an average with the cargo, are of less value to them.

(iv) John Newton had been a slave-ship captain. He became an Evangelical clergyman and an abolitionist. His account contradicts Penny:

. . . . in the day time they are upon deck; and as they are brought up, by pairs, a chain is put through a ring upon their irons, and this is likewise locked down to the ring-bolts, which are fastened at certain intervals upon the deck. . . .

I have seen them sentenced to unmerciful whippings, continued till the poor creatures have not had power to groan under their misery, and hardly a sign of life has remained . . .

With our ships, the great object is, to be full. . . . Their lodging-rooms below the deck which are three, (for the men, the boys, and the women,) besides a place for the sick, are sometimes more than five feet high, and sometimes less, and this height is divided towards the middle, for the Slaves lie in two rows, one above the other, on each side of the ship, close to each other, like books upon a shelf. . . .

. . . Let it be observed, that the poor creatures, thus cramped for want of room, are likewise in irons . . . which makes it difficult for them to turn or move, to attempt either to rise or to lie down, without hurting themselves or each other. . . .

. . . The ship, in which I was Mate, left the coast with Two Hundred and Eighteen Slaves on board; and though we were not much affected by epidemical disorders, I find, by my journal of that voyage, that we buried Sixty-two on our passage to South-Carolina. . . .

John Newton, *Thoughts upon the African Slave Trade*, 1788

The slaver's means of controlling his cargo

epidemical disorders: infectious diseases that spread quickly

B *The abolitionist argument*

John Wesley on the slave trade:

John Wesley was the founder of Methodism

I would to God it may never be found more: that we may never more steal and sell our brethren like beasts; never murder them by thousands. Oh, may this worse than Mohammedan, worse than pagan abomination be removed from us for ever. Never was anything such a reproach to England, since it was a nation, as having a hand in this infernal traffic.

It cannot be, that either war, or contract, can given any man such a property in another as he has in his sheep or oxen. Much less is it possible, that any child of man should ever be born a slave. Liberty is the right of every human creature. . . .

John Wesley, *Thoughts on Slavery*, 1788

C *The opposition to abolition*

(i) The abolition of the slave trade would destroy the West Indies Trade. What were they about to do? Did they mean to swallow all the property of the planters in order to gratify a humane disposition towards the Africans? Before they were humane to these, he thought they should be tender of their own subjects whom they had seduced to hazard their property in this trade.

seduced: persuaded
to hazard: to risk

Mr Molineaux in the parliamentary debate of 1789

(ii) If abolition . . . shall take place, our interest in the West-India islands must be at an end; seventy millions of property will wear away with time, and be sunk at last; the revenue will suffer an annual diminuation of three millions at least; the price of sugar, which is now become a necessary article of life, must be immediately enhanced . . . the necessity of additional taxes may puzzle the minister, divide the legislature, and distress the people. . . .

diminuation: reduction

William Beckford, *A Descriptive Account of the Island of Jamaica*, 1790

1 Equiano, Penny and Newton give three different accounts.
   (a) How do Equiano and Newton agree in their opinion of conditions on a slave ship?
   (b) Compare the accounts of Equiano and Penny. How do they contradict each other?
   (c) How do you explain the differences between the three accounts? Which is the most accurate? Give reasons for the choice you have made.
2 Read sources B and C.
   (a) What are Wesley's arguments against the slave trade? Were they likely to convince supporters of the trade?
   (b) How do the arguments of Molineaux and Beckford differ from those of Wesley? How effective are they?
3 The opponents of abolition were often humane and religious men. So were many of the planters who owned slaves. How, then, do you explain their support for the trade?
4 Use all the sources, and others you may find, to write your own account of the slave trade.

The slave trade was abolished in 1807 but slaves in British colonies did not get their freedom until 1833.

Adam Smith and the idea of Free Trade

In 1776 Adam Smith's *An Inquiry into the Nature and Causes of the Wealth of Nations* was published. Smith argued that the state should allow businessmen complete freedom to increase wealth without any restriction on their activities. Total free enterprise would benefit the state. As the businessmen increased their profits, national wealth would grow.

The idea of *laissez-faire* sprang from this. In trade it was the belief in Free Trade. Smith denounced all restrictions on trade because they slowed down wealth-making, and even prevented it. Trade could only grow, he suggested, if all barriers and restrictions were removed and the merchant had the freedom to sell in any market and to buy raw materials in the cheapest.

This proposal was very attractive to British industrialists mainly because the Industrial Revolution had given Britain the capacity to mass-produce iron and cotton textiles for a world market in which there were no competitors.

William Pitt the Younger encouraged trade by his treaty with France in 1786. This gave the British manufacturers access to French markets which had previously been closed to them. In 1812 the newly-appointed Prime Minister, Lord Liverpool, remarked:

The less commerce and manufactures were meddled with the more they were likely to prosper.

The battle for Free Trade

1 The Corn Law of 1815

The Corn Law of 1815 gave protection to the farmers and landowners from cheap imported continental grain. The cotton manufacturers in Manchester regarded this as an unnecessary barrier to trade. It prevented the European producers selling their grain to Britain and spending their profits on British goods. For the next thirty years the Corn Laws became the symbol of protectionism that the free-traders wished to remove. Industrialists and landowners lined up on different sides of the argument.

Despite this disagreement, progress was made. Many officials at the Board of trade were free-traders, and many of Lord Liverpool's ministers wanted freer trade.

In the budgets of 1824 and 1825 many high duties were reduced. William Huskisson, the president of the Board of Trade, eased the Navigation Laws to allow the colonies to trade directly with other countries. By the Reciprocity Act he was given the authority to negotiate commercial treaties with other countries in which there would be an agreed reduction of tariffs and controls. He also modified the Corn Laws.

2 The Anti-Corn Law League

The depression of the late 1830s and the 1840s drew attention to the Corn Laws, which were blamed for maintaining high food prices. In 1838 the Anti-Corn Law League was founded with the sole aim of obtaining their repeal. Its supporters believed that Free Trade would end the series of economic crises that had ruined trade. Prosperity and full employment would create a buoyant home demand.

The working classes turned to Chartism and the reform of Parliament. Chartists distrusted the manufacturers who backed the League claiming that repeal of the Corn Laws would be an excuse to lower wages.

Even the membership card makes a propaganda point. What is it?

Allow the food and raw-material producers free access to British markets, argued the Leaguers, and they would buy the products of British industry in return. Large sums of money were contributed to League funds. One Liverpool merchant said:

He had gladly given his £100 for the next year to accomplish the objects of the League; he had hopes he was promoting his own individual good to no small extent by extending free trade principles; he was not ashamed to avow his belief, that his £100 subscription would bring him back a hundred times £100, if the objects of the League should be attended with success.

Until 1843 the League's headquarters were in Manchester. It became a wealthy and powerful organisation. Its propaganda was spread by lecturers and through newspapers it owned or subsidised. The new penny post was used to send pamphlets and leaflets to possible supporters. League candidates fought by-elections. Great fund-raising

In cartoon A (below) and B (right)

PAPA COBDEN TAKING MASTER ROBERT A FREE TRADE W[...]
Papa Cobden – "Come along, Master Robert, do step out."
Master Robert – "That's all very well, but you know I cannot go so fast a[...]

bazaars, selling specially-embroidered handkerchiefs and scarves or pottery stamped with slogans, created publicity. The League was the first modern pressure group and it pioneered many of the tactics that pressure groups still use.

After 1841 it was represented in Parliament by Richard Cobden. In 1843 he was joined by John Bright, a Quaker cotton manufacturer from Rochdale. These two men were the League's chief spokesmen. Both were eloquent and effective speakers. Cobden understood the emotions that words could arouse.

I think it is better to use the word bread-tax than the corn law. A bread-tax is a good term to fix upon our opponents.

The activities of the League and the speeches of Cobden and Bright, prepared the way for repeal. In 1845 the Whig politicians, who depended on the votes of middle-class industrialists and traders, declared in its favour.

3 Sir Robert Peel and the Corn Laws

Sir Robert Peel became Prime Minister in 1841. He was leader of the Conservatives, the party of the landowners and the farmers. He was determined to solve the economic problems that caused unemployment, distress and Chartism.

To do this he adopted Free Trade policies. The main justification for tariffs was that they raised revenue. Peel discovered that less than 20 items produced 95 per cent of this revenue. In 1842 he reduced all duties on imported raw materials to 5 per cent and on foreign

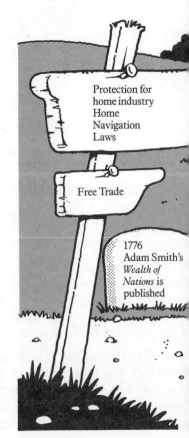

Protection for home industry
Home
Navigation
Laws

Free Trade

1776
Adam Smith's
Wealth of
Nations is
published

on Peel's difficulties in 1845

MAID OF ALL WORK IN TROUBLE.
"Well, Richard Cobden! They've been and given me
warning, and I shall lose my place thro' talking to you!"

manufactured goods to 20 per cent or less, introducing a three-year income tax to replace lost revenue. The duties on 750 items were affected. Three years later (1845) he renewed his income tax, reduced duties on sugar, timber and coffee, abolished all duties on exports and on imported raw materials.

However, Peel would not touch the Corn Laws. He knew he would be opposed by members of his own party. In 1842 he had modified them but many Conservative MPs were suspicious of him. There is a story that in 1845, after listening to a speech from Cobden, he screwed up his notes, turned to his neighbour and said: 'You must answer this for I cannot.' Peel had probably decided that repeal was inevitable some years before.

Realising the consequences, he did not want to be the minister who abolished the Corn Laws. In 1845, however, his hand was forced by the failure of the potato crop in Ireland and the poor corn harvest in England, both of which increased the need for imported grain. Using the Irish famine as his excuse he pushed the repeal of the Corn Laws through Parliament in 1846. Denounced by his own backbenchers, he was forced from office and the Conservatives split into two hostile groups.

1815
The Corn Law gives extra protection to British farmers

1838
Anti-Corn Law League is formed. Richard Cobden is its leading figure

1846
Irish Famine. Repeal of the Corn Laws

1849
Repeal of the Navigation Laws

86
illiam Pitt
e Younger
ake a trade
eaty with
ance

1824/1825
Duties on import of raw materials and consumer goods reduced. Prohibition of silk imports ended (budgets of 1824, 1825). William Huskisson relaxes Navigation Laws to give colonies greater freedom. Makes trade treaties with foreign countries.

1842/1845
Budgets 1842, 1845 reduced and abolished a mass of import and export duties.
Income tax introduced, 1842, to replace lost customs revenue.
Sir Robert Peel is Prime Minister.

1853/1860
Gladstone completes the move to free trade in his budgets 1853, 1860. Only 48 revenue duties remained.
1860 Free Trade treaty with France.

FREE TRADE ROAD

Questions

1 The Anti-Corn Law League believed in propaganda. Some of the points
made against the Corn Laws are referred to in the text. Make a note c
them. Here are some more.

> He had heard that tax called by a multitude of names. Some designated it a
> a 'protection'; but it was a tax after all, and he would call it nothing else. Th
> bread tax was levied principally upon the working classes. . . . It compelle
> the working classes to pay 40 per cent more, that is, a higher price than the
> should pay if there was a free trade in corn. . . .
>
> > Cobden's maiden speech in the House of Commons, 184

> We believe that the extension of commerce consequent on Free Trade wi
> knit nations together in bonds of fellowship too strong to be broken for th
> gratification of . . . warriors. . . .
>
> > *The League*, 13 July 184

Design a poster for the League to emphasise one or more of these
points.

2 Look at the two cartoons.
 (a) In cartoon A: (i) Where is Papa Cobden taking Master Robert?
 (ii) What is the meaning of Master Robert's reply? (iii) Is this an
 accurate view of Cobden's influence and of Peel's attitude?
 (b) What, according to Cartoon B, is Peel's problem?

The Great Exhibition, 1851

The exhibition was opened on 1 May 1851. During its 140 days ther
were over six million visitors. On the one shilling days, Monday t
Thursday, 4 400 000 paid their admission. In the last week of th
Exhibition attendances reached 100 000 a day. It was a great spectacle
Landowners took their tenants to London by special train, employer
sent their workers. Many came on special railway excursions from al
parts of the country.

The crowds behaved themselves remarkably well. The tensions o
the previous decade and of Chartism had vanished with renewe
prosperity. On the 'shilling days' workmen flocked to the machiner
section.

> Here every other man you rub against is habited in a corduroy jacket, or
> blouse, or leathern gaiters; and round every object more wonderful than th
> rest, the people press, two and three deep, with their heads stretched out
> watching intently the operations of the moving mechanisms. You see th
> farmers, their dusty hats telling of the distance they have come, with thei
> mouths wide agape, leaning over the bars to see the self-acting mules a
> work. . . .
>
> > Henry Mayhew, *1851 or the Adventur*
> > *of Mr and Mrs Sandboys*, 185

Visitors marvelled at the exhibits, gaped at the Red Indians and Africans also on show, and went away convinced of Britain's superiority. No other nation rivalled the machinery or the skill of the first industrial nation. It was a suitable beginning to twenty years of rising prosperity when Britain was the undisputed 'Workshop of the World'.

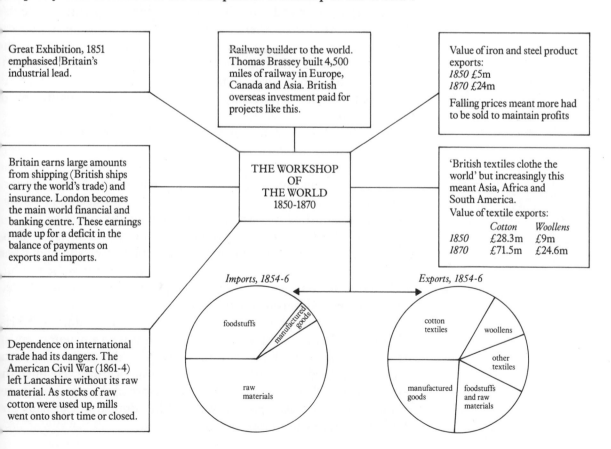

Great Exhibition, 1851 emphasised Britain's industrial lead.

Railway builder to the world. Thomas Brassey built 4,500 miles of railway in Europe, Canada and Asia. British overseas investment paid for projects like this.

Value of iron and steel product exports:
1850 £5m
1870 £24m

Falling prices meant more had to be sold to maintain profits

Britain earns large amounts from shipping (British ships carry the world's trade) and insurance. London becomes the main world financial and banking centre. These earnings made up for a deficit in the balance of payments on exports and imports.

THE WORKSHOP
OF
THE WORLD
1850-1870

'British textiles clothe the world' but increasingly this meant Asia, Africa and South America.
Value of textile exports:

	Cotton	Woollens
1850	£28.3m	£9m
1870	£71.5m	£24.6m

Dependence on international trade had its dangers. The American Civil War (1861-4) left Lancashire without its raw material. As stocks of raw cotton were used up, mills went onto short time or closed.

Imports, 1854-6

foodstuffs
manufactured goods
raw materials

Exports, 1854-6

cotton textiles
woollens
other textiles
foodstuffs and raw materials
manufactured goods

Iron and steel after 1850

Until 1850 steel was made by either the cementation process or the crucible process. The quality of steel from cementation furnaces was very uneven. Crucible steel was of good quality and was preferred by the Sheffield cutlery manufacturers. Unfortunately steel could only be produced in small quantities and it was therefore expensive.

Henry Bessemer was a successful inventor. During the Crimean War (1854–6) he was designing new artillery gun barrels. A material stronger than iron was required. In 1856 he revealed that he had succeeded in mass-producing steel.

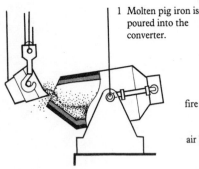

1 Molten pig iron is poured into the converter.

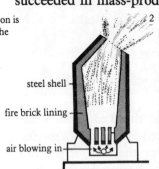

2 Oxygen is blown through the molten iron. The colour of the flame indicated the stage the process was at. This lasted twenty minutes to half an hour. The force of the blast blew about 18% of the metal out of the converter. A mixture of iron, manganese and carbon was added.

steel shell

fire brick lining

air blowing in

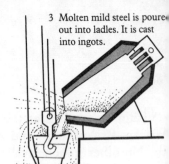

3 Molten mild steel is poured out into ladles. It is cast into ingots.

The Bessemer converter

Initially there was great interest. Converters were installed at the Dowlais ironworks and other ironmasters obtained permission to use the process. At Dowlais there was failure. The steel crumbled and was useless. Bessemer investigated and eventually discovered that if the iron ore from which the pig iron had been made contained phosphorus then it could not be converted into good steel. Most British iron ore contained phosphorus, the only exception being the haematite ores of Cumberland.

After this discovery the iron industry lost interest and in 1858 Bessemer set up his own steel works in Sheffield. Converters were slowly adopted by other concerns. In 1860 John Brown of Sheffield began to roll steel rails and in 1863 the London and North Western Railway began to replace its wrought-iron rails with steel. The railway company established its own Bessemer steel works at Crewe.

In 1867 William Siemens patented his open-hearth steelmaking process. This had many advantages over the converter. Although it was a slower process, the operator could control the quality of the product and scrap iron could be used. By 1900 over two-thirds of British steel was being made in open-hearth furnaces.

The problem of phosphoric ores was solved by Sidney Gilchrist Thomas and Percy Gilchrist in 1875. Thomas was an amateur chemist. At a lecture he heard the remark that there would be a fortune for the man who enabled steelmakers to use the phosphoric ores. He lined the converter with dolomite limestone. This absorbed the phosphorus out of the iron. This 'basic' process was rapidly adopted in Germany and the United States but more slowly in Britain.

The uses of steel

Steel was a superior material to wrought iron but it was 1878 before steel rails were cheaper. Railway companies then changed to steel. In 1877 Lloyds accepted steel-built ships for insurance purposes. There was a boom in the production of steel plates as wrought iron was replaced in ship-construction.

New locations

Two major new ironmaking and ironworking areas emerged after 1850. The haematite ores of Cumberland encouraged the development of Barrow. There were eight blast furnaces in 1866, eleven in 1867 and seventeen converters in 1872. Barrow's population grew accordingly:

1861   3135
1871   19 000
1881   48 000

The other boom town was on the East Coast – Middlesbrough. Rich in ore, the Cleveland Hills became the centre of a vigorous iron industry. The one blast furnace of 1850 had become 50 by 1860. There was a vast complex of foundries and puddling furnaces.

The great Middlesbrough concern of Bolckow and Vaughan installed converters and the first successful trial of the Gilchrist–Thomas process was at their works. Again, the population figures for Middlesborough reflect these industrial developments:

1851   7 631
1861   18 892
1871   39 284
1881   55 934

Neither district was on a coalfield.

Before the railway system was developed to its present extent it was always considered that the ironstone should be carried to the coal, but partly by increased facilities of communication, and partly by improved manufacture, it has in many cases been found more advantageous to carry the coal as coke, to the iron ore.

E. Riley, On the Manufacture of Iron, 1862

Ships and shipbuilding

The first working steamboat in Britain was William Symington's *Charlotte Dundas*. Built for work on the Forth–Clyde canal it had to be withdrawn because the canal company feared its wash would undermine the banks. Henry Bell's *Comet* (1812) was the first commercially successful steamship operating on the Clyde between Glasgow and Greenock.

All early steamships had paddles. In 1836 Francis Petit Smith patented the screw propeller.

Brunel's *Great Western* demonstrated that steamships could operate on the transatlantic passenger routes. His *Great Britain*, launched in 1843, was the first iron ocean-going ship. The use of iron plates enabled larger ships to be constructed.

At first steamships could not compete with sail because the engines available were inefficient and wasteful. Too much coal had to be carried at the expense of cargo. However, the development of the compound engine (1854), which used the steam twice, and later of the triple expansion engine, resulted in great fuel savings. Steamships were less dependent on coaling stations and could compete with sail on all routes even to Australia. The opening of the Suez Canal in 1869 allowed steamships to reach India and China.

British shipyards supplied the world with the new iron and steel steamships. In 1892 81.7 per cent of ship tonnage launched was built in Britain, and Britain exported a greater tonnage than was built in German and American yards combined.

Brunel's Great Britain *was the first iron ocean-going ship and the first to have a screw propeller instead of paddle-wheels*

Launched in 1858, Brunel's Great Eastern *was the largest vessel on the seas. It was too big to be profitable as a liner and ended its day laying undersea telegraph cables*

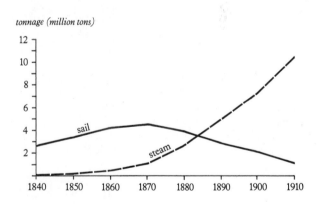

A busy scene in London docks, 1893, but sailing ships still predominate

The rise of steam – British steam and sail ships

	No. of sail-powered ships	No. of steam-powered ships
1840	21 883	771
1850	24 797	1187
1860	25 663	1524
1870	23 189	3178
1880	19 938	5247
1890	14 181	7139
1900	10 773	9209
1910	9090	12 000

1 By which date were there more steamships than sailing ships?
2 By which date was the tonnage of steamships greater than that of sailing ships?
3 How many ships of each type were there at the end of that decade?
4 What can you deduce about the capacity of the average sailing ship and of the average steamship?

Index

agricultural shows 23, 46
agricultural revolution 24
agriculture 22–41, 42–54, 134, 149, 160
  early eighteenth century 24–6
  new methods 26–31
  enclosure 32–41
  depression 42–5
  'high farming' 46–8
  competition 48–50
  'great depression' 51–4
Allen, William 226, 227, 228, 229
Amalgamated Society of Engineers 226, 238
Amalgamated Society of Railway Servants 231, 238
Annals of Agriculture 31
Anti-Corn Law League 253–5
Applegarth, Robert 226, 227, 228, 229
Arch, Joseph 231
Arkwright, Richard 62, 68–73
Ashley, Lord 169, 177, 178, 182, 184

Bakewell, Robert 28–9
Bamford, Samuel 199, 203, 204
banks 248
Barton Aqueduct 127, 128
Bell, Henry 259
Bertollet, C. L. 67
Besant, Annie 16–17, 233
Bessemer, Henry 258
Bessemer process 258
Birmingham 15, 16, 116, 132, 198, 206
Birmingham Canal 129
birth rate 10, 11, 12, 13, 16–17
Blanketeers, march of 198, 203
Blenkinsop, John 98, 139
Blincoe, Robert 170–1
Board of Agriculture 31–2
Booth, Charles 54
Boulton and Watt Company 65, 92, 96, 103, 108, 110
Boulton, Matthew 84, 85, 108–9
Bradlaugh, Charles 16
Brandreth, Jeremiah 203
Brassey, Thomas 150, 162
Bridgewater, Duke of 66, 98, 127, 128, 130
Bridgewater Canal 98, 127, 128, 140
Bright, John 254
Brindley, James 127, 128, 129, 130
Bristol 12, 15, 144, 207, 246, 247–8, 249

Broadhurst, Henry 237
Brunel, Isambard Kingdom 144–5, 149–50, 260
Buddle, John 88, 89, 93
Burns, John 237, 238
Burt, Thomas 237

Caird, James, journalist 45, 48, 51
Canals 30, 66, 81, 98, 127–37, 159
canal construction 134, 135, 136, 137
'canal mania' 132
Carron 80
Cartwright, Edmund 64
Cartwright, William 191
cast iron 74, 76, 77, 81
Cato Street conspiracy 198
Chain, Sir Ernest 17
charcoal iron industry 75–6, 78
Chartism 190, 208–16, 226, 253, 256
chemical industry 67
child labour 95–6, 166–71, 172–6, 182–4
chimney sweeps 172
Churchill, Winston 240–1
clover 26, 27
Coalbrookdale 76, 77, 81, 248
coal mining 88–100, 128, 133
  accidents 88
  output 90–1, 158
  problems and solutions 92–9
Cobbett, William 42, 43, 44, 45, 199, 202, 203
Cobden, Richard 254, 255, 256
coke smelting 76–7, 78
Coke, Thomas, Earl of Leicester 22, 32, 43
Colling brothers 28
Combination Acts 218–19, 220–1
Conservative Party 254–5
Conspiracy and Protection of Property Act 1875: 230
Continental System 247
contraception 16–17
Cook, Thomas 160
Cooper, Thomas, (Chartist) 215
Corn Laws 42, 46, 198, 199, 252–5
Cort, Henry 79–80
cotton industry 56, 57, 60–68, 111, 112, 140, 172–3, 198, 247
Crawshay, Richard 80, 85–6, 248
Crewe 161, 162
Criminal Law Amendment Act 1871: 230, 231
Cromford, Derbyshire 62, 72

Crompton, Samuel 62
crop rotations 26–7, 32, 34
croppers 191–2, 193, 197
Curr, John 96
Cyfarthfa ironworks 80, 85–6, 248

Darby, Abraham I 76, 77
Darby, Abraham II 77, 78
Darby, Abraham III 81, 84, 117
Davy, Sir Humphrey 95
death rate 10, 11, 12–14, 16, 17
Defoe, Daniel 15, 24, 25, 26, 58, 172, 248
Derby, Lord, Prime Minister 1866–7 217
Disraeli, Benjamin 217, 230
dockers' strike 1889: 234–5
Doherty, John 222
domestic system 56, 57, 58–9, 172
Dowlais ironworks 85, 86–7

electoral system 200–1
Ellman, John 28
emigration 18
Employers and Workmen Act 1875: 231
Enclosure 32–41, 42
  process 33
  benefits 34, 37–8
  opposition 38–9
  and the poor 38–9, 40–1
  and small farmer 41
Enclosure Acts 32–3, 35
Engels, Friedrich 166

Factory Acts 186–8
  1802: 172
  1819: 176
  1833: 177–8, 209
  1844, 1847, 1850: 182
factory conditions 173–7
  1816 Report 173–6
  1831 Report 176–7
  1833 Royal Commission 177
factory inspectors 178, 179–81
factory system 59, 62, 63, 65, 81, 173
family size 16–17
farm labourers 43–5, 53–4
fertilisers 30, 46–7, 48
Fielden, John 182
firedamp 92–3
fishing ports 160
Fleming, Sir Alexander 17
Florey, Sir Howard 17
flying shuttle 60–1

free trade 49, 252–5
French Wars, 1793–1802, 1803–
1815: 34, 42, 198, 218, 247
Frost, John 212, 213, 214
fustian 58, 59

Gagging Acts, 1817: 198
gas workers 232–3
Gauge Act 145
George IV 207
Gilbert, John 128
Gilchrist, Percy 258
Gilchrist-Thomas process 258, 259
gin-drinking 13–14
Gladstone, Herbert 239
Gladstone, William Ewart 230
Glasgow 16, 66, 246, 247–8, 249
Graham, Sir James 182
Grand Junction Canal 132
Grand National Consolidated Trade
Union 224, 225, 226
Great Britain 260
Great Eastern 260
Great Exhibition, 1851: 47, 256–7
Great Northern Railway 148, 149
Great Western 260
Great Western Railway 144–5, 154,
161
Greg, Robert Hyde 165, 169, 170,
178–9
Greg, Samuel 66, 164, 166, 168, 169
Grey, Lord, Prime Minister 1830–
4: 206, 207

Hampden Clubs 198, 199
handloom weavers 63–4, 195–6, 197
Hardie, James Keir 237–8
Hargreaves, James 61, 62
Hedley, William 98, 139
Hetton Colliery Railway 99, 139
Hornby v. Close 228
Horner, Leonard, factory inspector
179–81
Horsfall, William 194
hosiery industry 58, 61, 62
hospitals 12–13
Hudson, George 146–8
Hume, Joseph 221–2
'hungry forties' 210, 226
Hunt, Henry 204
Huskisson, William 252
Hyndman, H. M. 237

immigration 19–20
Immigration Act 1962: 20
Independent Labour Party 238
income tax 198, 254–5
Irish famine 19, 255
iron industry 74–83, 84, 91, 158,
258–9

Junta 228–9, 231

Kay, John 60, 61
Kay, Robert 60–1
Kelly, William 63
King, Gregory 10

Labour Party 237–9
Labour Representation Committee
238–9
'laissez faire' 181, 252
Lawes, Sir John 46
ley farming 27
Litton Mill 170
Liverpool 15, 16, 66, 115, 128, 144,
246, 247–8, 249
Liverpool, Lord, Prime Minister,
1812–1827: 252
Liverpool-to-Manchester Railway
66–7, 139, 140–3, 144, 148, 152–
3, 159
Lloyd v. Wilkins 238
Locke, Joseph 144
Lombe brothers 59
London 14, 15, 16, 17, 24, 25, 59,
123, 198, 246, 247
London and North Western
Railway 148, 161, 258
London-to-Birmingham Railway
144, 148, 149
London Working Men's
Association 209, 210
Loveless, George 224–5
Lovett, William 209, 212
Luddism 190, 191–7

McAdam, John Loudon 120–1
MacDonald, Alexander 237
MacDonald, Ramsey 239
mail coaches 125, 126
Manchester 15, 16, 19, 59, 66, 111–
2, 115, 128, 203, 204, 215
Mann, Tom 235
Marx, Eleanor 233, 237
Marx, Karl 237
Meikle, Andrew 31
Melbourne, Lord, Prime Minister,
1836–41: 214, 225
Mellor, George, (Luddite) 192, 193,
194
Mersey and Irwell Navigation 128,
140
Metcalfe, John 120–1
Midland Railway 147
migration 14, 16
mine drainage 92, 104, 105
mine transport 95–9
mine ventilation 92–4
miners,
unions 226, 231
strikes 218, 226, 239–41

Mines Act, 1842: 184
mines inspectors 184

Napier, Sir Charles 211, 214
Navigation Laws 245, 246
navvies 150
Neilson, James 81
New Model Unions 226–7, 228
'New Unionism' 232–6
Newcomen, Thomas 105–6
Newcomen engines 76, 84, 92, 105–
7, 108
Newport rising 210, 212–14
newspapers 127, 162
Norfolk four-course rotation 26
north-east coalfield 90, 92, 93, 98,
115–6
Northern Star 212

Oastler, Richard 176, 177, 182
O'Connor, Feargus 211–12, 213,
214, 215, 216
Oliver the spy 198, 203
open-field farming 32, 34, 36
Osborne Judgement 239
Owen, Robert 174–5, 176, 222–4
Oxford Canal 129

Palmer, John 125
parliamentary reform 198, 199, 202,
206–8, 209–11, 216–17
pauper apprentices 166–71, 172
Pease, Edward 139
Peel, Sir Robert, Prime Minister
1841–6: 222, 254–6
penicillin 17
Pentridge Rising 198, 203
People's Charter 209, 210
Perceval, Spencer, Prime Minister,
1810–12: 196
'Peterloo' massacre 198, 203–5
Peto, Sir Samuel Morton 150, 162
Pickard, Joseph 109
Pitt, William the Elder 246
Pitt, William the Younger 252
Place, Francis 221–2
Political Register 202
Political Union 206
Poor Law Amendment Act, 1834:
42, 209
poor rates 39, 40, 43
population 10–18, 24, 34, 46, 91
growth 10–15, 16–17
distribution 15–16, 17
age structure 18
postal service 162
Potteries 114, 115, 129, 130
power loom 63–4, 196
Poynton, Cheshire 47, 100–1
prices, grain 34, 42, 46, 49, 190, 219
'puddling and rolling' 79–80

Quarry Bank Mill, Styal 102–3, 164–70

Race Relations Act, 1966: 20
Railway Act, 1844: 154
railway gauge 139, 144–5
railway locomotives 98–9, 139, 142–3
'railway mania' 145–6
railways 46, 66–7, 81, 91, 97–9, 100–1, 136, 137, 138–62
  opposition to 141, 148–9
  construction 141, 142, 143, 149–51
  development 144–6
  amalgamations 147–8
  travel by 152–7
  effects 158–62
Rainhill Trials 142–3
Rawfolds Mill 191
Reform Acts, 1832: 207, 208, 209
  1867: 217
  1918: 217
  1928: 217
river transport 114, 115
roads 97, 114–5, 116–22, 128, 158–9
Rocket 143
Roebuck, John 108
Rothamsted research station 46
Rowntree, Seebohm 54
Royal Agricultural Society 46
Royal Commission on Trade Unions 228–9

Sadler, Matthew 176, 177
safety lamp 88–9, 95
Sankey Brook Canal 98, 128
Savery, Thomas 104–5
Scotland 10, 80, 91, 132
Secret Ballot Act, 1872: 217
selective breeding 28–9, 32, 34
Seven Years War, 1756–63: 246
Shaftesbury, Seventh Earl of, see Ashley
sheep shearing festivals 22–3, 32
'Sheffield Outrages' 228
shipbuilding 260–1
Sidmouth, Lord, Home Secretary 205
Siemens, William 258
silk industry 59
Six Acts 198
slave trade 248–51
smallpox 12
Smeaton, John 108
Smith, Adam 252

Smith, Francis Petit 260
Social Democratic Federation 237
South America 247
Spa Fields meetings, 1816: 198, 202
spinning jenny 61–2
spinning mule 62
Staffordshire and Worcestershire Canal 129
stage coaches 121, 123–7, 143, 158–9
steam engines 48, 49, 65, 77, 78, 84, 92, 96, 104–9, 110–12
steam-power 65–6, 91, 104–13
steamships 259–61
steel 82, 258–9
Stephens, James Rayner, (Chartist) 209
Stephenson, George 95, 98, 99, 139, 140, 141, 143, 144, 145
Stephenson, Robert 143, 144, 149
stocking knitters 195, 197, 203
Stockton-to-Darlington Railway 99, 138–9
strikes 219–21, 226, 227, 231, 233, 234–5, 239–42
Strutt, Jedediah 61, 62, 66
Suez Canal 260
Swindon 161
Swing riots 190
Symington, William 259

Taff Vale case 238
Telford, Thomas 81, 120–1, 125, 136
Ten Hours' Movement 176–7, 182
  opposition to 178–9
Tennant, Charles 67
textiles 56–9
  see also: cotton industry, silk industry, woollen industry
Thomas, Sidney Gilchrist 258
Thorne, Will 232–3, 235, 236, 237
Tillett, Ben 234–5, 237
tithes 33, 43
Tolpuddle Martyrs 224–6
Tory Party 206, 207
towns 14, 68, 91
  growth of 16
Townshend, Lord Charles 26, 30
trade 56, 61, 244–251, 257
trade clubs 218
Trade Disputes Act, 1906: 239
Trade Union Act, 1825: 222
Trade Union Act, 1871: 230
Trade Union Act, 1913: 239
Trade Union Congress 229–31, 237, 238

trade unions 190, 218–36, 238, 239–42
transport 12, 24, 46, 49, 66, 76, 90, 97–100, 114–137, 138–161
Trent and Mersey Canal 129, 132
Trevithick, Richard 98, 139
Triple Alliance 240
Tull, Jethro 30
turnips 26, 27
turnpike trusts 97, 116–22

unemployment 198, 199, 206, 237, 238
United States of America 49, 246–7, 258, 260

vaccination 17

wages 198, 211,
  farm labourers 43, 45, 53, 54
  weavers 64
  ironworkers 86
  children 170, 172, 173
Wales 17, 85–7, 91, 133
water frame 62, 63, 70
water-power 62, 63, 65, 66, 76, 77, 102–4, 110, 112, 166
water wheels 102
Watt, James 84, 85, 107–9
Webb, Jonas 28
Wedgwood, Josiah 117, 126–7, 129, 130
welfare state 17
Wellington, Duke of 207, 216
Wesley, John 251
West Indies 246, 247, 251
West Midlands 74–5, 91, 92, 116
West Riding of Yorkshire 25, 57, 58–9, 66, 111
Weston, Richard 26
Whig Party 206–7
Wilberforce, William 249
Wilkinson, John 84–5, 108, 117
William IV 207
Wilson, Benjamin, (Chartist) 211, 215
wool 51, 52
woollen industry 56, 57–9, 66, 110, 111
working conditions,
  textile mills 172–6
  mines 182–4
Worsley 128
wrought iron 74, 75, 77, 79, 80

Young, Arthur, journalist 22, 26, 29, 31–2, 34, 40–1, 119

Acknowledgements

The author and publishers wish to acknowledge, with thanks, the following photographic sources:

All Sport p. 20; BBC Hulton Picture Library pp. 14 left, 23 top, 30 bottom, 31 top, 31 bottom, 42, 55, 56 bottom, 68 bottom, 74, 78, 85, 89 top, 102, 108, 112, 113, 115, 117, 130, 134, 135 bottom, 138, 141, 142, 143, 145, 148, 151, 153, 155, 156 bottom, 157, 159, 161, 162, 172 bottom, 182, 219, 226, 237, 242, 243, 253, 254 left, 260 top, 260 bottom, 261; Bristol Corporation p. 247; British Library pp. 97 top, 199, 200 bottom; Cheshire County Record Office p. 118; Communist Party of Great Britain Library, The James Klugmann Collection p. 215; Courtesy of Dodington House, Gloucester p. 177; Mary Evans Picture Library pp. 12, 14 right, 75, 156 top, 233; Guildhall Library p. 21; Illustrated London News p. 172 top; Institute of Agricultural History and Museum of English Rural Life, University of Reading pp. 30 top, 48; Kirklees Museum p. 192; Kingston-Upon-Hull Museum and Art Gallery p. 249; Lancashire County Record Office pp. 119, 122, 135 top; London Museum p. 25; London Public Record Office pp. 205 top, 212; Manchester Public Libraries pp. 165, 168, 171 left, 171 right; Mansell Collection pp. 23 bottom, 35, 38–39, 44, 49, 51, 56 top, 64, 67 top, 68 top, 71, 79, 80, 81, 95, 99, 106, 125, 126, 136, 163, 173, 174, 179, 189, 191, 194, 196, 200 top, 201, 205 bottom, 214, 223 top, 225, 229, 232, 235 right, 254 right, 257; National Trust pp. 164 top, 164 bottom, 166, 167; Newcastle Upon Tyne, City Engineers Photographic Section pp. 94, 97 bottom; Robert Owen Museum p. 223 bottom; Post Office p. 124; John Topham Picture Library pp. 22, 28, 46, 50, 53, 61, 62, 67 bottom, 70, 82, 89 bottom, 96, 183 bottom, 183 top right, 206, 207, 224, 231, 235 left, 241, 255; William Wilberforce Museum p. 250.

The author and publishers wish to thank the following who have kindly given permission for the use of copyright material:

Associated Book Publishers (UK) Ltd for extracts from *English Historical Documents* Vol. XI, edited by A. Aspinall and E. A. Smith, Eyre and Spottiswoode, 1959; and *Class and Conflict in 19th Century England* by P. Hollis, Routledge and Kegan Paul, 1973; B. T. Batsford Ltd for diagram from *The Agricultural Revolution* by J. D. Chambers & G. E. Mingay, 1966; The City of Manchester Leisure Services Committee for extracts from the Gregg Papers; David and Charles Publishers, for diagram adapted from *The Canal Builders* by A. Burton 2nd edition, 1981; and diagrams adapted from *The BP Book of Industrial Archaeology* by Frank Cossons, 1985; Gateshead Libraries and Arts Department for material from J. Oxberry, 'Notes relating to the Coal

Mines and Coal Trade of Northumberland and Durham', 1916; Victor Gollancz Ltd for extracts from *The Making of the English Working Class* by E. P. Thompson; D. Gregory for adapted diagram from *Regional Transformation and Industrial Revolution*, Macmillan Publishers, 1982; Stainer & Bell Ltd for 'I had a little galloway' from *Down the Wagon Way* edited by Michael Dawney; Unwin Hyman Ltd for maps from *Agriculture 1730–1872* by J. R. S. Whiting, 1971.

The publishers have made every effort to trace the copyright holders, but if they have inadvertently overlooked any, they will be pleased to make the necessary arrangement at the first opportunity.